The
Family Guide
to Crime
Prevention

Also by Martin L. Forst

Civil Commitment and Social Control

Crime and Justice in America with Jerome H. Skolnick
and Jane L. Scheiber

The Family Guide to Crime Prevention

Manuel M. Estrella

Martin L. Forst

Beaufort Books, Inc.

New York / Toronto

Library of Congress Cataloging in Publication Data
Estrella, Manuel M.
  The family guide to crime prevention.
  1. Crime prevention. I. Forst, Martin Lyle.
II. Title.
HV7431.E8   362.8'8   81-2490
ISBN 0-8253-0036-3   AACR2

Published in the United States by Beaufort Books, Inc., New York. Published simultaneously in
Canada by General Publishing Co., Limited
Printed in the United States of America

First Edition
10 9 8 7 6 5 4 3 2

Design by Ellen LoGiudice

Contents

Introduction

Your valuable possessions have been taken, your heirlooms have been destroyed, or worse, you have been seriously injured. You are a victim and the damage has already been done. The time to fight crime is *before* it happens. Prevention is the best protection against the criminal.

This book is designed to give you knowledge about the latest methods of crime prevention. These methods, endorsed by law enforcement agencies everywhere, are now being practiced by citizens around the country. If you follow the measures detailed in this book, you too can better protect yourself, your family, and your home against the many types of crime that threaten you each day.

The chances of becoming a victim of crime depend on several factors: the motives and abilities of the offender, the efficiency of the police, and the specific measures that *you* take to prevent crime. What can be done to lower the likelihood that a crime will be committed against you or your family? After a thorough analysis of all factors, experts have come to a sobering conclusion — you, the citizen, must take the basic precautionary measures to protect *yourself* against crime.

What accounts for this situation? First, it is very difficult to change the criminal's motives, needs, or abilities. Criminologists don't know whether the offender commits a crime because of psychological makeup, social environment, or the high unemployment rate. Whatever the cause of crime, there is very little you can do to change criminal behavior.

The police are increasingly unable to control crime as we wish they could. On the average, only 20 percent of all criminals are apprehended leaving the rest free to find new victims. Police administrators used to believe that more patrol cars cruising the streets would deter potential criminals, but the crime rate does not go down in areas where police patrol is extensive. Patrol cars cannot cover all areas of town. An army of police officers is not feasible. Citizens are much better off cooperating and watching each other's property than relying on the police to do it for them.

The police are fully aware of their own limitations. As the National Advisory Commission on Criminal Justice Standards and Goals put it in 1973, "Criminal justice professionals readily and repeatedly admit that, in the absence of citizen assistance, neither more manpower, nor improved technology, nor additional money will enable law enforcement to shoulder the mounting burden of combating crime in America." Unless individual citizens take an active part in combating crime and in protecting themselves, their families, and their neighborhoods, the criminal justice systems throughout the country will fall further behind in their battle against rising crime rates.

You can lower the chances of being a victim because most crime is a matter of opportunity. If the opportunity exists, somebody will likely be there to take advantage of it. The goal of this book is to teach you how to take away the opportunity from criminals and lower your chances of being harmed.

To be sure, there are criminals, determined and clever, who will commit a crime no matter what precautions have been taken. There are others with such severe mental problems that nothing can be done to influence their behavior. If a person goes berserk and shoots people at random on a crowded street, there is little you or anyone else can do about it.

Fortunately, most criminals do not have an obsession to commit crimes. They will only engage in criminal activity if the opportunity exists; that is, if the crime is easy to commit and they think they can get away with it. They try to balance the risks with the potential gains. This book will tell you how to put the odds in your favor, to make the risks so great that the criminal will be deterred.

It will not only deal with crimes that present immediate physical danger (rape, burglary, mugging), but also with how to protect your property and avoid fraud. Though all crimes differ in many respects, they have one thing in common: They can be prevented if you remove the criminal's opportunity by taking the time and trouble to employ adequate preventive measures.

Get in the habit of thinking about protecting yourself. Heed the good advice of the President's 1967 Commission on Law Enforcement and Administration of Justice: "Every American can translate his concern about, or fear of, crime into positive action. Every American should."

Chapter 1

Residential Burglary And Theft

The crime statistics we hear every day make us realize that no one is safe from burglary or theft, no matter where we live. Consider the following FBI data from the 1978 *Uniform Crime Reports:*

- More than three million burglaries are committed each year in the United States, accounting for one-third of the reported serious crime.
- Every ten seconds a burglary is committed.
- Two-thirds of all burglaries, or over two million, are committed in houses and apartments.
- Since 1970, residential burglaries have increase more than 60 percent.
- Burglary is expensive! The average dollar loss per residential burglary is $526.
- Burglary is not only a big city crime. Recent statistics indicate that burglary rates have increased faster in the suburbs and rural areas than in the cities.

Burglary and theft are on the rise everywhere. It is up to us to protect ourselves, our families, and our possessions.

Burglary means entering into a house or apartment (residence), building, or vehicle with the intent of committing a crime inside. The crime most burglars commit is theft, also called larceny. Theft means the intentional taking of another's personal property. The typical case of burglary involves a person who enters an unoccupied residence to steal valuable possessions.

A burglar is an opportunist. He is concerned primarily with stealing valuables and leaving undetected. The opportunity for crime comes from the environment in which the burglar works. One way to think about burglary and its prevention is to examine the methods burglars use and the opportunities that they like to seize. In so doing, we can remove those opportunities and reduce the chances that a burglary or theft will occur in your residence.

Many burglars believe that certain areas of town have better opportunities for a successful crime than other areas. This belief is substantiated by government studies showing that certain areas of every American town or city do indeed have higher crime rates. Opportunities vary with the time of day or the day of the week. In suburban areas, for example, the majority of burglaries are committed between 10:00 A.M. and 4:00 P.M. on weekdays.

Opportunity also depends on the precautions you take to prevent crime. Unfortunately, the measures often employed by the average citizen are not adequate. Frequently, careless individuals leave obvious clues indicating that nobody is home or that entry into the residence would be quite easy. Many times doors and windows are left open or unlocked, or if locked, the locks are inferior and easily opened. It is the reckless citizen who becomes a crime statistic on the police blotter.

Potential burglaries depend heavily on the burglar's sophistication. Professional burglars are very clever, able to break into a house or apartment under almost any circumstances. This breed of criminal commits less than one percent of all burglaries. Other burglars break into a house hoping for a confrontation with the victim. Fortunately, most burglars are unprofessional and have no desire to encounter the victim. The most common burglar is a juvenile or young adult living in the neighborhood of the victim. According to the 1979 FBI *Uniform Crime Reports* 85 percent of all persons arrested for burglary in 1975 were under twenty-five years of age. These young burglars wait for the right opportunity and then strike. A three-day accumulation of newspapers or an open garage door is an enticement to the potential thief.

Burglaries are crimes of opportunity. Eliminate the opportunity, and you make the first step toward preventing a crime at your residence. Place obstacles in the burglar's path and he will move on to an easier target.

There is no way to make your residence 100 percent burglar-proof. However, by following the suggestions in this chapter, you can make entry so difficult that the burglar will go elsewhere to seek an easier victim. The one thing you do *not* want to do is to present the opportunity for crime. Why make things easy for the criminal? As Glen D. King, Executive Director of the International Association of Police Chiefs, has stated: ". . . the reason burglary is so popular is we make it so easy. Do yourself a favor — make burglary difficult."

Studies show that burglaries can be prevented by *deterrence, delay,* and *detection.* Basic residential security practices and strong locks are good deterrents because they eliminate the opportunity for an easy burglary. Nonvictims are more likely to have taken simple precautionary measures against burglary than victims. According to the 1978 *Uniform Crime Reports* in nearly a fifth of all burglaries, the entry was made without force — doors and windows were left unlocked.

Delaying the burglar for as little as four minutes is generally considered sufficient to prevent entry into a house or apartment. A burglar wants to avoid being caught and the longer it takes to force a door or window, the greater the risk. The burglar also wants to avoid making noise, such as breaking glass or smashing doors. In other words, he must avoid attracting attention.

The fear of detection is the third element of burglary prevention. The possibility of detection is increased if you can force the burglar to work where he can be observed or in such a way that he will have to make a lot of noise. Alarms on doors and windows, trimmed shrubbery, and watchful neighbors are all effective means of detection.

There are different levels of security, each taking some degree of time, trouble, or money. The rules for protecting your residence from most burglaries and thefts are simple and basic. You can reduce the chance of becoming a target for burglars by using old-fashioned common sense and good modern locks. *Precaution* is the watchword.

Law enforcement agencies describe two types or levels of security — minimum and additional. Minimum security is the prevention of entry by a burglar through your door or window except by destructive force. This level of security will prevent most burglaries, because most burglars will not break a door or window to gain entrance. The majority of the devices required to achieve this level of security will not cost you very much.

Additional security means preventing the intruder's exit through your door or window except by means of destructive force. This level of security reduces the possibility of theft of large household possessions, such as television sets and stereos. Most burglars, even the daring ones, will not want to break down your door from the inside or remove large items through a broken window.

DOORS AND LOCKS

Doors

The most common entry point in residential burglaries is the door. Your doors, therefore, should be made as secure as possible.

Though doors are made from many materials, the most common door used in houses and apartments is the hinge type made of solid core, hollow core, or composition woods. All hinge doors leading to the outside of the house should be solid core construction, approximately 1½ to 2 inches thick. Solid core doors offer the best protection against burglary and vandalism. Naturally, metal doors offer excellent protection as well, but many people do not like the way they look.

Hollow core and composition doors do not offer adequate protection. They can be easily battered down or bored open. The resulting noise and closeness of your neighbors will usually convince a potential burglar not to try this means of entry, but your home would be safer with a solid core hardwood door, especially if you live in an isolated area. If you already have hollow core doors and do not want to replace them, they can be reinforced with metal housing around the edges, which should be placed on the door before new locks are installed.

In hinge doors, wide gaps between the door and the door frame are very tempting to burglars, who often carry crow bars (also known as pry bars and jimmy bars) to pry doors open. If you do not want to buy a new door or pay a carpenter to shore it up, you should shield the gaps with angle iron fastened to the edge of the door with carriage bolts.

Glass doors do not provide adequate security. Some hinge doors have glass on the top half or glass panes throughout. While this may be attractive and provide a clear view of anyone outside, it does not give the necessary security against burglary or vandalism. Burglars can break the glass near the lock, reach in, undo the lock, and walk into the residence. Because breaking glass may cause too much noise, many burglars use glass cutters to make a small hole (big enough for an arm to go through) near the doorknob and gain access to the inside lock of the door.

Security screening or metal decorative grilles should be used on all wood doors with glass panels. If you feel that metal screening will ruin the appearance of your front door, you should at least use it on all other doors that lead outside — to the garage, backyard, or alleyways. This is particularly important for any part of the house where a burglar might conceal himself. Metal screens or grilles should be mounted with nonremovable screws.

Keys

Carelessness with house keys accounts for a substantial number of burglaries. Good locks do not provide security if someone else has your keys. There are several things you should do to maintain greater control of you keys.

First, never carry identification tags on your key ring. If your keys are lost, it is better to have them gone forever than in the possession of someone who has your name and address. A caller might identify himself as an employee in the store where you misplaced your keys and ask you to come and pick them up. He will probably be in a phone booth close to your home. As soon as you rush out to claim your keys, he will enter and clean out your house. If you do lose keys with identification tags on them, have all of your locks reset and get new keys. Although it will cost money, it could be cheaper in the long run.

Second, separate your house keys from your car keys. If you park your car in a commercial garage or parking lot, leave only the auto ignition key. By leaving your house keys as well, anyone could make a duplicate set and trace your address through the vehicle registration in your car.

You should never leave an extra house key in an obvious place. A burglar will not search the entire grounds looking for a hidden key, but if you put it in any of the traditional hiding places — under the doormat,

in the mailbox, over the door, or in a flower pot — you may as well
leave the door open for uninvited guests. Burglars routinely look in
these obvious "hiding" places.

Here are a few additional tips about key security:

• Do not leave your keys in your coat pocket when you check it or hang
  it up in a public place.
• Do not loan your keys to casual acquaintances.
• If you move to a previously occupied residence, change the locks on
  all of the doors. Having the tumblers reset and getting new keys can
  cost as little as $35.

Hinge Protection
Occasionally the hinges of the doors are installed on the outside of the
door rather than on the inside. In this case, the burglar has the opportunity to remove the hinge pins and pry off the door, even if it is locked.
Nonremovable hinge pins purchased at your local hardware store will
alleviate this problem.

There is another easy and effective hinge security measure which
you can adopt. As you open the door, you will notice hinge plates
attached to the inside of the door and the door frame. Remove the
center screw from the hinge plate attached to the door frame; then
remove the corresponding screw from the hinge plate attached to the
door. You must now replace that screw with a new headless screw.

Hinge security

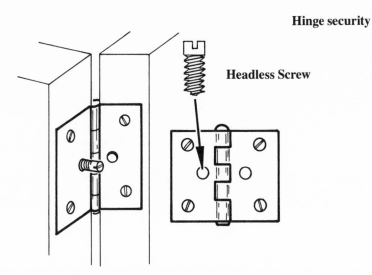

Headless Screw

Insert the headless screw into the hole leading to the door frame. Screw it in until there is approximately three-eighths to one-fourth inch protruding from the hinge plate. It may be necessary to drill out a small portion of the wood in the corresponding hole to allow room for the headless screw. When you close the door, the protruding portion will engage in the remaining screw hole leading to the door itself. Repeat this procedure on the bottom hinge as well. This process is called "pinning" the door. It will prevent a burglar from removing the hinge pins and sliding the door away from the frame.

Locks

Before considering the types of locks to put on your doors, note that an important aspect of crime prevention is knowing who is on the outside of the door without opening the door and jeopardizing your security. One device is a wide angle viewer (or peephole) located at eye's height in the center of the door. This inexpensive piece of hardware allows you to see who or what is on the outside of the door without allowing anyone to see you.

If you live in an apartment, you should have a two-way speaker and a buzzer system. Always find out who is ringing the bell to the entrance door of the apartment building before allowing them to enter. If you do not have a speaker system, try to persuade your apartment manager or owner to install one for you.

If your door has a mail slot in it, an interior hood will prevent anyone from looking into your house and still not interfere with mail deposits.

You should have some form of chain guard attached to your door. It will allow you to open the door an inch or so to see outside, and will prevent most people from pushing the door open against your will. Door chains come in various types and styles. The most common chaining device is attached to the door frame and the upper part of the door. A more secure chain guard is made of heavier gauge chain and is attached only to the door frame directly opposite the doorknob. Both ends of the chain are secured to the chain plate on the door frame, and the chain is looped around the doorknob to prevent unwanted entry.

To keep intruders out of your residence, you must lock it. This may sound obvious, but statistics indicate that one out of every five burglars simply walks into a home through an *unlocked* door or window. One of the authors of this book had his residence burgled because he was careless and lazy and did not adequately lock the front door while at the grocery store for a half hour.

Any lock is better than none — but you have to *use it.* Most burglars do not know how to pick locks. If they cannot get in quickly and quietly, they may well pass up your house or apartment and try to find one easier to enter.

Locks are expensive, but consider that all of the hardware on your house, including locks, can be valued at .5 to 1.5 percent of the total building cost. Locks make up 25 to 40 percent of this figure, depending on the type of building; they therefore represent only one-eighth to three-fifths of one percent of the complete building cost. This is not much of an investment when you consider that locks protect the entire building and its contents.

Different locks offer varying amounts of security. Unfortunately, most residential locks can be broken by an inexperienced teenager in less than thirty seconds. If you want to prevent illegal entry, you will have to purchase locks of good quality. The inside parts should be metal, not plastic. Plastic locks will melt under extreme heat. If there were a fire in your home, the lock would melt and it might be impossible to open. You could be trapped inside. It is a very good idea to shop around for the best quality metal locks. The extra time and expense is well worth it.

Springlatch Lock
The most frequently used lock for hinge doors is the springlatch (or the key-in-the-knob) lock. This type of lock does not offer good security. It can be easily forced open by breaking off the knob. Moreover, it is vulnerable to one of the burglar's most common tricks. The springlatch lock can be "slipped" (opened) with a narrow piece of plastic (like a credit card), a fingernail file, or a thin-bladed knife. The burglar pries loose the molding trim of the door, slips the credit card or knife blade in and depresses the bolt, opening the door.

Some springlatch locks are also equipped with a deadlatch, located directly next to the bolt. The deadlatch offers protection against slip-

Springlatch lock

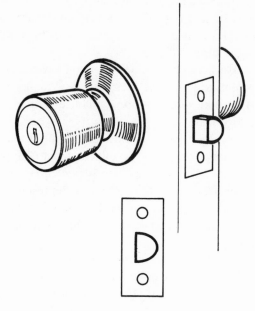

Springlatch lock with deadlatch

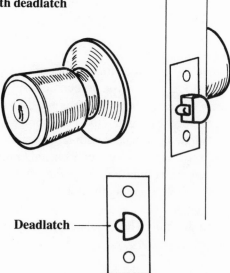

Deadlatch

ping the door. When the door is closed and locked, the deadlatch cannot be slipped by depressing it with the standard burglar tools. If you have a springlatch lock, you should make sure it also has a deadlatch with it.

Springlatch locks, with or without the deadlatch, are not good locks for doors leading to the outside of the house. They are not designed to withstand great pressure and can be forced open with very little noise by a fairly strong person using a pipe wrench, crow bar, or similar tools. For this reason, your springlatch lock should be supplemented with another type of lock.

Deadbolt Lock

The deadbolt lock, in both single- and double-cylinder models, has proven to be an excellent crime prevention device. It has been demonstrated that homes equipped with deadbolt locks have a much smaller chance of being burglarized than residences without deadbolts. These locks have proven so effective, many cities have passed ordinances requiring newly constructed houses and apartments to have them installed.

The single-cylinder deadbolt lock operates by a key from the outside of the door and a thumb screw from the inside. There is no knob on the outside of the deadbolt, so it cannot be knocked off to gain entry. Mounted flush through the inside of a solid core door, it cannot be slipped with a credit card or other standard burglar tools. For many reasons, it gives the best protection you can get from a standard lock. It provides your residence with minimum security, that is, no one can gain entry unless something is broken.

Single-cylinder deadbolt

outside view

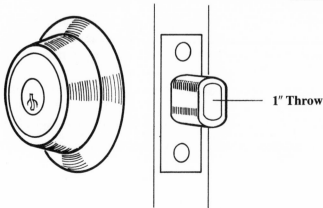

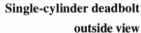
1″ Throw

Single-cylinder deadbolt lock (arrow points to thumb screw)

There are a few problems with single-cylinder deadbolts. They are not particularly useful if you have glass in your door or next to it. A burglar can break or cut the glass, reach in, turn the thumb screw and open the deadbolt from the inside. As mentioned above, either a solid core door or metal screening over the glass will prevent this method of entry.

The main problem with the single-cylinder deadbolt and its minimum security is if a burglar gets into your residence, he can easily get out again by turning the thumb screw on the inside of the door. You need a lock that will provide additional security by stopping the easy exit of the intruder.

A 1972 Department of Justice study on burglary has disclosed that other than ready cash and coin collections, burglars are most interested in stealing television sets, stereos, and radios. These are easily converted into money. Your goal is to prevent the burglar from opening the door from the inside and walking out with your large, expensive possessions.

The double-cylinder deadbolt lock offers this additional security. It requires a key (the same key) to open it from the inside as well as from the outside. There is no thumb screw. Double-cylinder deadbolts are particularly useful on doors with glass anywhere near the doorknob. If the burglar breaks the glass, there is no thumb screw (as on the single cylinder deadbolt) to turn, and he will have to knock out the glass, to let himself in. Even on solid core doors with no glass, the double-cylinder

Double-cylinder deadbolt

1″ Throw

deadbolt is beneficial. If a burglar breaks a side or rear window to gain entrance, he is less likely to carry out any of your large items through that same broken window. It is too noisy and too dangerous.

If you install a double-cylinder deadbolt, there is one very important safety precaution that you must take. Whenever you are at home and engage the deadbolt from the inside, be sure to leave the key in the lock or on a hook near the lock for ready use in an emergency. If the house catches fire, you want to avoid a frantic search for the key.

There are several important things to remember about any deadbolt lock:

- It should have a bolt that extends at least one inch in the locked position (a one-inch "throw").
- It should have a cylinder guard ring of hardened steel.
- It should have a steel insert or bearing in the bolt. This prevents sawing off the extended bolt.
- It should be installed in a solid core hardwood (or metal) door.

Deadbolt locks are expensive. Depending on the quality and the region, they cost between $15 and $30 per lock. Installation fees may run approximately $15 per lock. However, you do not have to pay a

Double-cylinder deadbolt lock (arrow points to one-inch throw)

locksmith to install them for you. You can do it yourself by renting the tools at a local equipment rental store. The lock mounting machines typically cost between $5 and $7.50 per day and it should take you about one hour per lock for installation. The rental equipment service man can give you proper instructions on the use of the equipment.

There is one thing to remember in mounting the locks. It is advisable that you do not use the small screws (one-half inch or so) that come in the lock package when installing the strike plate to the door frame. With short screws it is relatively easy for a burglar to kick in the door, breaking the door frame. You should use longer screws (two to three inches), purchased separately at the hardware store for less than one dollar. They are worth the added expense and make it very difficult for anyone to force the strike plate off the doorjamb and open the door.

Surface-Mounted Lock
Another kind of supplemental lock is surface mounted on the door. Surface-mounted locks are known by several names: drop deadbolt, rim lock, vertical deadbolt, or "jimmy-proof" lock. We recommend two surface-mounted locks known as the rim lock and the jimmy-proof rim lock. They are more desirable than the standard flush-mounted deadbolt described above for two reasons: They are less expensive and

easier to install. They do not have to be mounted through the *inside* of a solid core door (as with the deadbolt lock), but are mounted on the surface of the door. Since no special installation equipment is necessary, surface locks are easier to mount and the costs are lower.

The simple rim lock is installed on the surface of the door, and it has a one-inch bolt that engages the strike plate located on the door frame. The jimmy-proof rim lock offers somewhat greater security, since the locking bolts are vertical. The locking action results from mating the vertical pins in the lock with the rings in the strike (receiver) plate on the door frame. The vertical bolts make it more difficult to jimmy, as the name implies.

Either type of rim lock can be used on any hinge door (preferably solid core) where the strike plate can be fastened securely to the door frame. If you install any type of surface-mounted lock, be sure you use screws of sufficient length to secure properly the lock to the door and the strike plate to the door frame. Sometimes the screws that come with the lock are too short and can be knocked out if a heavy person throws his weight against the door. Use 1½- to 2-inch screws.

Surface-mounted locks are easier to install than flush-mounted deadbolt locks. However, if you are not handy with tools or do not have the time, a professional locksmith could install them for you at relatively little expense.

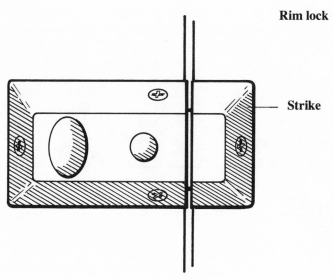

Rim lock

Strike

Jimmy-proof rim lock

Strike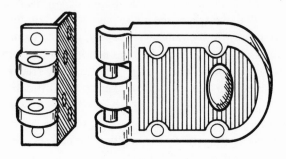

Rim lock (arrow points to throw)

A final note about springlatch, deadbolt, and surface-mounted locks. You might conclude that your doors will be weighted down with so many different locks that you will need a pocketful of keys to open them. This is not necessarily so. Consult your locksmith before you purchase any new locks. Tell him the manufacturer of the locks you currently have in your doors. He can inform you which brands of locks have the same type of key-way as those you already have. When you purchase new locks, you can have the locksmith re-key them with the key you presently use. If you buy locks at a hardware store and take them to a locksmith, it will cost approximately $7.50 per lock for re-keying. If you purchase the locks from a locksmith, the cost of re-keying will be much less.

French and Dutch Doors
French doors, or double doors, have an active and an inactive side. Both sides should be properly secured to prevent unwanted entry. Many homes with French doors use half-barrel slide bolts on the inactive door. These are inadequate, because they can be easily forced open.

French doors

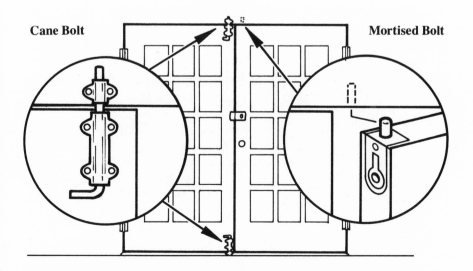

Cane Bolt   **Mortised Bolt**

French door lock   **Barrel bolt**

Double doors are best secured by properly mounted cane or full-barrel bolts. These should be one-half inch in diameter and approximately twelve inches long. They should be installed on both the top and the bottom of the inactive door. For greater security on double doors, a mortised bolt should be placed within the door at both the top and the bottom. When the active door is closed and secured, it is nearly impossible to disengage this type of lock.

For the active door, we recommend a surface-mounted lock, either a rim lock or jimmy-proof rim lock. You must remember that the lock installed on the active door will *not* provide adequate protection if the inactive door is not properly secured first.

On Dutch doors, the two halves of the door should be locked together with a cane bolt, full-barrel bolt, or mortised bolt. Moreover, at least one part of the Dutch door should be locked to the door frame with a deadbolt. The part not locked with a deadbolt should be secured in the same way as an inactive French door.

Sliding Glass Doors
Sliding glass doors present a major security problem if they do not have the proper locks and if special precautions are not taken to prevent their removal.

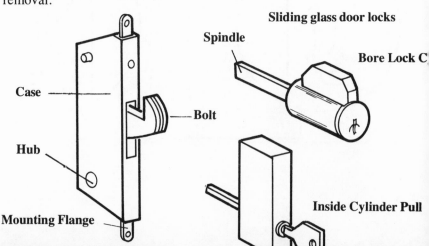

Sliding glass door locks

Spindle

Bore Lock C

Case

Bolt

Hub

Inside Cylinder Pull

Mounting Flange

There are easy and inexpensive measures you can take to keep your glass door from being forced open. One common trick which applies as well to windows is to place a long thin piece of wood (like a sawed-off broom handle) along the bottom track between the sliding door and the opposite wall. Make sure that the stick is cut so that it fits snugly in the track and keeps the active door tightly closed. By pounding a nail halfway into the stick, you can remove it easily from the track whenever you want to use the door.

A more sophisticated version of this trick is called the Charley bar. It is a steel bar placed in metal brackets between the active door and the opposite steel frame at the other side of the track. While the Charley bar is somewhat more secure than a simple broomstick, neither is sufficient to secure your sliding glass doors. Not only are sticks or bars relatively easy for the burglar to remove, but they do not offer additional security. If a burglar enters your residence, he can easily remove the bars and walk out with your household goods. These security measures should only be used in conjunction with locks.

There are several types of locks designed specifically for sliding glass doors and windows. One option we highly recommend is the slide bolt, which should be installed for minimum security. For additional security when your home is unoccupied, use a padlock to secure the active door to the slide bolt.

The best lock, however, for a sliding glass door is the deadlock, which utilizes a bore pin tumbler cylinder and opens with a key from the outside. The lock bolt should engage the strike plate snugly so that it cannot be disengaged by pushing and pulling the door. When the existing inside "pull" has to be replaced to accomodate the new deadlock, an inside cylinder "pull" is recommended.

Key locking device for sliding glass window

When a sliding glass door is installed, it is merely lifted into position. It can, therefore, also be lifted from its track and removed. One of the main objectives of securing your sliding glass door (or window) is to keep it from being pried up and out of the track. Burglars commonly gain entry into houses and apartments by lifting the glass doors off the runners.

It is very easy to prevent this method of entry. When the active door is open, screw a thin piece of wood (approximately one-fourth to three-eighths inches thick and two-thirds the width of the door) into the overhead runner; that is, where the door would be if it were closed. Unfinished molding strips from a lumber store should work well.

Another security measure that prevents the door from being pried or lifted out of its track is called "pinning" the door. Drill a downward sloping hole from the inside through the top track (channel) into the top portion of the sliding door frame. Be careful not to hit the glass door when drilling. One nick from the drill bit will cause tempered safety glass to shatter completely. Also be sure not to drill all the way through the door, or the intruder could push out the pin from the outside. The hole can be of any size, but we suggest about one-eighth inch in diameter. After the hole is drilled, place a metal pin (also one-eighth inch in diameter) into the hole. It would be advisable to attach the pin to a short metal chain and to secure the chain to the steel track. This method may be used for minimum security.

Other Doors

Basement doors and windows provide burglars with an easy way to get into your house because they are located conveniently at ground level and are often hidden by shrubs. Make doors and windows less inviting with metal grilles. Put an inside bar across the basement door so it cannot be forced open. Treat the door from you basement into the main part of your house as you would an exterior door. In other words, install a deadbolt or rim lock and *use* it.

In general, treat all exterior doors on the rear and sides of your house as possible targets for a burglar. Since these doors are less frequently observed from the street than your front door, you need to take extra precautions.

**Garage door security
inside view**

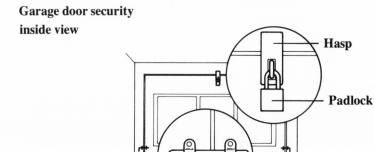

Hasp

Padlock

Cane Bolt

Garage Doors

Most garage doors can be pried or forced open with little difficulty. If there is an external center lock or even a sliding bolt lock on one side of the door, at least one side can be opened far enough for someone to enter.

Here are three measures that can be taken to secure a garage door:
1. Add another bolt and padlock to the opposite side if one already exists on the outside of the door.
2. Install a pair of cane bolts to the inside of the door.
3. Add a top center hasp to the inside of the door.

Adding another bolt and padlock to the outside of your door, or installing two if you have none, will prevent a burglar from prying open either side. The use of a proper padlock (described in Chapter 3) will deter a potential burglar, because he will most likely not want to use large bolt cutters in a driveway that is visible from the street. The main inconvenience with this method is that you may need an additional key for each padlock.

We suggest cane bolts be installed on the inside of the garage door. They should be placed on both sides toward the bottom of the door. Although cane bolts offer good security, they can be inconvenient because they must be secured from the inside, leaving access to the car only through the side door or the house. Security takes time, but the few extra minutes could save you a lot of grief.

For extra security, particularly if you go away for a vacation, you should install a hasp, secured to the top inside center of the garage door. Use a secure padlock to lock the hasp. With the hasp locked, it would be extremely difficult to open the garage door either from the inside or the ouside. Make sure your hasp is made of hardened steel; others of pressed steel are cut easily with a hacksaw. When a hasp is installed, none of the mounting bolts should be accessible to the burglar.

The garage doors should always be kept locked, particularly if your garage is attached to your house. A burglar in your garage can work on your house door without being seen from the street. He will even use *your* tools to gain entry. Make sure that you treat the entrance door from the garage into your house just as you would any exterior door. This door can be covered with sheet metal both for fire protection and for greater security against burglary.

WINDOWS

Each type of window presents its own security problem. In general, the chief aim is to eliminate windows being pried open. Most burglars avoid breaking glass because they are fearful of noise attracting attention.

Double-hung sash windows are usually found in older homes and apartments. These windows move up and down and usually have a simple sash lock that can be jimmied quite easily. There are a few relatively easy and inexpensive ways to secure these windows. One means of protection is a key-locking security sash lock. These should be mounted with extra long screws, which offer greater security because they cannot be jimmied open. It should be noted, however, that key-locking devices on all types of windows can be a fire exit hazard. If you are inside the house, always keep the key in the lock or on a hook near the lock. You should only take the key away from the lock if you go out of the house, particularly for more than a few hours.

Whether or not you decide on a key-locking sash lock, we recom-

Double-hung wooden window

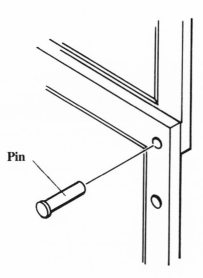

Pin

Key locking security sash lock

mend that you pin your windows. To do this, drill a hole (approximately one-eighth to one-fourth inch in diameter) that angles slightly downward through a top corner of the bottom window into the bottom corner of the top window. Place a metal pin or screw (the same size) into the hole. Now the window cannot be opened even if the sash lock is jimmied. Of course, a screw offers greater security; it cannot be pulled out easily if the burglar breaks or cuts open your window. However, the screw is also more difficult for *you* to remove. We recommend that whenever you are around the house, you use a metal pin. If you leave the house for a vacation, you should secure the windows with a screw.

You can also use this pinning method to open your windows a few inches for ventilation, without allowing them them to be forced open. Open your window two to three inches, but not so far as to allow an arm to reach in. Then drill another hole of the same size through the inside window frame and halfway into the outside window. Now the metal pin or screw can be placed in this hole to allow ventilation while preventing the window from being pushed up all the way.

A more drastic, though effective, crime prevention measure for windows is the use of bars or heavy gauge metal grilles. Though they are not particularly attractive and seem restrictive to many people, they should at least be used on the most vulnerable windows of your residence. The grilles should be attached with one-way screws or fastened from the inside. If the grilles are installed in the bedrooms, which is *not* recommended, *be sure* that they are designed to open from the inside, otherwise they can prevent escape in case of a fire.

Casement (Steel Sash) Windows
Casement windows are made of a metal frame or sash and generally open and close by means of a gear operating the handle, called the operator. They also have a locking device (latch) that secures the window to the center post or frame. Your main concern with casement windows is that they will be pried open. Never leave casement windows partially opened; they can be forced open easily from this position.

There are no real tricks to making casement windows more secure.

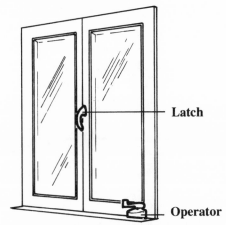

Latch

Casement (steel sash) window

Operator

You could remove the crank handle (the operator) from the operating mechanism when the window is not in use. This will prevent someone from prying the window open a little and then turning the handle to get it open the rest of the way. You could also pin it by drilling a small hole through the two latch sides and the latch handle. Then insert a small metal pin into the hole. This will prevent the latch (the locking mechanism) from being easily disengaged.

The best way to maintain minimum security on casement windows is simply to make sure that all of the parts are working properly and to use them. Check the operator and make sure it has no excess play. If it does, replace the worn hardware. The locking latch should also be working properly. Unfortunately, there is no good way to provide additional security for these windows.

Sliding Glass Windows
Sliding glass windows are usually made with a metal frame, and they should be protected in the same manner as sliding glass doors (see pages 28 – 30). The primary security objective for sliding glass windows is to keep them from sliding open or being lifted up and out of the track.

One way to prevent someone from sliding the window open is to place a metal or wooden dowel, such as a broomstick, in the tracks. This is a good temporary measure, but it should not be used exclusively, since the dowels are relatively easy to remove. Another way is to pin, as was described for the sliding glass doors. And finally, there are many products available for securing windows. Two devices we recommend are the anti-slide block and the slide bolt. These and many others can be purchased at your local hardware store or locksmith.

If you want to prevent your windows from being lifted out of the track, screws should be placed in the upper track (see page 30).

Louvre Windows

Louvre windows are difficult to burglar-proof since the individual panes of glass may be easily removed. In order to secure the panes, apply a two-part epoxy resin to each pane of glass. This will prevent a burglar from sliding the pane out.

Because these windows are difficult to secure, the use of metal grilles or grates is recommended. If they are installed in bedrooms, they must be designed to open from the inside.

No matter what type of window you have in your residence, they all present one main security risk: They can be broken or cut open very easily. Most burglars will not break a window for fear of attracting attention, but an increasing number of burglars are beginning to cut windows with glass cutters. This is a very quiet and effective means of gaining entry.

There are three basic preventive measures you can employ to counter this means of entry:

1. Use decorative metal bars, grilles, or screens.
2. Use a burglar alarm. This will be described in the next chapter.
3. Use some form of shatterproof glass.

If you live in an isolated area or have particularly vulnerable windows, it would be advisable to replace your regular windows with some form of safety glass. Safety glass falls into four categories: laminated glass, tempered glass, wired glass, and plastics. Any one of these types of glass will offer good security, but there is one drawback — they are very expensive. It costs between $5 and $15 per square foot, depending on the type and brand. Safety glass should, therefore, be used only on your most vulnerable windows. Consult your local glass dealer to find out how much it would cost to fulfill your needs.

Examples of metal bars and grilles

SECONDARY BARRIER (SECURITY CLOSET)

Outside locks are the first barrier in preventing burglary. A secondary barrier is a closet inside your residence that has been made secure to provide extra protection against burglary or theft. This secondary barrier, or security closet, should be used to keep your valuables in and burglars out.

To make a secondary barrier, you need a closet with a hinged swinging door and no windows. You cannot make one from a closet with sliding doors. The door must be solid core and open outward away from the inside of the closet. This type of door is almost impossible to kick in.

To secure your secondary barrier properly, install one or two single-cylinder deadbolt locks. Remember that the deadbolts should have a minimum length (throw) of one inch, and a hardened center core. Obviously, you must keep them locked when not in use.

With the door opening toward you, you will notice that the hinges are outside the closet and vulnerable to attack. If a burglar were to take out the hinge pins, he could pry open the door from the outside. Therefore, you must pin the door and door frame where the hinges are located. Follow the same procedure described under Hinge Protection on pages 17 — 18.

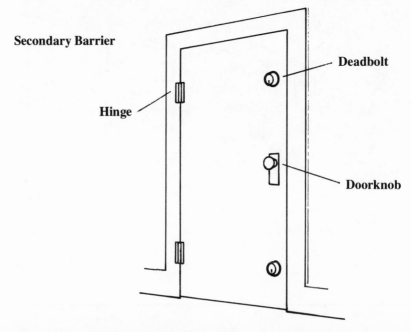

Secondary Barrier

Deadbolt

Hinge

Doorknob

EXTERNAL SECURITY

The outside appearance and landscape of your residence may be conducive to burglary or theft. If a person can hide in your yard or next to your home, he will be more likely to burglarize it. If it is dark or if he can hide in shrubs or bushes, he will have more time to pry open a window or pick a lock on your door. A house visible to neighbors or passersby puts fear into the potential burglar.

A well-lighted residence is a necessary step in burglary prevention; an intruder prefers darkness to avoid detection. In over half of all residential burglaries, the offender enters from the rear of the house, so all areas of the house should be well lighted, particularly the back. Wire mesh coverings over all external lights will help prevent the lightbulb from being broken.

For many of us, it is scary to return to a dark house; a burglary may be in progress. If you install a photoelectric cell in your outside lights, front and back, you will never come home to a dark house. The

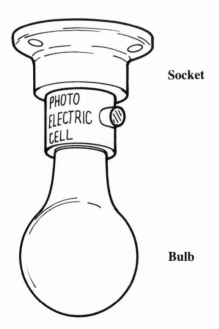

Photoelectric Cell

Socket

Bulb

photoelectric cell is light-sensitive, so it will automatically turn your lights on when it gets dark and will turn them off when it gets light. Many street lights operate in this manner.

We recommend a photoelectric cell that screws directly into the light socket, and then the light bulb screws into the cell. Photoelectric cells generally cost between $5.95 and $9.95 and can be purchased at almost any electronics or hardware store.

Keeping lights on at night is an inexpensive way to burglar-proof your house. Naturally, rates will vary around the country, but on the average a forty watt bulb burning out front for twelve hours costs only about four cents. A sixty watt bulb is good for the back of the house. The extra protection is well worth the price.

Bushes and trees provide privacy, but they also give a burglar a place to hide. A good idea is to plan your landscaping with both privacy *and* security in mind. Prune large trees near the house to prevent access to a second-story window. Keep shrubbery trimmed, to keep the view to or from any door or window. Trimmed shrubs also provide you, your neighbors, and patrolling police officers a view of trespassers and deny them a place to hide. See that the lawn and yard are well kept to give the home a lived-in look. Do not leave ladders or tools outside the house

Don't let bushes or trees block windows.

where a thief can get them and use them to enter your home. This is particularly important to remember if you go on vacation. Finally, gates and fences offer the first line of defense against unwanted entry. They should be properly built and maintained and they should be equipped with locks.

OPERATION I.D.

To combat the great increase in burglary rates, the tiny electronic engraving pen is an effective device. With this pen you can inscribe your driver's license number on all your valuable possessions and thus participate in a nationwide crime prevention program called Operation I.D.

Operation I.D. has reduced burglaries by as much as 75 percent in some communities. When Operation I.D. began in Monterey Park, California, in 1963 there was a severe burglary problem. A few years after the program was implemented, only three of the 4,000 participating residences had been burglarized. This figure compares dramatically with the 1,800 burglaries committed in the 7,000 nonparticipating residences.

If you do not own an electronic engraving pen, you can borrow one from your local police or sheriff's department. Some police departments will also send an officer or volunteer to your residence to mark your possessions for you. The marking pen handles like a ball-point pen and will etch metals, ceramics, plastics, or wood surfaces. After inscribing your driver's license number be sure to add the abbreviation for your state, such as CA for California or NY for New York. This helps authorities return property if it is transported across state lines. If you do not have a driver's license, you can get an official identification number from your state Department of Motor Vehicles, the agency that issues driver's licenses. Do *not* engrave your social security number on any of your property. Federal law forbids the release of any social security information, even to law enforcement agencies.

Operation I.D. provides good crime prevention for several reasons.

If you make your property readily identifiable to the police by marking it, you can help deter crime. Most people would be discouraged from stealing marked property because it is so difficult to "fence" (sell). Also, if something is stolen, it is easier to catch and prosecute the thief with identifiable goods.

According to the California Crime Prevention Institute, of the $400 million worth of goods stolen each year, less than 2 percent are ever returned to the rightful owner. Without some identifying mark or serial number, the police are unable to verify that the property has been stolen or to locate the lawful owners. Unclaimed property is either auctioned off or destroyed. By marking your property, you not only discourage theft, but you also greatly increase the chances of recovering your property if it is stolen.

There are a few general rules for marking your property. On large items such as television sets, stereo equipment, and appliances, engrave on the back side, in the upper right hand corner. Mark furniture on the bottom right-hand side. Bicycles should be marked on the top of the sprocket.

On small transistor items, such as pocket calculators and radios, scratch your driver's license or I.D. number on the back with a pin or needle. The vibrating of the marking pen may cause damage to delicate circuits. You can use this method to engrave your expensive cameras as well.

Small items, such as jewelry and silverware, are difficult to engrave and doing so might harm their appearance. Such valuables should be photographed up close. Take the photo on a plain white background and include your driver's license number next to the items. The police find it helpful if you place a small ruler next to the items.

The stolen property rooms of many police departments look like fur stores. Stolen furs cannot be returned to their rightful owners if the linings and labels are torn out and there are no identifying marks to prove ownership. You should, therefore, mark all furs with an indelible pen. You might prefer to mark furs with invisible ink, the kind that can only be seen under a special black light. Do not mark them on the lining or label, for the thieves will probably rip these out. Mark all furs directly on the backs of the skins, in several places. This same method should be used for other expensive clothing and for works of art.

Make a complete inventory of your personal possessions. The list should include the date each item was purchased and its original value. Save the receipts and the serial numbers of your more valuable items and keep them on the inventory list. Give one copy of the list to your insurance agent and keep another in a safe place outside your residence, such as a safe deposit box. Be sure to update your list every year or so to include all newly purchased items.

If a marked item is sold, you should delete your identification number by drawing a single line through it from the upper left to the lower right-hand corner. Do not attempt to remove the number in any other way, such as filing it off. In most states it is against the law to possess property with a serial number obliterated.

When all your possessions have been marked and you return the electronic engraving pen to your local police station, you can receive a sticker or decal to put in the window of your residence indicating that you are participating in Operation I.D. If a burglar sees this sticker and knows all of your possessions have been marked, he will be less likely to burglarize your residence. You should contact your local law enforcement agency as soon as possible about Operation I.D. It is free, takes very little time, and is well worth the effort.

WHEN YOU ARE AWAY FROM HOME

A vacation or a business trip should be a pleasant experience for you and your family. You should not have to worry about your home or property while you are gone. Yet a vacant house — or one that appears to be vacant — is a tempting target to a burglar. The reverse is also true: A residence that appears to be lived in, even if it is not, is a deterrent to burglars.

To make your time away from home more enjoyable and set your mind at ease, take the following precautions to reduce the likelihood that your residence will be burglarized or vandalized.

At Least One Day Before You Leave

1. *If* you know *and* trust your newspaper carrier, you should have your newspaper deliveries discontinued until you return. We recommend, however, that you continue to have your newspaper delivered and arrange with a trusted friend or relative to pick it up every day. The police have found that newspaper carriers occasionally commit acts of burglary or theft, or inform others that you are on vacation.

2. The same holds true for mail deliveries. We strongly suggest that you have a trusted friend or relative pick up your mail each day you are gone.

3. Make arrangements to have your lawn cut and watered. Have someone remove throwaway papers and circulars from your doorway and yard every day. If you take a winter vacation, arrange for someone to shovel the snow off your walkway, drive their car up and down your driveway, and walk around outside. This will convince burglars that someone is currently occupying the house.

4. If you have valuables in your residence, take them to your bank for storage in a safe deposit box or vault. Deposit any extra cash in your bank account.

5. Tell your local law enforcement agency when you plan to depart and return, and let them know the name, address, and phone number of the person taking care of your home.

6. Make sure any broken windows, doors, or locks are repaired.

7. Arrange with a neighbor or relative to watch your house and give them a key. Ask them to check the house periodically. Have them change the position of the drapes or blinds to give the appearance that someone is living there. Let them know where you are and how you can be reached in an emergency. Write their telephone number down so that you can check with them during your trip. Give them a description of your car and its license number.

8. Ask your neighbor to park his extra car in your driveway.

9. Remove all ladders, tools, lawn furniture, garbage cans, and so forth to your garage, basement, or storage shed.

On the Day You Leave
1. Turn down the volume control on the bottom of your phone so that it cannot be heard from the outside.
2. Make sure that you have closed and locked all doors and windows. Use all of the added security techniques that have been discussed so far, such as extra padlocks, Charley bars, and pins in windows.
3. Put window shades in their normal daytime position and make sure all main floor drapes, shades, and curtains are arranged so that your neighbors and police can see into your home.
4. If you are leaving a car or other vehicle in the driveway, make sure that it is locked.
5. An empty garage advertises your absence, so close and lock your garage door.
6. Set an electrical timer to turn some lights on and off during the evening hours. You might get several timers and set them consecutively so that when the lights go off in the living room, for example, they go on in a bedroom. This makes it look like someone is moving around the house.
7. Hook up your electrical timer to your radio. Tune the radio to a talk station and keep the volume rather low. This will create the impression of conversation.
8. Make sure that the last person out of the house checks all locks on doors and windows. Take a walk around the house to double-check that everything has been done.
9. If you have not already done so, leave a key with your neighbor or relative. Check to make sure that you have their phone number.

Here Are Some Don'ts
1. Don't leave notes indicating your absence.
2. Don't leave extra keys in obvious places such as the mailbox, under the doormat, and so forth.
3. Don't advertise your absence by putting a notice in the local newspaper that you are going away on vacation. Wait until you return for any report of your trip.
4. Some burglars are very creative: They read the newspapers for notices of weddings, funerals, graduations, christenings, and bar

mitzvahs, and then visit the family house during the ceremony. On such occasions, arrange to have somebody stay at your house.

Tips to the Baby-sitter
If you are going out for the evening and hire a baby-sitter, it is a good idea to make sure the sitter is as properly instructed in crime prevention as in emergency situations. Be sure to:

1. Leave a phone number where you can be reached.
2. Leave the phone numbers of the police and fire departments next to the telephone.
3. Leave your *home* address next to the telephone in case the baby-sitter must summon help in an emergency.
4. Familiarize the sitter with the premises for quick escape in emergencies.
5. Instruct the sitter on the proper use of all doors and windows and their locks.
6. Make sure all windows and doors are locked when you leave.
7. Advise the sitter if you are expecting any visitors or phone calls.
8. Tell the sitter to call the police if he or she sees anyone loitering in the area or is suspicious of any callers (in person or on the phone).
9.8Instruct the sitter not to open the door to any unknown persons.
10. Tell the sitter to remain on the premises unless given permission to leave.

WHAT TO DO IF YOU FIND A BURGLAR
IN YOUR RESIDENCE

The ordinary burglar does not want to hurt you — he only wants to take money or valuable property without interruption. But not all burglars are ordinary. Since they commit their crimes in a state of high tension, many burglars are capable of doing you or your family great harm if trapped, scared, threatened, or confronted. Never confront a burglar. Don't sacrifice your personal safety to save your property. Some burglars are also rapists, drug addicts, or mentally unbalanced. It is simply not worth the risk to antagonize a burglar in order to keep your possessions.

Call your local police whenever a stranger appears to be hanging around with no legitimate purpose. The police can examine the situation with no trouble to anyone. You are not bothering the police if you call them about suspicious persons; they want your cooperation and assistance. Get a license number if you can, but do not subject yourself to danger by approaching a strange person or car.

If you come home and see signs that your residence has been burglarized, the thief may still be inside. If he is, he will be very anxious to escape and he may use force to do so. Do *not* go inside. Leave the immediate area and call the police from someone else's phone. Do not enter your house until the police have checked it out for you.

If you are already inside and discover you have been burgled, do *not* touch anything or clean up. Preserve the scene of the crime until the police can inspect for evidence. There is less chance of collecting evidence such as fingerprints if you touch anything.

If you find a burglar in your home, try to get away and call the police. If you cannot get away, be cooperative. Do what the burglar says and do not try to attack him. Use force only if he attacks you. Then you should fight with all your might and use whatever means you have available to reasonably defend yourself.

If you wake up during the night and find a burglar in your bedroom, pretend to be asleep. Do not get up and try to fight him. You are better off letting him take your possessions and leave.

If you see a burglar, try to get one or two points of identification. General height, weight, and coloring are helpful, but the best identification is the nature and location of any scars or tattoos.

Never attack a burglar. He might be armed with a knife, screwdriver, or pry bar. If he has a gun, he may use it on you.

CONCLUSION

All available evidence indicates that most burglaries and theft are the result of citizen carelessness. If you do not take the necessary precautions, burglars and thieves will avail themselves of the opportunity to steal your belongings.

A 1972 study sponsored by the U.S. Department of Justice concluded: "The most important recommendation that we can make is that the ordinary citizen realize that, by a series of simple straightforward acts, he can affect the likelihood of his being burglarized." By using the crime prevention measures presented in this chapter, you can significantly lower that likelihood. Police officials estimate that burglary rates could be cut in half if citizens had even the slightest knowledge of the methods burglars use as well as the common sense precautions to counter them.

Chapter 2

Burglar Alarms

Because of the ever-increasing crime rate, you may be considering a burglar alarm for your home. If you have inquired about burglar alarms (called *security systems* by crime prevention professionals), you may be puzzled because of the wide variety available and their enormous range in price. You should ask: "Do I really need a burglar alarm in my home?" "Which alarm is best for me and my family?" This chapter answers these and other important questions and offers general rules to follow if you purchase a security system.

THE BENEFITS OF BURGLAR ALARMS

You will remember from the last chapter that one of the three keys to burglary prevention is detection. Detecting the burglar before he strikes greatly increases the chances of protecting your family and your valuables. Early detection also aids the police in apprehending criminals.

Burglar alarms have proved to be effective tools in the detection of crime. A March 1979 article in *Popular Science* magazine stated that a 1978 Portland, Oregon, study of burglar alarms found that alarmless homes were burgled six times as often as those protected by alarms.

Burglar alarms can provide other benefits such as increasing the value of your home and perhaps lowering insurance rates; expenditures for some alarm systems may also be tax-deductible.

Some burglar alarm systems can be modified to include other forms of security. In some, a fire alarm in a security system can be included at little added expense. If your burglar alarm has this fire prevention capability, we strongly recommend that you take advantage of it. You are more likely to be killed by fire than by criminals in your home. Other optional alarms that can be added to a few systems are: flood alarms for the basement, if a pipe bursts; food freezer alarms, if the temperature in your freezer rises above a predetermined degree; and electrical power failure alarms.

THE PROBLEMS WITH BURGLAR ALARMS

Most burglar alarms require major changes in the living habits of all family members. Owners of security systems are often quick to acknowledge that their alarms can be a real nuisance. When the alarm is engaged, you must enter and exit the house with great care or the alarm will sound. Such caution is particularly difficult for a family with active children. Teenagers who come home late at night must cooperate fully or the alarm system either will not work properly or will sound off to announce their return home.

False alarms pose a major problem. A nationwide survey by the *California Crime Prevention Institute* shows that more than 90 percent of all alarms are false alarms. They have become such a problem that police departments in many communities no longer allow citizens to connect their alarm systems to the police station.

Be sure to check local ordinances and police department policies governing the use of burglar alarms in your community. Different cities have different rules. Many police departments, for example, charge a fee each time police officers respond to a false alarm. In Portland, Oregon, operation permits are required for any alarm system that calls a police emergency number. The permit costs $8, but after four false alarms in one year the permit is revoked until the problem causing the false alarms is solved. It then costs $40 to obtain another permit. Subsequent false alarms result in even higher charges to the citizen. Police in some cities have adopted a ''No Response'' policy to deal with people whose security systems frequently sound false alarms.

DO YOU NEED A BURGLAR ALARM SYSTEM?

Everyone does not need a burglar alarm; some people need one more than others. There are several factors that determine whether you need a burglar alarm system.

Your valuables. Since the average burglary in the United States results in a loss of of only $526, it is hard to justify, on economic grounds, spending thousands of dollars on an elaborate burglar alarm system. A typical family may find the cost of a security system substantially greater than the financial losses from a burglary. If, however, you own many valuable objects, you need the extra protection a burglar alarm can offer.

Your neighborhood. In most areas the crime rate is not high enough to warrant spending substantial sums of money on a burglar alarm. If you live in a suburban area or a close-knit community with a small population, the use of high quality deadbolt locks and other basic precautionary measures should provide enough protection. The typical burglar is an unsophisticated juvenile who will enter only through an open door or window. Most burglars will not break anything to gain entry. In an urban area or any place where criminals are desperate and daring, however, the added security of a burglar alarm may be justified.

Your crime prevention capabilities. If you are able to take normal precautions to protect yourself and your residence by practicing the crime prevention techniques presented in the last chapter, you probably do not need a burglar alarm. Otherwise, you should consider one. If, for instance, your neighbors are too distant to help look out for your property, or your house is surrounded by trees and shrubs, burglars can avoid the normal means of detection. Moreover, if you have to be away from your home for long periods, you need extra protection. Prolonged absences give the burglar the opportunity to find out when a house is vacant, and his fear of detection is drastically reduced.

Your mental state. Generally, burglars will not enter a residence they believe is occupied. But if you *feel* particularly vulnerable in your home, a burglar alarm can give you peace of mind. You may live alone and feel vulnerable, or you may need to know that you have done all that is humanly possible to protect your family. Many people who own security systems sleep better at night simply knowing their alarm is turned on.

You should not forget, however, that salespeople from security companies may play on your fears. Try not to be swayed by their emotionalism or your anxiety. Use reason. Calculate the extra protection you are likely to get from a burglar alarm against the cost of the system. Overprotection does little good for you and your family; it is just an additional expense.

FACTORS TO CONSIDER WHEN CHOOSING A BURGLAR ALARM

When you are considering installing a burglar alarm in your residence, thoroughly study all available options. Burglar alarms come in many types and range enormously in price. Find out as much as possible about each system. Talk to people who have systems installed in their homes. Talk to representatives of several different alarm companies to find out what services each company will provide. Finally, talk to your local police department's crime prevention specialist.

Evaluate carefully what you can afford for a system and which one meets your needs. Burglar alarms range in price from a few dollars to several thousands of dollars. For minimal protection and expense, you can buy battery-powered alarms designed to protect one door or window. An elaborate security system to safeguard a mansion can cost

$10,000 or more. A complete security system will also entail a monthly service charge for maintenance and a fee for security guards in case of an emergency. The average family, however, can expect to pay between $250 and $750 for a burgular alarm system.

When calculating the cost of a security system, you should also take into account the ease of installation. It is relatively easy and inexpensive to install a good burglar alarm when a home is under construction. Costs of installation in an old two-story plaster house, on the other hand, may be prohibitive. Be sure that the alarm system you want fits the design and construction of your home.

Consider also the parts of your residence you want to protect. Is there only one entrance or are there numerous doors and windows? Naturally, the more potential entrance points for an intruder, the more complex and expensive your system will be.

Placement and appearance of the system are also important considerations. Some burglar alarms have unsightly wires and sensors that are objectionable to many people, while other alarms are housed in small, decorative wooden cabinets. Unfortunately, many of the most attractive systems are prone to false alarms.

Convenience is another consideration. If you have children or animals, certain alarm systems are unsuitable for you. A survey by *Consumer Reports* found that over half of the burglar alarms were turned off most of the time. Some owners *never* turned their alarms on because of the nuisance of frequent false alarms.

If you buy a burglar alarm, get one you can live with. An alarm that you keep turned off most of the time is a waste of money, yet buying an alarm that is easy to live with has its own problems. The most convenient alarms usually offer the least protection.

TYPES OF BURGLAR ALARMS

Most burglar alarms work on the same general principle. They provide some sort of sensing device that, when activated, detects an intruder and triggers an alarm. Burglar alarms alert you and the intruder, your neighbors, or the police of an unwarranted entry. They vary widely in complexity, cost, sensitivity, and effectiveness. After briefly outlining the types of alarms, we will describe each one in detail.

There are three basic types of burglar alarms.

I. *Perimeter Alarms*
    A. Hardwire
    B. Wireless
II. *Interior Alarms*
    A. Hardwire and Wireless
    B. Motion Detectors
       1. Sound (Ultrasonic)
       2. Heat (Thermal)
       3. Light
          a. Photoelectric
          b. Infrared
       4. Microwave
III. *Spot Alarms*

PERIMETER BURGLAR ALARM SYSTEMS

The perimeter alarm system is what most people think of when they hear the term ''burglar alarm.'' This type of system is called a perimeter alarm because it guards all entrances (doors and windows) into your home. Establishing a perimeter of protection is the most effective method to secure against unwanted entry, but the perimeter system can be expensive. If you have a good one installed with several accessories, it may cost several thousand dollars, depending on where you live, labor costs, and the construction of your home. If you install one yourself, a perimeter system can cost as little as $200.

The two types of perimeter alarm systems are hardwire and wireless.

Hardwire Alarm Systems
All hardwire burglar alarm systems consist of three basic components: detectors (sometimes called sensors), a central control box, and some

form of attracting device (a bell, siren, light). The detectors are located at each entry point around the house. Standard electrical hardwire links them together and leads to the central control box and the attracting device, which is usually a noisemaker. If a door or window is opened when the alarm is turned on, the detector will send a signal to the control box which will in turn trigger the noisemaker. The noisemaker alerts you and the burglar of the illegal entry. The control box can also be set up to send a signal to the police or to a private security agency instructing guards to respond to your alarm. The control box can also trigger a silent alarm which alerts only the police or a security agency so the burglar can be caught in the act. Usually, however, silent alarms are used only in businesses.

Hardwire systems have two main benefits. First, they offer the best security because they are hard to defeat. Second, they are more reliable; very little can go wrong with them if they are of high quality, installed properly, and well maintained. Moreover, provided you know how to operate the system, they seldom trigger false alarms.

Hardwire systems have some disadvantages. The electrical wires must be strung between each entrance point in the residence to the centrally located control box. If the wires are not concealed properly, they are unsightly and make the system easy to deactivate. But installing wires behind the walls and under the floors is, unfortunately, quite expensive.

Detectors (Sensors)

The detectors are basic to the entire alarm system. These devices guard the doors and windows of your home and trigger the alarm system when an intruder tries to enter. There are several types of detectors.

Magnetic detectors. The magnetic contact is the most common detector used in hardwire systems. It is also the most effective, versatile, and dependable. It consists of two parts, a switch and a magnet and is mounted on the door or window frame. The *magnet* is attached to the moving part of the door or window. Each part of the magnetic detector is enclosed in a weatherproof plastic case. The two parts of the detector are installed about one-eighth of an inch apart. As long as the doors and windows stay closed, the magnet is next to the switch and the switch contacts remain closed. If a door or window is opened and the magnet moves away from the switch, the switch contacts open and an electrical signal is sent to the control box that activates the noisemaker.

Mercury detectors. Mercury detectors are sensitive to motion. When the detectors are at rest, the switch remains closed and the electrical current is prevented from flowing to the control box. When the detector is moved, the mercury inside also moves, opening the switch and sounding the alarm.

Screen detectors. Special screens with unnoticeable wire detectors built into them are also available. These screens are usually used over windows, such as louvered windows, where magnetic detectors are impractical. If the burglar cuts the screen to gain access to the window, a signal is sent to the control box and the noisemaker.

Other detectors. There are a variety of other detectors that are not commonly used, including: the all-purpose contact, the button contact, leaf springs, and the door trip switch.

Control Box

The control box is the electrical heart of the hardwire burglar alarm. It contains the switch you use to turn the alarm on and off and the controls that relay the electrical impulses from the detectors to the attracting device. It also regulates the power source of the system. If the system is dependent on your house electrical circuit, the control box monitors the power source. If, for whatever reason, the electrical power source goes

Magnetic detectors   **Control box**

dead, the control box will automatically switch to the battery back-up power supply so that the alarm can still be activated. (A battery backup is not included in all control box models.) The control box also functions as the brains of the system, managing and operating all the accessories you decide to buy.

Because the control box is so important, it must be well protected. It should be placed out of the reach of children and animals protected from bad weather and difficult to locate so burglars cannot tamper with it. However, it should not be so inaccessible that you avoid periodically checking to make sure that it is working properly.

A burglar who can tamper with the control box can foil your alarm. To ensure that he does not find the control box, you should *not* buy one with a noisemaker inside. For the same reason, you should install the noisemaker as far away from the conrol box as possible.

We strongly suggest that the control box you consider have the following accessories:

Key activating switch. If the control box has a simple knob or toggle switch, the burglar will be able to turn the alarm system off if he finds it. The control box should therefore have a key activating switch so that only you can turn the system on and off.

Battery back-up system. The control box is powered by the electrical current from your house. If the electrical power fails or the lines are cut, the alarm system will be useless. The control box should therefore have a battery back-up system that can operate for at least twenty-four hours. We recommend gel-cell batteries with an automatic recharger instead of lantern batteries. Lantern batteries can run down, whereas gel-cell batteries with an automatic recharger will assure you greater reliability of standby power. Whatever kind of batteries you choose, be sure to check them periodically.

Test switch. The control box should have a test switch that will allow you to check the condition of the batteries, detectors, and their connections. You should be able to conduct the test without activating the noisemaker, so you do not arouse your neighbors.

Shunt switch. One major problem you have to confront is how to rig your control box so you can get in and out of your house without sounding the alarm after you turn it on. A common solution to the entry/exit problem is to install a shunt switch, both inside and out, somewhere near the front door. This key-operated switch, wired to the control box, will shunt out the detector from the front door whenever you turn the key. As you are leaving the house, you turn the key in the shunt switch, go outside, and lock your door. You then turn the key in the outside shunt switch and reactivate the alarm. When you come home, reverse this process.

A shunt switch is also a handy device if you have children. During the day you can shunt out the detector in the front door. The kids can come and go through that door as they please, while the rest of the house remains protected by the alarm. The shunt switch thereby helps cut down on false alarms.

Tamper-resistant switch. There are problems with the shunt switch, however. Because the key operates from the outside of the house, the shunt switch lock can be picked by a professional burglar. The shunt switch can also be pulled away from the wall exposing the wires to the control box; the wires can then be cut and the system rendered useless. To counter these problems, install a tamper-resistant switch. The tamper-resistant switch is spring-loaded and placed against something stationary, such as a stud of the house, to hold the spring closed. If the shunt switch is pulled away from the house, the tamper-resistant switch will also be pulled from its position, the switch contacts will open, and the burglar alarm will sound.

Delay switch. A better way to solve the entry/exit problem is to install a delay switch with an automatic timer. The delay switch will allow you to get in or out of the front door before the alarm goes off. Most delay switch timers are adjustable up to one minute. This will give you time to turn off the control box with your key.

Constant ringing drop. An essential part of any control box is the constant ringing drop. This relay increases the effectiveness of your system if the detectors are put back in their proper places. When the detector sends an impulse to the circuit in the control box, the relay makes a contact between the power source and the attracting device. The alarm will then ring until the constant ringing drop is reset. If a burglar shuts your door immediately after entering, the alarm will not shut off, even though the detectors are back in the closed position.

Alarm timer. When a burglar alarm sounds, your neighbors are aroused and the police may respond. If it is a false alarm and you are not home, the police may have to break into your home to shut off the alarm unless your control box is equipped with some form of alarm timer. This device will automatically turn off the alarm after a designated period of time.

Instant alarm mode. The control box should be equipped with an instant alarm mode that will bypass the entry and exit delay switch. On occasion, particularly at night, you want the alarm to ring the instant an intruder tries to enter. You do not want to wait thirty seconds or more before the alarm is activated. By that time, the intruder could be inside your bedroom pointing a gun at you.

Panic button. A final accessory that should be wired to every control box is a panic button. Panic buttons are usually placed in one or two strategic locations, most commonly right next to the bed in the master bedroom and by the front door. If an intruder somehow gets inside your home, you would simply push the panic button and the burglar alarm is immediately set off.

Attracting Devices

All alarm systems have an attracting device to alert you of impending danger. Usually, the attracting device is some form of noisemaker, such as a bell or siren. But a light can also be used, either alone or in addition to the noisemaker; or a silent alarm can be installed — one that is not heard at the residence, but instead notifies the police or a private security company.

Both bells and sirens are effective noisemakers, if loud enough. However, we recommend a bell for a variety of reasons: Neighbors may mistake the siren on an alarm for a firetruck or ambulance; a bell is traditionally associated with an alarm; and furthermore, sirens are prohibited in some communities.

A bell alarm may be difficult to locate in a neighborhood with tall buildings because the buildings can deflect the noise and confuse the police. In this situation, therefore, you should supplement your noisemaker with a flashing light above your front door. A blue or orange flashing light, similar to the ones on top of police cars, will easily attract persons responding to your alarm.

You should place one noisemaker inside your residence, situated where you can hear it from every part of the house, particularly from the bedroom at night. The best place for a noisemaker is probably in the hallway near the bedrooms or over the front door aimed at the bedrooms.

Install another noisemaker outside your home. Place it as high as possible to keep the burglar from reaching it and cutting the wires. Put the noisemaker in a weatherproofed steel box, with louvered openings, and make sure no wires are visible. All wires should come through the wall or roof and the box should have a tamper-resistant switch.

Attracting devices can be designed to signal several people or agencies. First, the attracting device should make a lot of noise around your residence. This noise will alert you, your family, and your neighbors of potential danger, and it should scare away the intruder.

Second, the attracting device can be hooked up to the police station. Direct connection to your law enforcement agency over leased telephone lines or by an automatic telephone dialer (to be discussed shortly) is allowed in some communities. Check with your local law enforcement agency to see if a police hookup is permitted in your area.

Third, the attracting device can be connected to a private security company. This connection offers you the greatest protection, but it is also the most expensive. Trained operators at the security agency monitor alarm signals around the clock. Most incoming alarm signals are recorded and printed on paper by a computer printer for a permanent record. The guard service also checks your alarm system and guards your leased lines against sabotage or electrical failure. Some private agencies will dispatch guards immediately upon receiving an alarm signal from your residence. The central station will also call the police for you.

Fourth, the attracting device can be channeled to your neighbors by an interconnecting system of alarms. If an alarm sounds in any of the wired homes, all of the neighbors in the system are alerted. They will call the police and rush to your house to assist you.

Finally, the attracting device can be aimed to a central point in an apartment complex or planned living community, where a security guard is constantly on duty.

Installation of Hardwire Alarms

Installing a hardwire burglar alarm by yourself has several advantages. Doing it yourself is less expensive. You can save from 50 to 75 percent of the total cost by ordering your own parts and doing all of the labor. Assuming that you are a skilled and careful worker, you will know the installation is well done. If you install the alarm yourself, only you will know about it, and you will not have to worry about dishonest employees. Security companies are not required to give lie detector tests to job applicants. If you are handy with tools and have some familiarity with electronics equipment, you can probably install your own hardwire alarm system. Preferably you should also be skilled in carpentry and painting, since the electrical wires in the system ought to be hidden in the walls, the attic, or beneath the floor.

The components for any type of alarm are available through mail-order electronics component companies specializing in security equipment. One of the biggest is Mountain West Alarm Supply Company in Arizona, but any mail-order firm will gladly send you a catalogue. If you live in a metropolitan area, you can also check the Yellow Pages of your directory for local firms selling this equipment.

If you install an alarm, hide all detectors (switches and magnets) as well as possible. Visible detectors are accessible to an intruder, and he can defeat the system by wrapping a piece of wire, a ''jumper,'' around the switch contacts. The guarded entry point can then be opened without sounding the alarm. Hide the detectors by recessing the switch contacts into the door, door frames, and window frames. Use a special type of detector called drill mount detectors, which can be placed easily into holes you have drilled with the appropriate size bit. Then put a thin layer of paste wood filler over the switch contacts and paint them.

The best time to install a hardwire burglar alarm system is when the house is under construction. Without walls, floors, or ceilings to contend with, it is much easier to run the wires through the house. It is also easier to recess the detectors into the doors and frames. Ease of installation means costs are kept to a minimum.

In a high crime area, we recommend detectors on every door and window. If your neighborhood is relatively safe, detectors on your home's most vulnerable entry points — those not in plain view or with poor locks — should be sufficient.

To allow ventilation while maintaining security, we suggest you install two magnets and one switch on your windows. The first magnet will make contact with the contact switch when the window is closed and locked. The second magnet should be placed several inches higher so the window can be opened high enough for ventilation, but not so high that a person can reach through the window and meddle with the system. This procedure can also be used for sliding glass doors.

We will discuss installation of burglar alarms by professional security companies at the end of this chapter.

Wireless Alarm Systems

A wireless burglar alarm is essentially the same as a hardwire system in that both guard the perimeter of the residence and both have the same components. But there is one major difference: As the name implies, the wireless system has no electrical wires connecting the various components. Instead, each detector is wired to a small radio transmitter placed near the detector. When the guarded entry point is opened, the detector causes the transmitter to send a radio signal to a receiver, which is housed in or near the control box. The receiver, in turn, sounds the alarm.

The wireless alarm system has several advantages. Although the basic components can be costly, this type of alarm is generally less expensive than a hardwire system because installation costs are minimal. Since the system has no wires, you do not have to tear up floors or punch holes in walls throughout your house.

The transmitters and detectors on a wireless system are portable. They can be attached to objects away from the house, like a separate garage, shed, or barn. They can also be placed on vehicles (cars, recreational vehicles, motorcycles) located anywhere near the house, as long as the transmission signals are within range of the receiver. Wireless portable transmitters are also easier to take with you if you move.

Portable transmitters make panic buttons much handier. The panic buttons of hardwire systems are stationary — built into the house. The panic button on the wireless system can be moved about. You can carry it with you wherever you go around the house or yard. If, for example, you are in the backyard and see a stranger enter your house, you can push the panic button to set off the alarm.

The effective range of the transmitter depends on several factors: the location of the receiver, the construction of the building housing it, and the make and quality of the equipment. Usually, the range of transmission is from 100 to 200 feet, though some companies claim that their transmitters are reliable up to 500 feet from the receiver.

Unfortunately, wireless systems have some disadvantages. To secure your house properly, you need a transmitter at each door and window. Transmitters cost from $35 to $75 each, so if you have numerous entry points the system can be quite expensive.

Radio interference poses a significant problem for the wireless system. A burglar can jam your system with radio signals that confuse the receiver and void the system. Accidental interference is a more common problem. Wireless alarms are frequently set off by radio transmitters from passing airplanes, police cars, taxi cabs, garage door openers, and CB radios. Some manufacturers have recently solved the problem of stray radio transmission by using numerous radio frequencies, making it highly unlikely that stray radio transmissions will set off the alarm.

Wireless systems are less reliable than hardwire systems. Hardwire systems use the electrical current of your house with battery standby. Wireless systems run exclusively from battery power, which is more likely to fail. The wireless system has no device to notify you automatically if the system is not working properly. A battery might go dead in a transmitter and you would not notice it. It is therefore essential that you frequently check the components of a wireless system. Batteries in particular should be tested every couple of months.

Installation of the wireless system is essentially the same as that of the hardwire system, although you avoid stringing electrical wires all over the house. There are a few additional suggestions to consider if you install a wireless system. Place the receiver in a central location, accessible to all transmitters. Do not locate the receiver behind any metal objects, such as a screen door or a heating unit; metal blocks the radio waves to the receiver. Be sure to test the operation of the transmitter and receiver before they are installed to ensure that the transmission signals are reaching the receiver. It is also a good idea to test the panic button. Start the test near the house and move progressively farther away, so you can determine the maximum distance before the system fails to operate. When testing your system, use a quiet noisemaker so you do not disturb your neighbors. Install the regular noisemaker after you are certain the system works properly.

A Direct Link for Help
Until now, we have assumed the burglar alarm will only signal people in the immediate area. The alarm will alert you of impending danger, summon help from your neighbors, and frighten off the intruder. If, however, you install an automatic telephone dialer, you can have a direct security link to the police, friends, neighbors, or a private security guard company.

An automatic telephone dialer is a device that plugs into a telephone. If a burglar sets off the alarm, the telephone dialer will automatically dial the police or any person you designate. A recorded message informs the police that there is an emergency at your address. Telephone dialers cost from $250 to $500.

Telephone dialers can be programmed with several taped messages for different phone numbers. You would probably want the dialer to call the police first. Whether the police telephone line is busy or not, the dialer would next call, for example, your friend around the block. By the time the dialer gives its recorded messages to several people, someone would most likely be at your house to give you aid. Most dialers are wired so that once the burglar alarm is sounded, the dialer cannot be stopped from completing its calls merely by shutting off the alarm. If you want to stop the dialer and prevent false alarms, it should have a dialer-abort switch hidden on or near it.

Some telephone dialers come with two channels — one for burglary and one for fire. If the burglar alarm detects an intruder, the telephone dialer will automatically call the police. If the fire sensors detect smoke or heat, the dialer will call the fire department.

Automatic telephone dialers are not legal in some communitites and their use is severely restricted in others. In Portland, Oregon, and Evanston, Illionois, for example, it is illegal to hook up a telephone dialer to police emergency numbers. Be sure to check local ordinances and police regulations before you buy a telephone dialer.

We generally do not recommend the use of automatic telephone dialers. Since they are seldom used, they frequently malfunction when needed. The message on the recording can become so garbled that the police cannot understand the address of your residence. Moreover, the telephone dialer can be disconnected by cutting the telephone lines to your house. No calls, including the ones coming from the dialer, will leave your home. To counter this defect, the new dialers have a built-in line monitor device that measures the voltage on the phone line. If someone cuts your phone line and the voltage drops below normal, the alarm will sound. The attracting device should alert your neighbors who will call the police for you. Of course, the line monitor can lead to false alarms, if, for example, a storm blows the telephone line away from your home.

The best type of perimeter alarm is professionally installed and hooked to a central station by a leased telephone line. This system will cost between $800 and $8,000. Additionally there is a monthly charge of $20 to $125 to lease the telephone lines and to keep private guards on call. If the alarm is triggered, a coded message is sent to the central guard station. There, a guard decodes the message, prints out the nature of the emergency, and immediately sends security guards to your home. At the same time, the guard service informs the police that a burglar alarm has sounded at your address.

A leased telephone line is harder for a burglar to sabotage. If an intruder tampers with it, electronic surveillance equipment will notify the agency's office. At a minimum, security personnel will call the police. If you have paid for the service, guards will be immediately dispatched to your residence.

INTERIOR BURGLAR ALARM SYSTEMS

Interior alarm systems are designed to detect an intruder if he gets past the perimeter of a residence. Interior alarms operate on the theory that a burglar must walk through certain key points in your house to get to you or your valuables. Interior alarms are therefore placed at one or more strategic locations, such as the living room or the hallway leading to the bedrooms.

In general, perimeter alarm systems provide better security than interior alarm systems. But a combination of perimeter and interior alarms will offer you the greatest security.

Hardwire and Wireless Detectors

Hardwire and wireless interior alarms are exactly like the perimeter systems just described, except that the detectors for the interior system are placed inside the house. Interior systems of some type have been used throughout history. The Japanese, for example, used "nightingale floors" in the eighteenth century. Because Japanese nobility were afraid enemies would sneak up during the night, they intentionally installed creaky floors to alert them of danger. Modern interior systems work on the same principle. If an intruder gets into your home, he will have to walk down a hallway or up stairs to get to your family. The detectors are placed strategically under your rugs or mats (called pressure mats). If anyone steps on them, the alarm will sound. Pressure mats can also be placed under windows and near doors.

Hardwire and wireless perimeter alarms can be adapted easily for interior protection. All of the components are the same. It is simply a matter of placing detectors in key points throughout the house.

Motion Detectors

The most common interior alarms work by detecting the motion of an intruder. Motion detectors erect an invisible barrier around the interior of a room. If anyone enters the room, the alarm will sound. The greatest benefit to the motion alarm is its simplicity for the home owner. To install most motion detectors, all you do is plug them in. You do not have to string wire all over the house or set transmitters on all windows and doors. Motion detectors are therefore better for apartment use. The tenant can take the motion detector with him when he moves.

Inconvenience is the main problem with motion detectors. There can

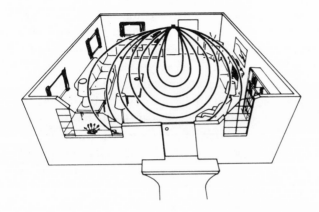

Motion detector burglar alarm

be absolutely *no* motion in the room when the alarm is on. Children or pets roaming around the house at night will cause false alarms. You cannot have the alarm set when you are working around the house during the day, nor can you have it in your bedroom at night.

Despite disadvantages, motion alarm systems are the fastest-selling home burglar alarm. They are marketed all over the country, even at large retail stores like Sears, and are priced for the average family, ranging from $200 to $500.

There are several types of motion alarm systems, differing whether they detect motion by sound, heat, light, or microwaves.

Sound (Ultrasonic) Systems
Sound systems detect intruders by measuring changes in ultrasonic waves. A transmitter sends out high-pitched ultrasonic waves on a specific frequency and a receiver picks up the waves. When someone enters the guarded area and the pattern of sound is altered, the receiver detects the change and sets off the alarm. The sound detectors don't actually ''hear'' the burglar, but detect his motion. Ultrasonic alarms are compact and can be disguised easily. Some models are designed to look like a large book, which, when placed on your bookshelf, are difficult for the intruder to locate.

Although ultrasonic alarms have many advantages over perimeter systems, they also create many problems. Ultrasonic alarms are relatively easy to defeat. In the older models, the intruder need only unplug the alarm to render it useless. The newer models have remedied this defect by providing battery back-up power inside the unit. The alarm will continue to sound even if the burglar pulls the plug.

Lack of battery backup would not be a serious problem if the units could be locked up, inaccessible to the burglar. But to be effective the units must be in plain sight. Even an alarm disguised as a book is easy to find when it sounds, since the noisemaker is contained inside the unit. Some newer models, however, have detached noisemakers. One noisemaker should be centrally located inside the house; the other should be placed outside the house so your neighbors can hear it.

False alarms are common with ultrasonic alarms. Even the slightest noises may disrupt the transmitted sound waves and set off the alarm. The ultrasonic alarm cannot distinguish between a burglar and a ringing telephone, air conditioner, or noisy heater. The biggest source of false alarms comes from children or pets roaming the protected area. Sounds from outside the house can also sound the alarm. You should place the alarm in a quiet and protected area, blocking out most external noises.

Ultrasonic alarms are not recommended for people with sensitive ears. Even if you do not hear the ultra-high-pitched noises, you may get headaches. This problem applies to pets as well. Even if your pet is in the garage or backyard, he may howl continuously when the ultrasonic alarm is turned on.

Ultrasonic alarms do not work well in rooms with plush furnishings, such as thick carpets, long drapes, and soft chairs. Since soft materials absorb sound, the ultrasonic sound waves sent from the transmitter will have difficulty reaching the receiver. An ultrasonic system works best in rather sparsely decorated areas, like hallways or entryways.

The delay timers on ultrasonic units do not provide sufficient security. The delay timer allows you to get in and out of the house before your own motion will sound the alarm. The delay must last from twenty seconds to two minutes. But the delay also gives the burglar as much time as it gives you. He will have plenty of time to look around the house and defeat the alarm before it can sound. The burglar will also have time to reach your bedroom and threaten your life by the time the alarm has sounded.

Ultrasonic alarms are expensive if you want to protect an entire house. Full protection would require two or three separate units, costing from $200 to $300 each. For that amount of money, it would be better to buy a good perimeter system. Perimeter systems offer better security and are easier to live with.

Heat (Thermal) Systems

Heat systems detect intruders by measuring any new or changing source of heat in the guarded area. The heat sensor detects a burglar's body heat and sounds the alarm. The heat alarm has several advantages over the ultrasonic system. It has only one unit, containing the thermal detector, whereas the ultrasonic system requires both a transmitter and a receiver. Heat systems are also less prone to false alarms. They are designed to adjust to gradual temperature changes, so that the alarm will not sound, for example, as your room heats up with the morning sun.

Heat systems have some drawbacks. Like ultrasonic systems, they cannot be used if you have animals loose in the house; the body temperature of a dog or cat will trigger the alarm. A heat alarm is also generally more expensive than an ultrasonic system, ranging in price from $200 to $400.

Light Systems

There are two types of light systems: photoelectric and infrared. Photoelectric systems have a transmitter and a receiver. The transmitter sends out a tiny beam of light across a doorway or hallway that the receiver monitors. If anyone crosses through the beam of light, disrupting the transmission, the alarm will sound. This is the type of detection device you have seen countless times at store entrances.

We do not recommend the photoelectric system as a residential burglar alarm. Of all the motion detectors, it is the easiest to defeat. The beam of light from the transmitter to the receiver is visible, especially at night. To foil the system, the burglar merely has to shine a flashlight (or any light source) into the receiver. He can then walk through the beam without sounding the alarm.

The infrared light detector is superior to the photoelectric detector as a residential burglar alarm. Because infrared light from the transmitter is invisible, a burglar is more likely to be caught by surprise and he will have a harder time avoiding the system. The infrared system also has pulsed signals. Assuming a burglar knew where the transmitter and receiver were located, he could shine an infrared flashlight into the receiver, defeating the alarm. With a pulsed infrared light, however, he would need an identical transmission source, which he is unlikely to have.

You can adjust infrared light transmission signals to be wide or narrow. A wide beam protects a larger area than the photoelectric eye. A narrow beam can be aimed a few feet off the floor, giving animals freedom to roam at night without sounding the alarm. Infrared transmitters and receivers come in several models. They are frequently designed as light sockets so that they are difficult for an intruder to spot, and they cost from $225 to $450.

Microwave Systems
The microwave system contains both a transmitter and a receiver. The transmitter emits high frequency microwave radiation and the receiver measures the bounce of the waves off objects in the guarded area. Any motion in the protected area will alter the pattern of the waves. The receiver will detect the change and sound the alarm.

The microwave system has one main advantage over the ultrasonic system. Microwave radiation cannot be heard by humans or animals, so there is less chance of headaches and howling pets. However, we generally do not recommend microwave alarms for residential use. They are extremely sensitive and prone to false alarms. Microwave radiation can travel through walls and pick up motion outside the house. Passersby on the sidewalk, cars in the street, animals in the front yard — all may disrupt normal microwave patterns in the house and activate the alarm. The alarms are also sensitive in the house. A bird hopping in its cage or a fan turning in the hall can make the alarm go off. Finally, they are expensive. Prices range from $750 to several thousand dollars.

SPOT BURGLAR ALARMS

Spot burglar alarms are individual, self-contained units that protect one spot (door or window) in a residence. If an intruder does not enter through the spot you have protected, you will not know he is inside until it is too late.

Since the spot alarm protects only one door or window, it will take several of them to secure an entire home. Therefore, spot alarms are best for an apartment with only a few entry points. They are also useful while you are on vacation. You can place them on the door of your motel or hotel room at night for a greater sense of security. The primary benefit of spot alarms is their low price, which ranges from $2.50 to $50.

Spot alarms provide the least security for you and your family. Most spot alarms can be set only from the inside of the house, providing some protection when you are home. If, however, you go out for the evening or are on vacation, you will not have an alarm to deter an intruder or signal your neighbors.

Since the spot alarm is a self-contained unit, it must be mounted next to the door or window it is protecting. Almost as soon as the alarm sounds, most burglars could easily disarm it. If the batteries are weak or the bell is not loud, you may not even hear the alarm for the few seconds it is sounding. The alarm may scare off an unsophisticated teenager, but not a seasoned criminal.

Spot alarms can be a valuable part of your security if they are used properly. Some spot alarms offer very tight security when used in addition to another alarm system. Proximity detectors create an electrostatic field around the protected object. A person who puts his hand near the object will disrupt the electrostatic field and trigger the alarm. A proximity detector should be used in conjunction with a perimeter alarm system, in case the burglar is clever enough to defeat your first line of defense.

How to Make Your Own Spot Alarm
You can make your own spot alarm with little trouble, probably from

spare parts you already have around the house. Called a trip alarm, it is designed to protect one door or window.

You need the following parts for your trip alarm:

1. A six-volt dry cell battery. (A twelve-volt battery is fine, but it is more expensive.)

2. A door bell or a horn from a car.

3. A set of automobile points (old ones are fine).

4. Several feet of light electrical wire, cut into three equal pieces.

5. A small piece of flat plastic (about one inch long and 1/6 inch thick) to be used as an insulator.

6. About five feet of old fishing line (two-pound test is sufficient).

To set up the alarm, you must first hook the battery, bell, and points in a series with the electrical wire. (See diagram). Lead a wire from one post of the battery to one of the bell hookups. Attach one end from another piece of wire to the second bell hookup and secure the other end of the wire to the arm of the points (position A). Fasten one end of the third wire to position B on the points and run it to the second post on the battery. (Note: If you do not have the insulator inserted between the

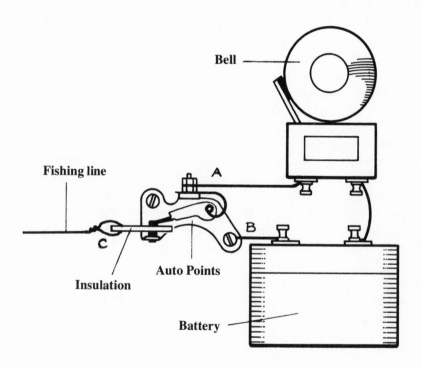

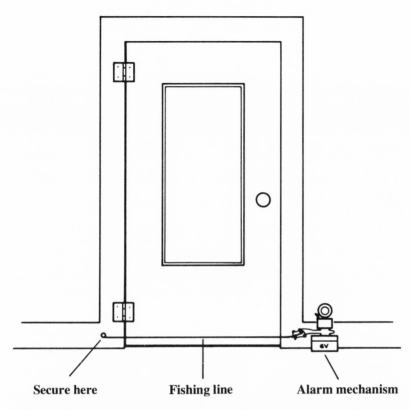

| Secure here | Fishing line | Alarm mechanism |

contacts of the points at position C, the bell will ring.) Next drill a small hole through one end of the plastic insulator.

To install the alarm across the door, securely fasten the alarm mechanism to the door frame inside the house, close to the floor and on the side where the door opens. Tie one end of the fishing line through the hole in the insulation and put the insulation between the contact points at position C. Pull the fishing line tight across the door (without pulling the insulation away from the points), and secure the loose end of the line to the inside of the door frame, near the lower hinges. Now, if someone enters, the opening door will hit the fishing line and pull the insulator out from the contact points. When the metal points touch, the electrical current will pass from the battery to the bell, and the alarm will sound.

THINGS TO REMEMBER IF YOU BUY A BURGLAR ALARM

If you decide to buy a burglar alarm, you should carefully consider the kind of system you need, the company you deal with, and the contract you sign.

The System

The rapidly increasing demand for security equipment has resulted in many fly-by-night companies that put out inferior products. We strongly reommend that you first determine the degree of security you desire and then purchase the best quality of system to fit your needs. Products that don't work well offer little protection; they are a waste of money. To avoid inferior products, make sure the equipment you are considering meets the highest standards of the Underwriters' Laboratories, an independent, nationwide organization for the testing and screening of electrical products.

Any alarm system you buy must give off a noise loud enough to attract attention. An alarm system is worthless if you sleep right through it. We recommend that the noisemaker emit a noise of at least ninety decibels, preferably one hundred.

All burglar alarms should be properly installed. A suitable location for burglar alarms will help prevent false alarms, ensure proper functioning, and lower the chances that the alarm will be defeated.

Regular testing is a must. Your alarm will not do you any good if it malfunctions. Often, particularly with the less expensive systems, you cannot tell if your alarm is working properly if you do not test it. Test the batteries of your system every couple of months. Check and test the operation of the other parts of the system every few months, and replace old parts.

No matter what type of system you buy, you should fully understand how it works. Be sure to get written instructions for the use and testing of the system. If you have the alarm installed, the security expert will be happy to give you complete instructions. Have the entire family listen to the instructions. All family members must cooperate to ensure

that the system provides the highest possible security. Family cooperation will also prevent false alarms. Finally, learn the pros and cons of
each system you are considering. Check *Consumer Reports* for an
objective appraisal of each alarm and talk with people who already
have systems in their homes. Find out which system is best for you.

The Company

If you buy an elaborate, expensive perimeter system, you may decide
to have a burglar alarm (security) company install the system for you.
There are several ways to make sure you are dealing with a reputable
company. Call the Better Business Bureau or your local law enforcement agency to find out if the company you are considering has had any
complaints lodged against it. Contact Underwriters' Laboratories,
which distributes a nationwide list of approved companies. Check with
the consumer protection division of your local district attorney's office
or with the state attorney general. You can also write to the Security
Equipment Industry Association (SEIA) or the National Burglar and
Fire Alarm Association for suggestions about firms in your area. If you
contact a company, obtain a list of personal references. Call former
customers to see if they are pleased with the quality of work and service
they have received.

The company you select should be an established firm with a proven
record of service and performance. A company representative rather
than an authorized repair center should service your alarm system. All
employees of the alarm company who have access to your house or
equipment should be bonded. Choose a company that will provide a
manufacturer's guarantee against defective parts and is qualified to
sell, install, and maintain the same system.

After you have chosen a company, call to make an appointment with
a representative. Get the name of the representative and make sure the
person who arrives is the one you expect. It is advisable to secure
estimates from several different companies to make sure you pay the
lowest prices offered. Dealing with several different companies also
exposes you to a wider variety of alarm systems suitable to your needs.

The Contract

The alarm company you deal with should make a written proposal and give you a copy of the contract you will be signing. Read it thoroughly. Have your lawyer look at it if it is hard to understand. Never sign a contract that does not list all of the areas to be protected and does not itemize the equipment to be installed. The company should also give you a design proposal covering the areas of your house to be protected. Check to see that the items listed in the contract match the items covered in the design proposal.

Your salesman may tell you your system will reduce your insurance rates, but do not take his word for it. Call your own insurance agent to find out for sure. No reliable firm will give a lifetime guarantee. If your company offers one, be suspicious and call the Better Business Bureau.

You should insist on a contract that specifies continuing maintenance and service. The contract should specify in a maintenance schedule how often the company will service your system and the costs of the service. If your alarm system has to be repaired at the alarm company, find out what company will give you a "loaner" alarm while yours is out of the house.

Finally, you should realize that you do not have to purchase an alarm system to be protected. You can also lease one. Leasing a system has advantages. The company that leases it to you is responsible for maintaining it. The thought of losing a potential customer will motivate the company to do a good job.

CONCLUSION

If a burglar alarm is of good quality, installed well, and used properly, it can be a valuable tool in preventing crime and providing greater peace of mind to the owner. Yet, security systems can also be a nuisance; they are prone to false alarms and they may substantially alter your living habits. We suggest that you carefully evaluate your security needs before investing in a burglar alarm system. Talk with people in your neighborhood who have had a burglar alarm installed and try to determine whether, given your personal circumstances, you would use one enough to justify the expense.

A burglar alarm is not designed to take the place of the security measures outlined in the previous chapter. If you have a limited budget, we believe your money would be best spent by installing high quality locks on all doors and windows — and making sure you use them.

Chapter 3

Vehicle Theft

Vehicle theft is one of the most prevalent crimes in the United States. Every day vehicles of all kinds are stolen, some for kicks and some purely for profit. In this chapter we concentrate on the two most common types of vehicle theft: car and bicycle theft. But most of the tips we offer can also be used to protect other vehicles such as trucks, motorcycles, and recreational vehicles.

CAR THEFT

Car theft is big business. According to the *Uniform Crime Reports* over one million automobiles were stolen in 1980; that's one every thirty two seconds. More than two hundred cars are ripped off every day in New York City alone. Since cars are becoming more expensive, the incidence of car theft is likely to increase in the future.

The likelihood of your car being stolen depends primarily on you. Car theft, like most offenses, is a crime of opportunity, whether it is committed by a thrill-seeking teenager or by a professional. When you take away the thief's opportunities, you also reduce your chances of being victimized. The well-protected car is passed up for an easier target.

Who Is the Car Thief?

Car thieves can be categorized as amateurs or professionals. Approximately 75 percent of stolen cars are taken by amateurs. Sometimes called "temporary users" by criminal justice experts, amateurs are generally young, most typically juveniles out for a joyride. FBI statistics show that over 60 percent of all persons arrested for car theft are under age eighteen, and many are under age sixteen — too young to obtain a driver's license. The joyriding juvenile has no intention of keeping the car or profiting financially from the theft. Normally he abandons the car after a few hours, and it will usually be recovered in a short time.

Young people steal cars for a variety of reasons. Because the automobile represents a status symbol to the young set, teenagers sometimes steal cars to drive to school and impress their peers. They also steal cars just to drive around. The simple act of cruising around is relaxing to young people; it gives them a feeling of freedom and independence. Whatever their motives, amateur car thieves have one thing in common: They act when the opportunity arises, such as when a car is unlocked or the keys are left in the ignition.

Professional thieves, responsible for roughly one-quarter of all car thefts, intend permanently to deprive the owner of his property. Most pros are in business strictly for the money — usually to profit directly from the sale of the car or its parts. Often the profits are staggeringly high. A good professional car thief can routinely make between $100,000 and $200,000 per year. Professional car thieves often work in rings and are frequently associated with organized crime. Only organized crime can finance the huge budget needed for large and sophisticated theft operations.

Professional thieves work fast. In one experiment conducted by the Commonwealth of Massachusetts, a reformed car thief was timed breaking into twenty cars. His average time was forty-three seconds — three to get into the car and forty to take out the ignition and start the car. Another professional thief, recently convicted of heading a nine-state auto ring, told a Senate permanent investigations committee, "At the time of my conviction, I could steal almost any American-made car in less than ninety seconds and could steal most cars in forty to fifty seconds."

Professional car theft appears to be growing, in part because of the ever-increasing profits and the encroachment of organized crime. One indication of the growth of professional car theft is the decline in the percentage of cars recovered. In 1963, for example, 91 percent of all stolen cars were recovered. By 1978 the recovery rate had plunged to only 61 percent.

Professional car thieves can be broken down into three subcategories. Pros who steal cars for resale — to make a fast buck — are the most common type. Frequently, they belong to a well-organized ring that is set up to disguise stolen cars and sell them to waiting customers. These professionals often go for late-modeled, high-powered cars, typically Cadillacs, Lincolns, Mercedes Benzes, and Jaguars. However, professional car thieves will steal anything "on order." One gang operating out of New York City specialized in stealing luxury cars with little mileage, called "cream puffs." The ring would obtain fake registration, replace the serial numbers, change the appearance of the car, and then sell it to customers at discount prices. Another ring in Dallas specialized in stealing Chevelles and Corvettes from shopping centers and apartment house parking lots. After altering the identification numbers and giving the car a new look, the thieves resold the cars to dealers or at public auctions. If you have the right contacts in some parts of the country, you can put in an order for any type of vehicle you want. You can probably have your car delivered to you faster than a legitimate dealer can provide one, and at discount prices.

The second subcategory of professional thief does not intend to resell the entire car as a unit, but to strip it down and sell its parts. In 1979 law enforcement officials told members of the Senate Governmental Affairs Committee that thousands of stolen cars are taken to "chop shops," which dismantel the cars and sell the parts to legitimate garages and body shops. Getting new parts from factory distributors often takes weeks and requires expensive assembly work. Chop shops thrive, therefore, because they provide twenty-four-hour service and supply assembled units ready for installation. A garage or body shop can order a part from a chop shop, whose operator will then order that a car with that part be stolen. The chop shop gets the stolen car the next day and takes out the part the customer needs. Both the chop shop and the garage make money on the transaction. The FBI currently has over six hundred theft rings and chop shops under investigation.

The third type of professional thief intends to profit indirectly from the car theft. This pro steals a car to use in another crime. In preparing for a "big job," usually a robbery, the professional criminal must find suitable transportation and also prevent the police from identifying him through his license plates. Stealing a car is a common solution. The FBI estimates that approximately 5 percent of all stolen cars are used to commit another crime.

Why Should You Be Concerned?
You may not feel particularly concerned about automobile theft, in part because the chances of your car being stolen are relatively low. Even if your car were ripped off, you may have insurance to pay for a new one. Nevertheless, you should seriously try to prevent the theft of your car for several compelling reasons. You will face endless inconvenience if your car is stolen, particularly if it is not immediately recovered. Also, the theft may occur under conditions that leave you stranded, possibly late at night in an isolated area. Police reports take a lot of time, and if the thief is caught you may have to go to court. Filling out insurance forms is also a big hassle, and often you don't receive payment for months.

The direct and indirect financial costs are also good reasons to guard against car theft. The damage done to cars stolen, but later recovered, averages about $200. When cars that are not recovered are entered into the equation, the average loss due to car theft is $2500. Figuring in recovery efforts, paperwork, and cash payments, stolen cars cost insurance companies more than $3 billion each year. The criminal justice system also pays heavily for the car thief. Law enforcement spends millions annually for the apprehension and conviction of car thieves. Even more dollars are spent maintaining car thieves in prison. Roughly 28 percent of the inhabitants of federal prisons were convicted of interstate auto theft according to the Federal Bureau of Prisons. In addition, thousands of car thieves are incarcerated in state and local jails and prisons. The next time you complain about high insurance rates and taxes, think about what you have done to prevent car theft.

Preventing harm to others is perhaps the most important reason to guard against car theft. Many stolen cars are used in the perpetration of other crimes, causing injury to innocent victims. Moreover, a car thief driving a stolen vehicle is two hundred times more likely to be in an accident than a person driving his own car. In 1979, over 150,000 stolen cars were involved in accidents; more than 20,000 people were injured or maimed and more than 600 were killed in the smashups. It would weigh heavily on your conscience if your neglect in preventing car theft resulted in injury or death to innocent victims.

General Precautions

You can lower the chances of having your car stolen in a variety of ways, some of which require very little effort and don't cost a thing. The general precautions we present are particularly important to observe at night, since that is when two-thirds of all car thefts occur. Of utmost importance is never to leave your keys in your car unattended. This may sound like elementary advice, but statistics show that 40 percent of all stolen cars had the keys left in the ignition. You should remove your keys for other reasons too. It is illegal in most communities to leave keys in an unattended car. Furthermore, you can be held legally responsible for any damages caused by your stolen car if you left the keys in the ignition. Also, never leave your car with the engine running, even for a moment. Thieves often hang out at fast-food stores or quick-stop markets waiting for a ''fish'' to leave his car idling. And don't hide a spare key under the floor mat or over the sun visor. That's as foolish as leaving a house key under the doormat.

Another safeguard of primary importance is never to leave your car unlocked. Over 80 percent of all stolen cars were unlocked at the time of the theft. A paramount reason for locking your car whenever you leave it is that you will usually have to remove the keys to do so. Locking your car also prevents robbers from hiding behind your front seat waiting for you to return. And third, although locking your car doesn't guarantee against theft, it definitely lowers the probabilities. A locked car will prevent the vast majority of thefts, particularly by joyriders. Though a locked car won't necessarily stop the professional thief, it may make him so uncomfortable with his work that he will look elsewhere. Get into the habit of locking your car, even if you will be away from it for only a few minutes.

Avoid leaving your keys with parking lot attendants, who often work in league with theft rings. If you must park where you are required to leave your car keys, leave only the key to the ignition. If you leave your house keys attached to the same chain, the parking lot attendant or his friends may make duplicates and use them later to burglarize your home.

Your parking habits also determine the probability of your car being stolen. If you have a garage, keep your car locked inside, especially at night. If you have two cars but your garage is too small for both, leave the less valuable one outside. If neither one fits inside the garage, park the more valuable car next to the house and block the driveway with the other. Thieves like to work in dark and isolated areas; don't give them what they want. Whenever you park away from home, leave your car in a well-lighted and busy location. In parking lots or public garages, try to park near the toll booth or where your car is most likely to be seen by passersby.

Antitheft Devices

Stopping a professional car thief is impossible if he really wants your car. You can, however, deter most amateurs and perhaps frustrate and delay many professionals so they will pass up your car and look for an easier target.

You have at your disposal a wide array of antitheft devices offering successive lines of defense: Some prevent the thief from getting into your car; some prevent him from starting it; and some prevent him from driving it away. No one antitheft device is foolproof; only a combination of systems can offer maximum security.

In this section we describe and give the advantages and disadvantages of some of the most common antitheft devices. Luckily, some of the most useful and effective antitheft devices are also the least expensive. Unless a specific company or distributor is mentioned, most of these devices are available through regular electronics supply houses or auto parts stores.

Door locks. Your first line of defense is preventing the thief from getting into your car. Most thieves enter a locked car by lifting up the

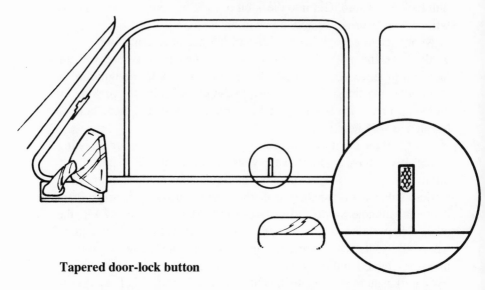

Tapered door-lock button

inside door-lock button with a coat hanger twisted through the top of the window. For a couple of dollars you can replace the standard door-lock buttons with the slim, tapered kind that are impossible to pull up with a piece of wire (see illustration). For added security, a locksmith can sell you deadbolt locks designed specifically for cars.

Alarms. Another way to prevent your car from being broken into is with alarms that sound when anyone tampers with the car's doors or windows. There are two types of alarm systems. For as little as $20, you can buy an alarm system that activates the car's horn. This alarm is also easy for a mechanically inclined person to install. A different type of alarm sets off a loud siren or bell under the hood. If you install one of these alarms yourself, it will cost as little as $30; having one installed will generally cost between $75 and $100. Better alarm systems are much more expensive. A Babaco alarm, the best car alarm system, runs from $100 to $400. This alarm, difficult to defeat, is used by thousands of sales representatives who carry samples of expensive merchandise in their cars.

Car alarms have several disadvantages. Good alarms are relatively expensive compared to other antitheft devices. Experience shows, moreover, that people who buy car alarms don't use them as often as they should. People frequently forget to turn them on, or simply don't use them if they are going to be away from the car for a short period. Many people avoid using the system because of false alarms. Another major disadvantage is the relative ease with which most alarms can be defeated by the experienced thief. The professional might, for example, open the hood and quickly pry off one of the battery cables to quiet the alarm; after disconnecting the alarm, he would replace the battery cable and proceed as usual. Alarms that work from the pressure switch on the door (the button that operates the dome light) are even easier to defeat. If the thief quickly closes the door behind him, the alarm turns off. If you install an alarm, be sure it is the type of system that once activated will continue to sound for at least two minutes. Alarms have one final problem. They do not prevent a thief from starting your car or driving it away once he gets inside. What are you going to do when the alarm sounds? Will you go out to stop or arrest the thieves? What if there are several of them or they are armed? You can call the police, but by the time they arrive the thieves will be long gone with your car.

Steering wheel locks. If a thief does break into your car, your second line of defense is preventing him from driving it away. One way to accomplish this is to lock your steering wheel. Most new cars come equipped with steering wheel locks, but if you drive an older model, you can purchase a separate, specially designed steering wheel lock for between $10 and $30. A steering wheel lock may be either one in an armored collar that locks the steering wheel and the brake pedal together, or it may be one that goes around the steering wheel and locks the gearshift into place. It would take a tungsten carbide-coated hacksaw more than ten minutes to cut through either one of these locks.

Rotor removal. Another way to prevent your car from being started is simply to lift up the hood, pry off the distributor cap, and remove the rotor. Even professional thieves are unlikely to carry a spare rotor that will fit your car specifically. This is probably one of the most effective antitheft tactics, and it doesn't cost a penny. However, this procedure is a nuisance, particularly if you are running errands or making frequent stops. This method is probably best used in high crime areas at night or when you leave your car for a long time, for example, in an airport parking lot for several days.

Electrical cut-off switch. An effective, yet more convenient method of preventing a thief from starting your car is with an electrical cut-off switch. When activated, this switch cuts off all electrical power from the battery to the coil or the distributor. The engine will turn over, but the thief cannot start the car without first shutting off the switch. You can install this device yourself for as little as $3.50. Obviously you should not mount the switch in an easily noticeable place, such as in the glove compartment or under the ignition switch. Hidden deep under the dashboard is the safest spot.

Gasoline shut-off system. A new type of antitheft device stops the flow of gasoline to the fuel pump. The less expensive type of gasoline shutoff system does nothing to prevent the thief from starting the car, but he will be stopped short as soon as the gasoline left in the carburetor is used up. This system has serious disadvantages, and we do not recommend it. It does not prevent the thief from driving the car away. Even if he drives only a few blocks, he may have enough time to find the hidden switch, turn it off, and return the flow of gasoline to the engine. The thief may also be able to drive your car to a deserted location where he and his accomplices can quickly strip the car of its parts. A better system, costing as much as $175, prevents the thief from starting the car in the first place. This system, controlled by a five-digit code entered through an eighteen-button keyboard mounted under the dashboard, was designed originally to prevent drunk drivers from starting their cars. It now functions as an effective antitheft device because even if the thief has the keys to the car, he will be unable to get it started without knowing the code.

Motion-sensor system. Finally, a different sort of antitheft device, one that detects the jostling or tilting of a vehicle, acts as a third line of defense. These motion-sensitive systems are particularly useful against professional thieves, since 40 percent of all cars stolen by pros are simply towed away. The most expensive motion-sensor systems, costing about $100, come with hardware, sensors, wires, and sirens. If you already have a standard alarm system, you can add motion-detection capabilities by attaching a motion-sensor switch to your existing system. Motion-sensor switches that mount easily under the hood sell for as little as $5 at some electronic supply stores. You can also buy a less complicated and expensive motion-sensor system, one designed originally to prevent the theft of costly Mag wheels. This vibration-sensitive alarm links your car's wheels to its horn or siren, and when the car is jacked up, a switch triggers the alarm and sounds the horn.

Protecting the Contents and Accessories of Your Car
Car thieves often do not want to steal an entire automobile, but only its valuable parts, accessories, or contents. Known in the trade as "car boosters" or "car clouts," these thieves strike fast and make off with batteries, CB radios, car stereos, or anything valuable that can be easily removed from the inside of the car.

Most of the advice we have given to deter the car thief will also hinder the car booster. By always locking your car and buying tapered door locks, you will keep most amateur thieves out of your car. A few additional tips, however, should further reduce the chances that you will be victimized by a car booster. Never leave packages, luggage, or other tempting items — no matter how worthless — exposed in your car. A thief walking by won't know the value of the packages, and he may be unable to resist breaking into your car to find out. At the very least, you will suffer the cost and inconvenience of having the damage to your car repaired. Lock all valuables in the trunk. However, you will be pressing your luck if you keep expensive items in your trunk for any length of time. Experienced thieves assume valuables are stored in the trunk and that is the first place they look.

Electronics equipment such as stereos, tape decks, and CB radios are special targets of car boosters. Using a lock specifically designed for electronics equipment is one means of protection. You can also install an electronic equipment alarm. The sensors on the alarm work independently of other alarm switches, giving you double protection. We recommend that you install your electronics equipment on a slide mount. Whenever you park for an extended period or in an area where you are likely to get ripped off, you can quickly slide the equipment out of the bracket and store it in the trunk of your car or in your home.

Because CB radios have proved so popular with thieves, a few companies now offer new models that are much more difficult to steal. The transceiver of the new models is mounted in the trunk of the car. All of the necessary controls (speaker/mike, channel selection, volume, etc.) are situated in the handset, which can be hidden under the seat or easily detached for storage in the trunk.

BICYCLE THEFT

Bicycle sales have increased sharply during the past several years, due largely to skyrocketing gas prices and the physical fitness boom. As sales have increased, so have bicycle thefts. The growing demand makes stolen bicycles easier to sell and, since bicycles are getting more expensive, theft is more profitable. If you follow the preventive measures outlined in this section, the chances of your bicycle being stolen will be significantly reduced.

General Precautions

You should register your bicycle with the local law enforcement agency. This is advisable because it is illegal in most communities not to have it registered, and registration acts as a deterrent. Experience has proved that thieves are less likely to steal registered bicycles. They do not want to get caught with a bicycle that the police can easily trace, and a registered bike is harder to sell. If your bike is stolen, registration increases the chances that it will be recovered. The vast majority of stolen bicycles returned to their owners are registered. Getting a nonregistered bicycle back is next to impossible; the police can't return what they are unable to identify.

In the past, the police put the registration or license number on a small piece of sheet metal and strapped it to the back of the bicycle. But because this type of license was easy to snip off, the police now more commonly imprint the registration number with a metal stamp directly into the metal frame of the bicycle. Far more stolen bicycles are now returned to their owners because these indented registration numbers are so difficult to obliterate. If the police in your area do not imprint the registration number on your bicycle, you should engrave your driver's license number in several places on the frame. (See the section on Operation Identification in Chapter 1.)

An essential precaution is *always* to lock your bicycle, no matter where you park it. Unlocked and unattended bicycles are invitations for thieves. In an informal departmental experiment, Oakland, California's police department left unlocked bicycles in a downtown area. The bicycles lasted an average of twenty seconds! Most bicycles are stolen directly from the owner's property — from an open garage or the front yard. Strangers walking by are tempted when they see an unattended bicycle in easy reach. It is also important, therefore, that you keep your bicycle inside a locked garage or home when it is not in use.

A person who is determined to steal your bicycle can do it, but the right preventive measures will deter most thieves from choosing your bicycle. The rest of this section outlines the most common means of securing your bicycle — a padlock and chain or cable, and the new locks designed specifically for bicycle security.

Padlocks

Padlocks come in a number of shapes and sizes, designed for several levels of security. Some padlocks (for example, "shell" or "warded" padlocks) are designed primarily for nuisance protection; they are useful for keeping children out of toolboxes or liquor cabinets. But inexpensive locks are easily broken and not suited for protecting an expensive bicycle.

Any padlock, no matter how expensive, can be defeated. But good padlocks will buy you time, and time is your ally. Thieves don't want to work ten or fifteen minutes to open a lock. They would rather move on to easier pickings.

A padlock used to secure a valuable bicycle should therefore meet certain minimal specifications. First, to be resistant to bolt cutters and hacksaws, the shackle of the padlock must be at least 9/32 of an inch thick. (See illustration.) Of course, the thicker the shackle the better. The shackle must also be made of case-hardened steel. Look for the word "hardened" imprinted on the shackle. Alloyed-steel shackles offer even greater resistance to cutting and sawing. A padlock can also be opened by prying the shackle loose, as thieves often do with a "shackle popper." To lower the likelihood of prying or popping, get a double-locking shackle — one that locks both at the "heel" and the "toe" of the lock. A "shrouded" shackle, that is, one where the case of the lock surrounds the shackle, will also make the use of a shackle popper much more difficult.

The case of the padlock must be resistant to smashing and pounding.

A laminated case, one with a series of metal plates riveted together under thousands of pounds of pressure, provides the greatest security. Laminated locks are stronger than solid metal ones in the same sense that a piece of plywood, made of several sheets of thin wood pressed together, is stronger than a comparable piece of solid wood.

Finally, a padlock with precision tumbler locks gives the greatest protection. Compared to a "warded" lock with only a handful of working parts, a four-pin-tumbler lock of similar appearance has at least nineteen precision parts. Machined by precision tools, the pin-tumbler lock provides a larger key selection to prevent accidental key duplication, and guards against picking by a screwdriver, pin, or other metal objects.

The lock specifications just described are for the maximum security needed with expensive bicycles ridden by older children and adults. For younger children's relatively inexpensive bicycles a combination lock may be preferable; it offers less security but it has no keys that the child can lose.

Chains and Cables
You will need to choose a chain or a cable to use with your padlock. We recommend a chain because it offers greater security. Cables have tremendous pull strength — they are used to hold up bridges — but compared to a good chain, they are less resistant to cutting and sawing. To match the strength of the padlock, the chain should be at least 9/32 of an inch thick and made of case-hardened, alloyed steel. The links must be welded together, not twisted, to prevent prying them apart. The chain should be five to six feet long so that it can secure both front and back wheels and the frame to a solid object.

Cables do have some advantages. One is that they are cheaper. A good chain costs between $15 and $20, whereas a comparable length of cable sells for only $5 to $7. Cables are also much lighter, which is important to avid cyclists. Next, they are more convenient because they are easy to coil up under the bicycle seat or in a backpack. Finally, cables are more functional for special security needs. For example, the parts on children's dirt bikes are frequently stolen. Special long cables have therefore been designed to go through the bike's frame, seat, handlebars, and both wheels. A comparable length of chain would simply be too unwieldly to use.

Whether you choose a chain or a cable, it is important to fasten your bicycle next to a solid object, not to something that can be easily cut. When securing your bicycle, remember to keep the chain or cable as high off the ground as possible. If you don't, the thief can use the hard ground as an anvil to smash against with a hammer or as one side of the leverage for a pry bar or bolt cutter.

Specially Designed Bicycle Locks

A new type of lock designed specifically for bicycles, particularly for light, multispeed bicycles, has recently been marketed. The best of these locks are Superlock, which normally sells for $17.95, and Kryptonite and Citadel, which each retail for $28. These locks are preferable to a padlock and chain. First, they are lighter. Whereas a high security padlock and chain weigh roughly five pounds, a special bicycle lock weighs only two pounds. Second, they are more conve-

Special bicycle lock

Special bicycle lock

nient and easier to handle. Some locks even come with attachments to hold the lock to the frame of the bicycle when riding. Third, they are in roughly the same price range as a good padlock and chain; some special locks are even less expensive. And finally, the security offered by these new locks is just as good, if not better, than that which a padlock provides. The new locks are shrouded to prevent prying or popping, and they are considerably thicker than the links on a high-security chain.

These new bicycle locks do have some drawbacks, however. The space around which the lock must fit is relatively small, which limits you to locking your bicycle to small objects, such as a signpost or a small tree. Moreover, these locks are designed for quick-release front wheels, like those found on expensive ten-speed bicycles. If you cannot quickly take off your bike's front wheel, you must leave it unsecured in the hope that nobody takes it, or you must buy an extra piece of cable to secure the front wheel to the frame.

CONCLUSION

Stopping the professional thief is next to impossible, but by following the common sense precautions outlined in this chapter, you can significantly lower the chances of your vehicle being stolen. Cars and bicycles — all vehicles — should be well locked and secured when not in use, and they should not be left in areas where theft and vandalism are most likely to occur. For people who are particularly worried about having their cars stolen, a wide variety of anti-theft devices is available, many at reasonable prices. Used in combination, these antitheft devices provide the best possible protection.

Chapter 4

Street Crime

"Crime in the streets" is more than a catchy phrase we read in the newspapers; it is a social reality that threatens us all and is one of the foremost fears of Americans. Statistically, four of every ten Americans feel unsafe in their everyday environments and are "highly fearful" that they will be victims of murder, rape, robbery, or assault. In a *Los Angeles Times* 1981 survey, almost half of those polled indicated that their greatest fear was becoming the victim of a violent crime.

This is a justifiable fear. FBI statistics indicate that a violent crime is committed every thirty seconds somewhere in the United States. The rate of violent crime has been climbing steadily over the past several decades, outpacing the increase in property crimes such as burglary and theft. Recent statistics show that this trend continues unabated. In 1980 violent crime rose by 11 percent. Robbery, one of the fastest-growing offenses, rose 13 percent in the country as a whole and a staggering 19 percent in cities of more than one million inhabitants according to the *Uniform Crime Reports*.

Whether you are the victim of a street crime is, to some extent, a matter of chance. You might be standing in the wrong place at the wrong time when someone goes berserk and flails away with a knife or club. You might be spotted by a desperate mugger only seconds before he decides to attack. The vast majority of street crimes, however, are crimes of opportunity and, by taking preventive measures, you can reduce your chances of being victimized. This chapter has two goals: to inform you about the characteristics of street crime and criminals so you can reduce the likelihood of being attacked, and to advise you how

94

to protect yourself in cases of suspected danger and actual encounter.

WHAT IS STREET CRIME?

Street crime is an informal label popularized by the media and covers a host of offenses; it is not a formal legal category. Because of the diversity of these offenses, it is difficult to find a common thread among them. For the purposes of this book, however, we define street crime as any offense committed in public space against the person (as opposed to property) and usually committed by a stranger.

This chapter concentrates on only a handful of the many categories of street crime: specifically, those that are most frequently committed and pose the greatest potential for violence and injury, although the advice we give is also applicable to the prevention of other types of street crime.

Aggravated assault — that is, an unlawful attack to severely injure another person — is the most common street crime, accounting for over half of all crimes of violence in the country. The motive for this crime is usually not to acquire money, but simply to harm the victim. However, your chances of being randomly attacked on the streets are quite small. In only 20 percent of the reported aggravated assaults are the victim and the assailant strangers. Most assaults take place during arguments between friends or acquaintances, often when one or both are drunk.

Robbery is defined by the FBI's *Uniform Crime Reports* as taking or attempting to take anything valuable from another person by intimidation, force, or violence. There must be a personal encounter between the offender and the victim. When people think of robbery, they often envision masked bandits robbing a bank and fleeing in a getaway car. In fact, bank robberies make up only one percent of all robberies. The biggest single category is street robbery, which accounts for almost 50 percent of the total.

Robbery is broken down into two subcategories. Armed robbery, often called a holdup, means that the offender possessed or used a weapon, usually a gun or knife. Armed robbery is unfortunately quite common; in almost half of all robberies, the victims surrendered their property at gunpoint. Strong-arm robbery means taking another person's belongings by force or intimidation, but without a weapon. Strong-arm robbery is often called mugging by the general public, although that term has no formal status in law.

Purse-snatching is normally classified as theft or larceny, which means the unlawful taking of another person's property without force or intimidation. Theft is defined and further explained in Chapter 1 (pages 12 – 48). The typical purse snatcher rips the purse out of an unsuspecting victim's hand and darts away before she realized what has happened. This crime often takes place with such speed and skill that the victim is rarely injured. However, purse-snatching can easily turn into robbery. If the victim resists and tightly clutches her purse, the thief may knock her down, drag her along the street, or hurt her — that is, use force or intimidation to complete the crime.

Rape can also be classified as a street crime, but because rape is such an important topic, with unique aspects of prevention, it will be treated separately in the next chapter.

WHO IS THE STREET CRIMINAL?

Understanding the street criminal — his background and motivations — is an important part of crime prevention. It will help lower your chances of being picked as a target, but, perhaps more importantly, it can minimize your chances of injury if you are confronted on the streets. No two individuals are alike. How street criminals behave depends on their personality as well as on the category of crime they commit. Nevertheless, extensive statistical data and years of research have led to useful generalizations.

Experts used to look to medicine and psychiatry to explain why criminals preyed on innocent victims in the streets. But in the past few decades criminologists have realized that social and economic factors are of greater relevance in understanding street crime. Studies conducted at the State University of New York concluded that a one percent increase in the unemployment rate accounts for a 5 percent increase in the crime rate. It is not surprising, therefore, that the vast majority of people arrested for street crimes are young (75 percent are under twenty-five years of age) and come from ghetto areas, where unemployment among young people is highest, education is of the poorest quality, and poverty abounds. Existence in ghetto areas is often harsh and brutal; people more readily solve their problems and attain their goals by resorting to force. Children grow up in what one criminologist calls a "subculture of violence."

Yet criminologists believe that most street criminals know the difference between right and wrong as well as the next person. What distinguishes the street criminal is his ability to invent excuses for his behavior and find exceptions to acceptable ways of treating people. The street criminal is able to dehumanize his victim, to see him as an object rather than a person, and can therefore harm him without feeling guilty. The street criminal may even view the victim as his enemy and derive pleasure out of inflicting injury.

Robbery is the crime you will most likely encounter on the streets. The victim and the offender are strangers in over 90 percent of all robberies. Robbers can be grouped into one of two categories. The first, which we call the professional, is the most common. The professional is in business for the money. Robbery is his livelihood, his means of survival. The professional robber selects his victim carefully, looking for an "easy mark." He is not careless or foolhardy; he carefully calculates his odds and then acts. The professional robber has a game plan, and he believes the victim knows the rules of the game. If the victim cooperates, the crime will be over in a moment and no one will be hurt. Although injury is not his goal, the professional robber will use force or violence if necessary to carry out the crime.

The second category of robber also wants to get away with the victim's money, but robbery is used to mask his real goal — to injure the victim. This type of robber, whom we call sadistic, wants to humiliate the victim, prove the victim's inferiority, and in some cases cause his death. Fortunately, the sadistic robber, by most estimates, comprises only 10 to 15 percent of all robbers, but the extent of gratuitous violence seems to be growing. A recent study of robberies in

Philadelphia found that roughly half of the victims were hurt and 30 percent required treatment or hospitalization. Some of these injuries were brought about by the victims' resistance, but a large number also resulted from unprovoked attacks on passive victims. Unfortunately, it is difficult to tell if you are facing the professional or the sadistic robber at the beginning of an encounter.

PLAYING THE ODDS

Every person on the streets, even the most cautious, is a potential target for crime. Yet some people, unknowingly or unconsciously, set themselves up to be victims. Studying criminal encounters in a new science called victimology, experts have identified several of the factors that increase a person's vulnerability to criminal attack. Any one factor by itself may be insignificant, but in combination these factors definitely increase a person's chances of victimization. We will explore these factors, showing you how to reduce your chances of encountering street criminals.

Whether you are alone. Street criminals want to lower their likelihood of meeting resistance, of being identified, and of getting caught. To put the odds in your favor, do not offer them a lone target by going out by yourself any more than necessary. The buddy system offers security. If you don't have friends or relatives to help you, there are other alternatives. Many civic organizations provide volunteers to escort people, particularly the elderly, on shopping expeditions. Contact your local police or district attorney's office for information. If you use public transportation, arrange for a friend to meet you when you get off or get off first and walk with the crowd. If you get off last, you can become isolated and more vulnerable to attack.

What time you go out. The most dangerous time to be on the streets is at night. Your chances of being victimized then are three times greater than during daylight hours, when observation and identification of the criminal are easier. The hour you are most likely to be attacked is 11 P.M. We are not suggesting that you never go out after dark or never go out alone, but if you do, be extra cautious. If you are walking, stay on a well-lighted route. If you are driving, park near bright streetlights so your car will not be in the dark. It is also a good idea to carry a small flashlight in your pocket or purse to help you find your keys or to use when you approach your car or residence.

Certain times of the month are also more hazardous than others. Professional robbers and purse snatchers know that paydays are often on the first or fifteenth of the month, or on Thursdays or Fridays. They also know when social security, unemployment, and welfare checks are sent out. In short, they know when people are more likely to be carrying large sums of money on the streets. We recommend that you arrange to have your paychecks or social security checks sent directly to your bank for deposit. This will also prevent the theft of your money from your mailbox. If your employer pays in cash go directly to the bank with fellow employees, who can serve as protection.

Where you go. Street crime generally occurs in areas where the offender is able to isolate his target and thus lower his chances of resistance and detection. Likely areas are not necessarily on the outer limits of the city. Deserted side streets, whether downtown or near residential neighborhoods, appear to be the most dangerous areas of the city. Most robberies and purse snatchings occur in the downtown area, usually within a block or two of the commerical arterials. And one recent study of robberies of the elderly found that nearly one-third of these robberies are committed in the immediate vicinity of the victim's home and another third occur in the victim's neighborhood.

Additional dangerous locations are large parks and parking lots because they are difficult to patrol and offer many hiding places for would-be muggers. Parks are particularly dangerous at night. Areas in public buildings hidden from surveillance — stairways, elevators, corridors, and roofs — are hazardous. Avoid alleys, paths, shortcuts, thick shrubs, and trees. Public transportation is getting more dangerous each year. It offers criminals a steady flow of potential victims.

If possible, plan your route to avoid high crime areas, or, if necessary, take a taxi. Even on heavily traveled steets and on sidewalks in crowded areas, walk on the outside edge of the sidewalk, away from building entrances and alleyways. When waiting for public transportation, don't stand too close to the edge of the loading area. Purse snatchers sometimes reach out the window and grab a purse as the train or bus is departing. Sit in front near the driver when you ride the bus.

How you dress. People who are victimized by street criminals are often victims more than once. It is as though they send off a message that they are easy scores. How they dress is one way they emit signals. People who stand out from the norm, from what is normal in that area, are most likely to be robbed. Anyone who wears expensive or showy jewelry on the streets is an obvious target, as is the business executive in the three-piece suit walking in a slum area. Clothing that can hinder your movement or self-defense is another signal. For example, women who wear high-heeled shoes or tight skirts quickly catch the watchful eyes of muggers. Large grocery bags or packages piled high in your arms are other impediments to self-defense and attract the attention of would-be robbers and purse snatchers.

When you are out on the streets, dress in a manner that will not attract unwanted attention. Try to blend in with the crowd. Don't wear flashy clothes or jewelry in areas you are not familiar with. Dressing for crime prevention also means wearing functional clothing. It is hard to run or maneuver in high-heeled shoes. If you go out for a stroll, we suggest you wear low-heeled shoes with laces, such as tennis or jogging shoes. We also suggest that you do not wear anything around your neck. Scarves, chains, and necklaces are easy to grab and can be used to choke you.

Your behavior. How you behave on the streets also sends signals to street criminals. Muggers can size up your potential as a victim in a matter of seconds. Studies show that people who are not aware of their surroundings and do not pay attention to where they are going are more susceptible to crime. Being drunk in public also significantly increases your chances of being mugged or attacked, since you are less able to protect yourself.

Research conducted in 1980 by communications expert Betty Grayson reveals that even the way you walk draws the attention of potential muggers. Using a hidden camera, Grayson videotaped one hundred pedestrians, each for seven seconds, the time it takes a mugger to size up a victim. She then visited Rahway State Prison in New Jersey and showed the tapes to prisoners who had been convicted of assault or robbery. The prisoners were asked to rate the muggability of each pedestrian; they consistently agreed that some were more muggable than others. Eventually, Grayson isolated the factors that correlate with muggability. In essense, the most likely targets had unnatural strides or movements and were slow or clumsy — all of which suggested to the muggers that these people could not easily avoid or defend themselves against attack.

In high crime areas, particularly at night, walk with purpose and at a steady pace. Stand up straight and keep your head erect. Try not to appear as if you don't know where you are or where you are going. If possible, be familiar with your route and pay continuous attention to your destination.

How you carry your money. People set themselves up as prime targets by the way they handle or carry their money. The professional mugger often knows when someone is carrying a large amount of cash. Some people are even kind enough to display it in public; they unthinkingly pull out their wallets to pay and flash a wad of bills. To a desperate mugger, this can be an invitation to commit a crime. Even if people don't display their money openly, they often give clues that they have a lot on them: Men constantly pat their hip or breast pockets to make sure their wallets are still there; women frequently look in their purses to see that nothing is missing.

Do not carry large sums of money in public. If you feel insecure without a lot of money, buy the necessary amount of traveler's checks. However, it is not a good idea to carry no money at all. Many muggers are desperate and short-tempered. If you have nothing to give them, their frustration may turn to aggression. We therefore suggest that you carry a second wallet containing five or ten dollars, some old identification that does not give your current address, and some old photographs. You should keep this wallet in its normal place (purse or hip pocket), and keep your valuables (money, credit cards, and identification) in a separate place.

Men who decide to carry only one wallet should carry it or a money clip in the front pants pocket or inside jacket pocket. The hip pocket is the least safe place to keep it. Other valuables should be in a separate pocket. If you are especially concerned about theft, a money belt offers the best security.

Women preferably should not carry a purse. It is much safer to carry your valuables in your pockets. If you do carry a purse, you should still keep your most valuable items — money, keys, identification — in a separate location. One company markets a small pouch, for example, that attaches to the inside of your clothing. When carrying a purse, keep it close to your body, gripping it under your arm or in your hand. Do not wind the strap around your neck or wrist. If someone grabs the purse, you may be knocked to the ground and injured. Whenever you wear a coat or shawl, keep the purse underneath. If you are carrying packages or books, put your purse between them and your body. Your purse will be hidden from view and harder to snatch.

Both men and women can avoid flashing money around by careful planning. Try to determine before you go shopping how much you are going to spend. Before you leave home or get out of your car, take out enough money to cover the bill and keep it in your pocket. Use this money to pay instead of opening your wallet or purse in front of strangers.

SENSING DANGER

Knowing where and when crimes are most likely to occur is necessary, but you must also be able to sense danger; you must be "street wise." Although this is partly intuition, it also comes from education. You must learn when dangerous situations are unfolding around you and how to deal with them.

As we emphasized before, don't walk heedlessly down the street, especially in high crime areas or at night. Be alert and aware of your surroundings at all times. Notice any changes in conditions that increase the prospects of danger. On routes you travel frequently, notice the location of stores or businesses that stay open late at night or buildings with doormen. Remember the whereabouts of police and fire stations, and police call boxes and public telephones.

Try to see as far down the street as you can. If you notice anyone suspicious, wait for other pedestrians to come by and walk near them, or take another route. Avoid eye contact with people who loiter in public places. Avoid persons who are intoxicated or high on drugs, and at night stay clear of liquor stores or bars where drunks often congregate. Groups of men or juveniles just standing aound can mean trouble. If there is a crowd of suspicious people in your way, cross the street to avoid them; at least walk around rather than through them.

Use your intuition. If can be one of the most important factors in avoiding street crime. Social conventions are unimportant if you suspect danger. A request for a cigarette may be just that, or it may be an opening to a conversation you don't want. If you feel uneasy, follow your intuition. Don't play the other person's game; reply briefly and firmly, and go on your way. Courtesy is fine, but you must think of your safety first.

Whenever you approach your home, have your keys out and ready to use, especially if you live in an apartment building or house where strangers might be in close proximity to your front door. Once inside, immediately close the door behind you. Some robbers wait for unsuspecting people to open their doors, then barge in to commit their crime. If you are dropped off by a friend or come home in a taxi, ask the driver to wait briefly until you get safely inside. You can flash a light on and off to indicate that you are safely inside.

If you think you are being followed, don't hesitate to find out. Look around and see who is there. Cross the street, walk a few seconds, and see if you notice the same person apparently following. If you sense danger, consider your options and the situation. You can look for someone to help you. Naturally, a police officer, fireman, or private security guard would be ideal. But you might also approach a stranger and ask to stay near him until help comes. Look for a safe place to go, such as an open business. Restaurants, theaters, hotels, gas stations, and convenience stores, for example, are often open in the evening. Use a police call box if one is handy. In some cities, you can call an emergency number on a public phone without inserting a coin. Call your local police department to find out if you have such an emergency number in your community.

If help does not seem near, staying in the middle of the street provides some safety. Few muggers are brazen enough to attack you in view of passing cars. If you are walking near parked cars, look for one that is unlocked (with the buttons in the unlocked postion); climb in, lock the doors, and honk the horn until someone comes to rescue you. If you are carrying a lot of money, you should drop your wallet or purse in the mailbox. Technically, this is illegal, but it happens all the time in big cities, and the postmaster is usually quite cooperative about returning your possessions.

If you are being followed in a residential area, run to a house that looks occupied (with lights or TV on) and pound on the door. The homeowner may be suspicious and reluctant to open the door; if so, you will have to explain the situation as best you can. Even if the resident does not let you in, he will probably call the police.

If you sense that danger is imminent, you should try to attract the attention of people in the area. One way to do this is to scream as loud as possible. But don't yell nonsense; people might think that you are just another "crazy" on the streets. Don't even yell "help" or "police." People who want to avoid trouble — and there are many of them — will turn a deaf ear. Yelling "fire" is your best bet; it will draw the attention of people who would otherwise hesitate to get involved.

You can also use any of several mechanical devices designed to attract attention or summon help. A good police whistle, costing no more than two dollars, is one such gadget. To be useful, it has to be kept handy. Wear the whistle on a key chain or bracelet. If you want to wear it around your neck, use a breakaway chain so an assailant cannot choke you with it. The main problem with the whistle is that you need a mouth and plenty of air to make it work. If you are too scared to blow or if the attacker has his hand over your mouth, the whistle is useless.

If, for whatever reason, you cannot blow a whistle, an air, or freon horn is a good substitute. The air horn consists of a cylinder about three inches long with a little plastic horn attached to the top. It is lightweight and fits comfortably in the hand. To be effective, the air horn has to be accessible, so you should not carry it at the bottom of your purse or pocket. If you are in an unsafe area or you think you are in danger, carry it in your hand.

IF YOU ARE CONFRONTED BY A STREET CRIMINAL

The old adage "an ounce of prevention is worth a pound of cure" may sound trite, but it is never more true than when applied to street crime. If through carelessness your house is burglarized or your car stolen, you can at least replace your property. But if you come face to face with a robber, you are in serious trouble. At the very least, your valuables will be taken. You also run the risk of being attacked, and the encounter could cause psychological trauma, physical injury, or, possibly, death.

If you are confronted by a street criminal, continue to think about prevention, but the goal of prevention is now avoiding serious injury. The following advice will help you increase your chances of walking away from the confrontation without getting hurt.

Remain Calm. Although it is a tall order, you must try to remain calm. At the beginning of the encounter, you cannot be sure of the person's mental state or his intentions. An experienced robber may not be unsettled by your nervousness, but many muggers are jittery, and the slightest miscue can cause them to behave irrationally. Avoid sudden movements and don't raise your hands unless the person starts to attack you. Keep your hands out of your purse or pockets. If you start to remove your wallet, tell the robber what you are doing. Obviously, retaining your composure is even more important if your assailant is brandishing a gun. Losing control of your emotions can cost you your life.

Do not resist. Resisting a street criminal, at least at the beginning of the encounter, increases the chances that you will be injured. There are several levels of resistance, all of which are to be avoided. Passive resistance — simply not acting or not acting fast enough — can be dangerous. Many robbers and purse snatchers openly state that they have resorted to violence when their victims were not responsive enough. If you are ordered to produce your purse or wallet, do so without hesitation.

Screaming for help is also a form of resistance. Although we recommended screaming if you sense danger is near, we generally do not advise it if you are confronted by an assailant. If you yell, the offender has two viable choices: He can run away in fear of getting caught, or he can silence you. If the offender has planned his crime properly, you will be isolated from other people and at a physical disadvantage, in which case he is likely to try to silence you. He may simply put his hand over your mouth to keep you quiet, but he may also hit you or use a weapon. This is simply too great a risk. You should not scream during an encounter unless you are positive that help is near, or unless it becomes apparent that the assailant is going to attack you despite your cooperation.

Running away is another tactic we recommended if you sense danger. But again we do not advise it during a confrontation unless the assailant is next to you, unless you are sure safety is near, or unless you are being attacked. Statistics show that running increases your chances of being hurt. An extensive review of police files by the Denver Anti-Crime Council revealed that running away or attempting to run away during a robbery increases chances of injury five times.

Do not attempt active physical resistance, at least initially, because, again, you are more likely to get hurt. The Denver Anti-Crime Council study showed that people who resisted robbers were 3.7 times more likely to be injured than those victims who cooperated.

Resistance increases the likelihood of injury for several reasons. Most street criminals do not particularly want to hurt you, but if you use force, you justify their meeting force with force and intensifying the attack. Your resistance allows the attacker to dehumanize you, to believe that you deserve the punishment you are getting. Many street criminals are angry and frustrated, and some are mentally unbalanced. Your resistance may give him the provocation he wants to vent his anger on you or to trigger irrational violence.

Communicate. Often street crime takes place very fast; the entire episode is over before you know what hit you. Other encounters may last a few moments. The criminal may try to talk to you or give you instructions. If he tells you to hand over your wallet or purse, by all means do so immediately. But if he appears to be at all rational, try to say something like, "Go ahead and take the money, but would you please let me keep my identification." Making this request can accomplish two things. It shows the mugger that you know the rules of the game and intend to follow them. You are not going to put up any resistance, and he will not have to resort to violence. In addition, it will also set the mood for the rest of the encounter. You have shown the assailant that you have control over your emotions, and are thinking rationally. The mugger is likely to respond in the same way, completing the crime without using force.

If the encounter takes more than a minute or so, you should try to communicate with him some more. Try to talk to him in a normal way. Acknowledge the frustrations in his life that are making him break the law. Tell him you understand how tough it can be to be out of work and desperate for money. Don't make any disparaging remarks about his lack of courage or morality.

At the same time try to emphasize your own humanity. Tell him your name, making up a false last name. Say that he reminds you of your brother, or your son if you are old enough to have a grown child. Tell him that you used to be unemployed and desperate. If your communication appears to anger the offender, stop talking immediately. Don't say anything that will allow him to dehumanize you. Don't speak in a whining voice or beg for mercy, which would be playing into the hands of a sadistic criminal. Don't speak contemptuously and don't say anything antagonistic such as ''I'll never forget your face.''

Use tricks or ploys. Finally, if it looks as if the offender intends to attack you, consider using a ploy or a psychological trick to lower the chances of injury. An elderly person, for example, might tell the offender that she has a bad heart and might have a heart attack. A woman of childbearing age can tell the criminal that she is pregnant. You can also break the criminal's game plan by resorting to a physical ploy. You could, for example, become hysterical, throwing yourself on the ground, kicking your feet, and acting as if you are in a world of your own. If there are people around to come to your aid, you might pretend to faint and fall down. These acts make it harder for the robber to get the money he wants and they may summon people to your aid. But, perhaps more importantly, they are not likely to be perceived as willfull resistance and therefore the offender is less likely to vent his anger on you.

Self-Defense
Despite your cooperation and fast talking, the offender may decide to

attack you. You are probably not sure how you would react if someone grabbed you from behind or approached you from the front and attempted to choke you. You might be able to collect your wits and defend yourself or you might be too terrified to act.

Self-defense is as much mental as it is physical; you are defenseless only if you think you are. The first step toward successfully defending yourself is a commitment that you can and will do so if necessary. Making that commitment builds self-confidence, which is more important than learning a handful of self-defense techniques.

The fear of being assaulted has prompted many people to enroll in self-defense courses: karate, judo, kung fu, and the like. We encourage everyone to take such courses, although their primary benefits are mental rather than physical, at least for the short-term student. Self-defense classes build self-confidence; they teach you to be more assertive and independent. People, especially women, often underestimate their strength and capabilities in self-defense. These classes change their attitudes so that they are less willing to play the role of the victim. If you don't consider yourself a victim, those around you are also less likely to.

Nevertheless, you would only be fooling yourself if you thought a few karate lessons would enable you to battle the average street criminal. A quick course in the martial arts will not compensate for the size and strength advantage of most muggers, nor will it provide a defense against a knife or gun. Years of dedication and training are necessary to become an expert in the martial arts, and few people are willing to work long enough to become proficient.

If you are attacked, the first thing to remember is not to try to outfight the assailant. His strength and experience with violence will put the odds heavily in his favor. He will have to defend himself against you and the level of violence will escalate.

For the amateur, the key to self-defense is *simplicity*. Your best bet is to follow your instincts and learn a few basic self-defense techniques. A pat answer to the question of what type of self-defense you should use does not exist; you must decide for yourself what you would do. Violence may be repugnant to you, but it is important to consider carefully how you would defend yourself under various circumstances *before* the occasion arises. Do not worry about fighting fair if you are in a battle for your life. Use whatever defenses you can muster.

Some of the self-defense techniques we describe are designed to inflict pain, but the first goal of self-defense is not victory; it is escape. The idea is to incapacitate the attacker momentarily so you can break free and run for help. By running away, you show the attacker that he is superior, that he has won the battle. You also show him that he doesn't have to fight harder to defend himself. If a person runs after you to continue the attack, however, you will have to resort to more drastic measures. Scratching and gouging often work. Biting is also effective because of the strength in your jaws. Kicking is generally better than hitting because a foot can deliver a blow eleven times more powerful than a fist. Attack the person's most sensitive areas: eyes, ears, nose, upper lip, testicles, throat, kneecaps, and instep. It is important to note that some self-defense techniques can be lethal. The throat is especially sensitive, and if you strike someone hard in the front of the throat, the larynx will swell up, causing suffocation. Use these defenses prudently.

If the attacker approaches you from the front and grabs your wrists, move your arms up and out, putting pressure against his thumbs. Even if he is much stronger, this tactic should break his grip. If the person tries to hit you, follow your instincts and put up your arms to block the blows. If he has a knife, use your purse or rolled up coat to shield yourself from the blade. If the attack continues and you cannot escape, it is best not to stand back and attempt to hit or kick the person's vital areas. Hitting or kicking from a distance is difficult because the person will move away fast or parry your blows. You can do the most damage by moving close to him.

If you are being choked from the front, first try to break the hold and get away. Lift your arms up and around the outside of the assailant's arms, with your palms facing each other. Then thrust your hands as hard as you can into the assailant's elbows, pulling away at the same time. If you want to try to disable the assailant, attack his groin area. If you are right-handed, take one step forward with your left foot, rotate your hips, and thrust your right knee as hard as you can into the assailant's crotch, aiming for his testicles. Start with the right foot and reverse the process if you are left-handed.

If you are attacked from behind and the assailant puts his arm around your neck, you should first maneuver to get some air. Turn your head in the direction of his elbow; the space at the crook of his elbow will allow you to breathe. To attempt an escape, grab onto one of his fingers and bend it back with all of your might. He will either let you go or have his finger broken.

If you cannot get away, we recommend that you stomp down with your heel as hard as you can onto the top of his foot. Since it takes only fourteen pounds of pressure to break the bones in the foot, even a small person should be able to cause the offender considerable pain. As a last resort, you should reach down with your hand and grab the person's testicles. A hard squeeze or pull will send the assailant into a state of shock.

You must bear in mind, however, that in defending yourself you should use only the amount of force necessary to protect yourself from injury. Under the law you cannot use force or violence to injure another person when your personal safety is not threatened. If you do, you can be sued for the damages you cause. Whenever you are fighting for your life, anything goes. But it is illegal, for example, to use deadly force against a purse snatcher.

If the attacker has hurt or injured you, let him know. Tell him if you have a broken bone or are bleeding. Even exaggerate your injuries. Showing pain will make it harder for the attacker to dehumanize you and treat you like an animal. It will prevent him from denying to himself the extent of the damage he is doing. He should cease the attack.

If you realize that you cannot offer any significant defense, you will simply have to endure the beating. In that situation, your best bet is to lie on the ground with your knees tucked up into your stomach and your arms covering your head. You are still going to feel pain, but by protecting your vital organs, you are less likely to suffer serious or permanent injury.

Guns

Some people feel that a firearm is the answer to self-defense, but for several compelling reasons, we do not recommend that you have a gun, either on your person or in your home. Gun possession might reduce the *fear* of crime, but it has little impact on its incidence. Although the percentage of families owning a gun for self-protection has been steadily rising (from 37 percent in 1965 to 52 percent in 1980), the national crime rate has more than kept pace. In each of the four major geographic areas (Northeast, Midwest, South, and West), moreover, gun ownership varies significantly. Seven out of ten southern households report owning guns, compared with only three out of ten in the Northeast. Yet the crime rate is increasing just as fast in the South as it is in the North. In fact, violent crime is more common in the South in large part because of the ready availability of guns.

Owning a gun increases your chances of injury. People who own guns often do not know how to use them effectively, especially in a crisis situation. Most people soon stop taking target practice and gradually let down their defenses. Their aim is poor and they are mentally and physically unprepared — the gun is at the bottom of a purse or briefcase or hidden deep in a drawer full of clothes. Even if the gun is accessible, many people find it difficult to shoot another human being. If you hesitate for a moment, the criminal can wrestle the gun away and use it against you. Over half the police officers killed by firearms are shot with their own guns. If a criminal can take a gun away from a trained officer of the law, imagine how easily he can take it from you.

Guns are also dangerous because they are much less likely to be used for their intended purpose of self-defense than in the killing of a friend or relative, especially when one party is drunk or in a rage. Having a gun around the house or on your person makes violence a ready solution to personal conflict. You are four times more likely to be killed by a relative during an argument than by a criminal during a burglary or robbery.

Finally, guns are dangerous because they often prove fatal to innocent victims. The handgun around the house is six times more likely to accidentally kill its owner or a member of his family than it is to repel a burglar. Each year in the United States two thousand people are accidentally killed by firearms. Many of the victims are children who play with guns lying around the house; some are simply innocent bystanders caught in a shootout. Perhaps the most common type of accidental killing occurs when someone who owns a gun awakes during the middle of the night and thinks he hears a burglar in the house. Nervous and still drowsy, he gets the gun and shoots the figure in the dark only to find that the victim is not a burglar, but his spouse or child. People do occasionally defend themselves successfully with a firearm, but by possessing a gun, you are much more likely to be involved in a personal tragedy than to avert one.

Other Weapons
If you are in a fight for your life, you can use a variety of objects other than a gun to defend yourself. Many of these are items that you carry with you every day, and they have the advantage of being unobtrusive, not immediately perceived as a weapon by the assailant.

Almost any small, sharp object, such as a fingernail file, rattail comb, or ball-point pen, can be used as a defensive weapon. A sharp pencil held tightly in your fist makes a particularly effective weapon. Place the pencil in your hand with the pointed end sticking from between the fingers of your clenched fist and the blunt end against the palm of your hand. When you are close to the attacker, thrust hard at his vital areas.

Hard, blunt objects, such as a cane, book, or briefcase, also make good weapons in emergency situations. You can also pick up a rock or stick. Do not try to strike the assailant over the head with these objects. Instead, grab the weapon as tightly as you can and jab or poke in the vital areas with short, hard strokes.

Even your keys can be used as a weapon. If you are attacked in a parking lot, for example, hold your keys in your fist, with the pointed ends protruding from between your fingers. Do not punch at the assailant with your fist, but rake the keys across his face or throat.

Tear Gas. One of the most popular new self-defense aids is tear gas. When sprayed into a person's face, this chemical causes temporary blindness and breathing difficulties, incapacitating the attacker so that you can escape unharmed.

We generally recommend that you carry tear gas, especially if you live or travel in areas where street crimes are likely to occur. Tear gas is convenient and easy to use. It comes in small canisters about three inches long, and is usually effective when sprayed up to ten feet away from the attacker. It is relatively inexpensive, costing between five and ten dollars per canister. Tear gas will not kill anyone. A squirt in the face is not lethal to the assailant, nor can it be used to kill you if the attacker grabs it out of your hand. In short, tear gas provides you with a new dimension in self-defense and is much less dangerous than a gun.

Our recommendation that you carry tear gas is, however, contingent upon three conditions. First, comply with the laws in your state. — some states ban the use of tear gas by civilians on the theory that it would be used more often by criminals than law-abiding citizens. If your state prohibits tear gas, do not carry it. Other states permit the civilian use of tear gas, but only after rigid requirements have been met, such as completing an authorized course or passing a state-sponsored test. And still other states allow almost free access to tear gas, with minimal restrictions or licensing requirements. Contact your local police department about the laws in your state.

Second, you should take a course in the use of tear gas, even if not required by law, because improper use of this spray can have serious consequences. If you use tear gas when not necessary for your defense, you can be sued for the resulting damages. Moreover, if you use tear gas in the wrong situation, such as when an attacker is armed with a gun, you increase your chances of being injured. Knowing when and how to use this chemical is, therefore, of utmost importance, and the best way to learn is from a qualified professional. Courses are frequently given by law enforcement agencies at community colleges and adult education programs, and even in some retail stores. Call your local law enforcement agency for details.

Third, you should possess tear gas only if you fully understand its many limitations. Perhaps the biggest danger you must guard against is a false sense of security. Tear gas does not lower your chances of attack because the would-be offender doesn't know you are carrying it. No matter what the situation, you are always in serious trouble when facing a street criminal. Even when armed with your tear gas canister, *avoiding* an encounter must remain your primary goal.

You must also realize that tear gas is not the ultimate weapon. It is useless, even dangerous, in many situations. Using tear gas on a person armed with a gun, for example, is courting danger, and may cause the assailant to use his gun.

Another limitation is that tear gas is not always reliable. Occasionally the canister is defective and the chemical cannot be sprayed. Often the canister is not used for a long period, and when needed simply fails to work. If the wind is blowing in your direction, moreover, the chemical will drift back into your face and disable you.

Tear gas can also be dangerous because it is not always effective. Even when it does hit the target, it does not always produce the desired effects. There are two types of tear gas on the market: CN and CS. CS gas normally takes between twenty and thirty seconds to work, and sometimes longer if the weather is especially cold. An angry assailant can do a lot of damage in that amount of time. CN gas, which we recommend, works in about two or three seconds, but it also has a drawback. It is not as potent as CS gas, and there is a greater chance it will not disable the offender, particularly if he is drunk, on drugs, or mentally unbalanced.

If you attempt to use tear gas and fail, you may be worse off than if you had done nothing at all. An attacker perceives tear gas as an offensive weapon even though you use it in self-defense. When you are aggressive, you increase the chances that the attacker will escalate the violence and cause harm you might otherwise have avoided.

IF YOU HAVE BEEN VICTIMIZED

If you are the victim of a street crime, you can do several things to increase the chances of catching the offender. Assuming you are not seriously hurt, you should call the police *immediately*. Use a police call box or a public telephone and dial the standard emergency number if your community has one. You must act fast; the police have a good chance of apprehending the offender if the crime is reported within two minutes of its occurrence. After several minutes arrest is much less likely unless you can provide a detailed description of the assailant.

Try to remember what the person looked like. Do not waste time studying his clothing, particularly his jacket or hat, because he will probably change clothes soon after the crime to avoid being caught. Concentrate instead on his physical appearance: his height, weight, age, race, hair, and eye color. Next look for one or two distinguishing features, such as scars, tattoos, or birthmarks. The more detailed the description, the more likely the police are to apprehend and prosecute the offender.

When the incident is over, see which way the assailant goes. Notice if he enters a building, apartment house, or store. Try to see if he boards public transportation. If he gets away by car, try to get the car's make, year, and license number. All this information is valuable to the police.

If your wallet has been taken or your purse snatched, look in the nearby bushes, litter cans, alleys, and public rest rooms, because these are the most likely places the thief will discard your belongings after he has removed the valuable items. It might also be a good idea to contact your postmaster to find out if your purse or wallet has turned up in any mailbox; a kindhearted thief might relinquish your identification.

CONCLUSION

With crime on the rise, it is important to be street wise, to know self-defense techniques, and to have the confidence to use them. It is equally important, however, not to become paranoid. We hope you will use the information in this chapter to give you confidence on the streets, to enable you more accurately to judge situations, and to make your plans accordingly. Taking a leisurely stroll on a nice day is fun and good exercise; it should continue to be.

Chapter 5

Rape and Sexual Assaults Against Women

More than 60,000 rapes are reported every year in the United States according to the 1980 *Uniform Crime Reports*. Thousands more go unreported. Every eight minutes a woman is raped somewhere in the country.

At the very least, rape is frightening, degrading, and brutal, often causing severe physical injury as well as psychological scars that remain with the victim for the rest of her life. Rape is an indignity that assaults the self-respect of all women.

Women's groups urge us to focus on the underlying issue of rape — the dominance of men and the inequality of sex roles in our society. Rape victims have not been treated fairly nor with sufficient respect by male-dominated criminal justice system. Husbands, friends, doctors, nurses, and police often have little sympathy for and too much misunderstanding about rape victims. The victim herself is usually unprepared mentally and physically for the ordeal during and after the rape.

Giving advice about rape is somewhat difficult because it usually reads like a list of "don'ts." Yet most of this advice is realistic under the present circumstances. Rape will decrease when there is greater equality and mutual respect between the sexes. But what about now? Women must recognize reality even as they work to change it.

116

We do not preach a double standard for men and women. Any person at night walking in an isolated area increases the chances of becoming a victim of crime. Men, as much as women, should restrict their behavior to lower the chances of their being victimized.

In rape prevention, women have special problems to overcome. They delude themselves that this vicious crime could not happen to them — that "nice" women do not get raped. The rapist is not so discriminating; he will violate any women, no matter her age, race, social status, or neighborhood.

Yet some women are more likely to be victims than others. Young women are more likely to be victims than older women, lower-class women more than upper-class women, and students more than professionals.

Victimization also depends, in large part, on the preventive measures that women take. You can deprive the rapist of the opportunity to commit his crime in the same way you minimize the opportunities of a burglar, mugger, or bunco artist. This chapter outlines and discusses measures to save you from becoming a rape statistic. How you handle rape prevention will be based on your needs, values, and attitudes, but it is important that you become informed *now*, before it happens.

WHAT IS RAPE?

Rape is usually defined as sexual intercourse with a female, not a spouse, accomplished without her consent. The law in most states provides that a husband cannot technically rape his wife. Should he force sexual intercourse, he could be convicted of assault but not rape. Moreover, the legal definition of rape normally does not extend to men raping men or women raping anyone.

For rape to occur, there must be some penetration, however slight, of the vagina by the penis. Without penetration, there is no rape; the charge against the attacker would be attempted rape or some other type of sexual assault. Rape does not require the attacker to ejaculate. Moreover, the law differentiates between forced vaginal penetration (rape), oral penetration (sexual perversion), and anal penetration (sodomy). It is not legally rape if a man forces a women to masturbate him or if he penetrates her vagina with any object other than his penis.

Most states have also defined rape as sexual intercourse with a woman who is incapable of giving her consent, such as a insane or unconscious woman. There is also a legal category called unlawful sexual intercourse or statutory rape, which makes it unlawful for a male to have sexual intercourse with a female under a certain age, usually about sixteen, even if she gives her consent.

In this chapter we will discuss rape in general terms — as sexual intercourse imposed on a female against her will. The preventive measures presented here will serve a woman to ward off any attacker: a total stranger, or an aggressive husband.

RAPE STATISTICS

Rape statistics are not absolute; many rapes are never reported to the police. Estimates of unreported rape vary greatly. The President's Commission on Law Enforcement and Administration of Justice estimates only one rape in four is reported, the FBI only one in ten. Frederic Storaska, author and lecturer, has interviewed many women who have not reported rapes and believes that only one out of every one hundred rapes is reported. No matter which guess is most accurate, rape remains a relatively unknown crime. Nevertheless, the following statistical information can be useful because by knowing the facts, you can lower the odds of becoming a victim of this dreadful crime.

Our information about rape and rapists comes from the FBI, which compiles official police reports, and from criminologists doing research throughout the country. Criminologists really do not know how to interpret the dramatic rise in the number of reported rapes. Perhaps there have been more actual rapes over the last several years, but it might also be that more women are coming forward and talking to the police.

Women remain reluctant to report rape to the authorities for several reasons. Some feel the police will not believe them. Police label *unfounded* those cases in which they do not believe the victim. The extent of unfounded cases varies somewhat, as low as 2 percent in New York City, but for most jurisdictions it averages about 15 percent of all reported rapes. These cases usually involve a victim and an offender who know each other or have had sexual relations in the past. Since most rapes take place between people who know each other, many women do not want to go through the trauma of reporting a rape by someone they know when they can expect that the police will classify it as unfounded.

Women also do not report rapes because they realize our criminal justice system does a poor job of apprehending and convicting rapists. 1978 FBI statistics show that police make an arrest in 51 percent of the alleged rape cases compared with 79 percent for murder, and 63 percent for aggravated assault. Even if the police apprehend the rapist, the victim many not be satisfied with the results. For every 100 who are caught, 76 are prosecuted. Of these 36 are acquitted or have their charges dismissed. Of the other 40 many are found guilty of a lesser offense (such as simple assault), or plea bargain their case down to a relatively minor crime. Only six (15 percent) will go to prison — a state-level institution where convicted offenders are sent for one year or more. The rest are put on probation, go to jail — generally a county or city institution where convicted offenders are sent for one year or less — or are given psychiatric help. And these are only averages.

When women hear the word rape, they often think immediately of rapist-murders like the Boston Strangler or the Los Angeles Hillside Strangler. There are no reliable statistics on the number of rape-murders because these crimes are treated statistically as murders, not rapes. From the available evidence, it appears that rape-murder is a very rare crime. Frederic Storaska and author Susan Brownmiller both agree rape-murder accounts for less than two percent of all murders in the country. Furthermore, such incidents comprise less than one per-cent of all reported rapes. Considering the number of unreported rapes, the chance that you will be murdered by a rapist is very slim indeed.

If you are raped, the odds favor escaping injury beyond the sexual assault. In 1969 the National Commission on the Causes and Prevention of Violence conducted a 17-city survey of rape and other violent crimes. According to *Crimes of Violence,* their staff report, three-quarters of the victims of reported rape were not physically hurt. Of the remainder, the greater number were injured by the assailant's fists; less than 2 percent were injured by guns and an even smaller percentage by knives or blunt instruments. While teaching at the University of Pennsylvania, Israeli sociologist Menachem Amir conducted a study of rape in Philadelphia. He found that 30 percent of the rape victims received brutal beatings or choking. An additional 50 percent were beaten, but, he claimed, not seriously enough to require medical treatment. A different study conducted in a Philadelphia hospital found that 18 of the 50 victims (36 percent) were assaulted as well as raped, although the term assaulted is undefined.

Rapists attack women of any age. Police departments receive reports of raped children as young as four or five and women in their eighties and nineties. Some age groups are more susceptible, however. The Institute of Sex Research, at Indiana University, sketched a composite rape victim averaging 24 years of age. Only 3 percent of the victims were over 51 years old. Amir arrived at the same conclusion in his study of rape in Philadelphia. There, the age group most vulnerable to attack was 12 to 29. Women between 15 and 19 comprised 25 percent of all reported rape victims. In Brenda Brown's 1974 study titled "Crime Against Women Alone," she found that students accounted for 27 percent of all rape victims in Memphis.

It is sometimes heard that many women who are raped are "asking" for it or are "loose women." In Amir's study nearly 20 percent of the rape victims had police records, mostly for sexual offenses, and another 20 percent had reputations for being free with their sexual favors. Many of the rapes in Philadelphia began with the victim meeting the offender in an atmosphere that allowed many men to believe that sexual intercourse would result. This raises a new concept in criminology — victim precipitation. The victim is not responsible for the crime, but there may be complicity. In such cases an illegal act has been committed, but it must be determined how the crime might have been avoided if the victim had behaved differently.

Because victim precipitation is a new concept, it has no standard definition. As definitions vary, so do the statistics about it. The National Commission on the Causes and Prevention of Violence defined victim precipitation as follows: "When the victim agreed to sexual relations but retracted before the actual act or when she clearly invited sexual relations through language, gestures, etc." Because of this restrictive definition, the National Commission found that victims precipitated rapes in only 4.4 percent of the cases.

Amir used a less rigid definition that included "risky situations marred with sexuality, especially when she [the victim] uses what could be interpreted as indecency in language or gestures, or [does something that] constitutes what could be taken as an invitation to sexual relations." With this wide definition, Amir found victim precipitation a factor in as many as 40 percent of the rapes. It was most frequent when white males rape white females. Such cases often culminated in rape after the victim and the offender met in a bar or at a party, and the offender took the victim home.

For many women the fear of rape has racial overtones, but the statistics consistently show that the rapist and his victim are almost always of the same race. The National Commission study found this true in 90 percent of the cases. A specific analysis of the commission's statistics shows: 60 percent black male/black female, 30 percent white male/white female, 10.5 percent black male/white female, and 0.3 percent white male/black female. Amir found essentially the same pattern with even lower percentages for interracial rape. Reporting problems occur again with these facts. Many minority women claim the amount of rape by white men against black women is substantially underreported because criminal justice agencies are dominated by white men.

Most women associate rape with strangers accosting them on the street or breaking into their homes at night. This, however, is not an accurate picture. The National Commission found 53 percent of all rapists were total strangers to their victims. Of the black intraracial rapes, Amir discovered 40 percent of the victims were raped by men they did not know; of the white intraracial rapes, 35 percent of the victims were attacked by strangers. But in Washington, D.C., a study indicated that only one-third of the rape victims were attacked by strangers.

The statistics are deceiving because they are based on the number of reported and founded cases. Frequently, the police will dismiss those cases in which the victim and the offender know each other. The statistics therefore show a higher percentage of rapes by strangers than actually take place. A more accurate estimate of the chances of being raped by a total stranger is given by Storaska. He breaks down the relationship of the rapist and the victim into three categories. In about 35 percent of the rape cases, the victim is raped in a dating situation. Very few of these cases are reported. Roughly 35 percent of the rapists are someone the victims know: a friend, boss, co-worker, fellow student, or friend of a friend. Most of these rapes also remain unreported for a variety of reasons. Finally, Storaska believes that about 30 percent of the rapes are committed by strangers, although the rapist may have seen the woman several times. This category of rape is reported to the police more often than the other two.

Many rape statistics are commonplace and fairly predictable. The majority of attacks occur in the evening and night hours, and more attacks occur on the weekend than on any other day of the week. Rape also increases during the summer months.

Where do most rapes take place? Most studies arrive at a similiar conclusion — rape occurs in the victim's environment. The Queen's Bench study in San Francisco found in 38 percent of the cases the attacker approached his victim by illegally entering a home, school, or business. Brown's Memphis study showed that 34 percent of all rapes occurred in the victim's residence, generally by illegal entry. Amir's study found 56 percent of the rapes occurring in a home. The 17-city survey by the National Commission found that 52 percent of all rapes occurred in the home. Other prominent places for rape were open spaces, cars, and commercial establishments.

The statistics on rape vary by region. In a comparative study of rape in Boston and Los Angeles, for example, patterns differ. Los Angeles has more rapes occurring in cars and with groups of men raping hitchhikers. Since men in groups are intimidating and powerful, rapes in Los Angeles are less likely to involve weapons. In Boston, the rapist is more likely to be alone, armed, and illegally entering an apartment.

WHO IS THE RAPIST?

If you could tell which men are rapists by looking at them, life would be much less complicated. This cannot be done. You may think of the rapist as a crazed sexual psychopath with a suitable leer, but only a small percentage of sex offenders fit this mold. The typical rapist has no readily identifiable appearance or psychopathology. One of the authors conducted a study of convicted rapists placed in a mental institution as a result of their crimes. There were no observable differences between the personalities of convicted rapists and the average man on the street. For your safety, you must accept the working assumption that every man you meet could be a rapist.

Amir searched the files of the Philadelphia police department and the FBI, reviewing 1,292 rape cases. He found that rapists tend to be young men; the average age in Philadelphia was 23, but the age group most likely to commit rape was between 15 and 19. The FBI confirms this image. Sixty-one percent of the rapists in the United States are under 25 years of age.

The rapist is no stranger to the criminal justice system. Just under 50 percent of the rapists in Amir's study had previously been arrested and booked for a crime. Rapists are likely to live in what criminologists call a "subculture of violence," stressing a "macho" personality and solving their interpersonal problems by force rather than negotiation and compromise.

The rapist's method of operation dovetails with his criminal lifestyle. Rape is not a spur-of-the-moment crime. Amir revealed that 71 percent of the rapes were planned and another 11 percent were partially planned. The attacker could have planned the rape with a specific victim in mind — someone he knows or has frequently seen — but it is more likely that the offender decided to rape a women, any available woman, with the specific victim left to chance. The Queen's Bench study asked seventy-five convicted rapists why they had selected their particular victims; nearly two-thirds said they chose the woman because she was "available and defenseless."

Psychiatrists and criminologists have attempted to classify the rapist by different types. Some experts believe that there are five types of rapists, some three, and others only two. We really do not know. Rapists exhibit a multitude of life-styles, attitudes, values, and opinions.

Judging from extensive research, there appears to be an underlying trait that characterizes most rapists, particularly those who attack strangers. This rapist has ambivalent feelings toward women. He loves and hates them at the same time; idolizing them, he is compelled to dominate and humiliate them. Rape is more than an act of sex. It is an act of power, aggression, dominance.

Most rapists are emotionally unstable. They have always craved female affection, but there is a pattern of rejection from mothers or other women in their lives. They hate women and are quite capable of severe physical abuse if given the opportunity. They want to dominate women and show that they are superior. The act of raping a woman is humiliation by itself, but the rapist frequently goes further. Amir found that many victims were insulted and humiliated beyond the rape.

During an interview in a San Francisco newspaper, the Nob Hill rapist described some of his feelings about women. "Partially it's an act of hostility, partially it's rejection, partially it's an act of reaching out and having your hand slapped and having it happen so much and so long that you become bitter. Some [people] strike out by killing, some strike out by raping, and some strike out by armed robbery." The Nob Hill rapist took out his frustration and anger by raping and beating anonymous women.

The Queen's Bench asked a sample of rapists their responses to their victim's struggling, screaming, or trying to talk their way out of the situation. Almost half of the rapists said they felt angry, and a third said they felt good, powerful, or comfortable because of the resistance. Rapists look, either consciously or unconsciously, for an excuse to hurt and humiliate women beyond the rape itself.

Other rapists are bullies with little respect for the feelings of other people, particularly women. They are chauvinists and see women only as sex objects. In the Queen's Bench study one-quarter of the rapists claimed that their victims were chosen because they were "loose women." They believe women are teasing them and actually want to engage in sex. A refusal must be met by force.

Rape is frequently committed by gangs. Amir found that in 43 percent of the cases the victim was raped by two or more assailants. As cited in John MacDonald's *Rape Offenders and Their Victims*, a study in Toronto concluded that 50 percent of the rapes were committed by groups. A Washington, D.C., study, "Rape in the District of Columbia," found 30 percent. A Denver study put the group rape rate at 18.5 percent.

Rape, like most other crimes of violence, usually involves alcohol. A study by the Queen's Bench, an organization of women lawyers in San Francisco, found that 61.6 percent of the rapists had been drinking immediately before the assault. There was also a higher percentage of *completed* rapes among offenders who had been drinking just prior to the attack. Those who had been drinking completed 80 percent of the rapes they attempted, compared to 58 percent by the nondrinkers.

In addition to police statistics, victim surveys also provide information about rape and rapists. A victim survey is an anonymous questionnaire given to a large sample of people, many of whom have not reported their assault to the police. We get a clearer picture of sexual assault as a common event in the lives of young women. A study by Kirkpatrick and Kanin at Indiana University illustrates that male sexual aggression is common on the college campus. One-fifth of the females in the survey reported that they had suffered "forceful attempts at sexual intercourse in the previous year." Six percent had to deal with "aggressively forceful attempts at sexual intercourse in the course of which menacing threats or coercive infliction of physical pain were employed." Seven out of ten of the most violent episodes involved women in regular dating or engaged relationships.

PLAYING IT SAFE

Although you are always a potential target of a rapist, there are ways to lower the chances of attack. Most of the precautions you can take have already been detailed in Chapter 1 and Chapter 4. In this chapter we present additional tips to help avoid sexual assault.

On the Street

Be aware of your surroundings at all times. When walking down the street or toward your car, notice if anyone is following you. As you approach your car, make sure no one is near. Notice the men who get on buses or subways, or those curiously lurking around shrubs and bushes.

Be suspicious. If you detect something strange, try to figure it out. For example, people fill up seats on a bus or subway in a routine way. Riders will generally sit in seats surrounded by empty ones. If you are alone on a bus seat and a man walks by several empty seats and sits down next to you, this is cause for suspicion. You should wonder about his motives.

When walking on the street alone, you should dress with crime prevention in mind. Appearance is an important factor in rape. If you dress in a provocative manner, men may see you as a sex object. Although this attitude may offend you, it exists and it must be recognized. We recommend that you avoid clothing that will substantially increase your chances of sexual assault.

At Home

You are more likely to be raped in your home than in any other location. Between one-quarter and one-third of all rapes occur in the victim's residence, usually following an unlawful entry. Following proper home security procedures is therefore imperative.

Never put your first name, Miss, or Ms. on your mailbox or door. Your last name should provide sufficient identification for the letter carrier. Remember, the Boston Strangler found many of his victims by scanning apartment mailboxes looking for women's names.

Any dog, no matter how small, provides excellent protection for the woman who lives alone. A Pekingese can be as effective as a Doberman pinscher in scaring off the potential rapist (or burglar). Rapists do not want to attract attention. They want to have control over all aspects of their crime. Although they may be able to get you to comply through threats of force, they cannot control a dog. See Chapter 7 for details on watchdogs.

If you live alone and strange males come to your door, try to give the impression that a man is around. You might call in a loud voice, "I'll get it, John," This may give the potential rapist the impression someone is at home to protect you. Also, avoid letting moving men or repair men know that you are alone.

Keep yourself out of dangerous areas. Do not go into an isolated laundry room in your apartment building alone, particularly at night. If necessary, wait and have a friend accompany you.

The Telephone

Train yourself to answer the telephone with a certain degree of suspicion. Rapists and burglars admit spending hours devising ways of finding easy targets.

If a man calls with the wrong number, never give him your name and phone number. Ask what number he is trying to reach. Sometimes men claiming to be poll takers ask personal questions. Refuse to give any information, particularly of a personal nature. If a man calls to give you a credit card from a particular store after you answer some personal questions, do not divulge any information. If you want the credit card, go to the store and apply in person.

If you list your full name in the telephone book, you leave yourself open to crank calls. Ask the telephone company to put only your first initial (or first two initials) with your last name.

When it is necessary to give your phone number to people from agencies or businesses unfamiliar to you, give them your daytime office number if you work. Also, be sure your fellow employees understand that they should never divulge any information about you without your permission.

In Your Car

Always lock your car doors. This applies when you are driving, sitting in it, or leaving it. Try to park in a well-lighted and conspicuous place as close as you can to your destination. Be especially wary of airport and shopping center parking lots. Rapists can loiter there and follow potential victims to their cars.

When you return from shopping, look in the back seat before getting in. Rapists frequently hide there and surprise women after they get inside. Have your car keys ready, particularly at night, and get in as soon as possible and lock the doors.

If you think you are being followed by a car, do something evasive — change directions, speed up, make a U-turn. If it appears clear that you are being followed, honk your horn and drive for help. It is best to drive to a police station. Nobody would follow you there. You could drive to a gas station and ask the attendant for help. Do *not* drive home, or the person following you will discover where you live. If you are driving in the country, head for the nearest home, and keep your horn on all the way. If possible, write down his license number, and get it to the police.

Sometimes the car behind you will flash its lights. Do not pull over if this happens to you. It is not the police. If a police officer wants to pull you over, he will turn on his red or blue flashing light and siren.

When driving, you may see a car on the side of the road with its hood up. You may be tempted to help someone with car trouble. We suggest you play it safe. Some men pretend to need help, hoping women will stop. If you want to help, telephone the police or highway patrol.

If a man tries to get into your car at a traffic light, quickly look both ways, honk your horn, and, assuming no cars are coming, drive away. Do not worry about breaking the law. Your most important consideration is safety. If a man does get into your car, never go to a secluded area unless he has a weapon and threatens your life. Try not to let the man tie you up even if he has a weapon; you would be too vulnerable to serious injury, or death. If you are in a populated area, attract attention by driving through a red light, running into a parked car, or going up on a curb. Do anything to avoid going to a secluded area where you may be raped or seriously injured.

Hitchhiking

Hitchhiking is not safe. Ten percent of all *reported* rapes involve female hitchhikers. If we calculate the unreported rapes as well, this figure would probably be much higher. Take a bus, borrow a car, ride with a friend. If you insist on hitchhiking, you should bear in mind the following tips to lower your chances of being raped.

Do not hitchhike alone. You are safer hitchhiking with a male friend than with another female, but always have someone with you. Do not accept a ride from a man, especially one who stops his car when you do not have your thumb out. If riding with one man is bad, riding with more than one is worse. Never get into the back seat with a group of men.

If you accept a ride with a man, there are several things you should notice before you get in the car. Look in the back seat to see if anyone is hiding. Check that the door handle on your side works; this is important if you need to escape quickly. Notice if the man is exposing himself and make sure that both his hands are in plain view. Do not accept any rides if you see evidence that the driver has been drinking, such as beer cans on the floor. For obvious reasons, it is a bad idea to ride with a drunk driver even if you feel safe from sexual assault. Do not ride with anyone who has changed directions when he saw you hitchhiking. Always ask the driver where he is going before you get in. If he says something like, "I'll take you wherever you want to go," you should wait for another ride.

Once in the car, there are several rules to follow. Know exactly where you are going and how long it takes to get there. If the driver starts going in the wrong direction, insist on being let out immediately. Never get dropped off exactly where you want to go, particularly if you are going home. Otherwise, strange men will find out where you live. If the man makes sexual advances toward you, follow the rules outlined in the next section.

On Public Transportation

You run the risk of sexual assault whenever you ride on public transportation. Sometimes you only have to contend with a man rubbing up against you or with his wandering hands, but you could be confronted by a rapist.

If a man intentionally touches you in a sexual manner, there are a few things you can do. Many women's groups advocate saying in a loud voice something like, "Get your hands off me, you disgusting pig!" The theory is to embarrass the man so much he will stop this undesirable behavior. We do not advocate this method. You should be concerned about yourself and getting out of an unpleasant situation, but we recommend that you just move to another part of the bus or train. In most cases these men are harmless and would not do anything serious if you embarrassed or humiliated them, but why take the chance? It is just as easy and effective to move away.

Waiting for a bus, especially at night, can be risky. Avoid waiting on isolated streets by walking to a more populated bus stop. Once on the bus, sit in the front near the driver. If anyone bothers you, ask the driver to drop you off at a safe place.

When you are waiting for a train or subway, stand near the change booth or ticket taker. Get into the first car with the motorman, or into a car with a conductor or a security guard. Once in the car, stay alert. This is no place to take a nap. Try not to be alone in a car with a man or a group of men. Know where your exit is, whenever possible. Near your destination, walk to the closest car near your exit. If the train approaches a station and a gang is about to get on, exit just before the door closes so they cannot change their minds and follow you. Push your way off if necessary, or run to another car. If you are being bothered, do not get off at your regular stop unless it is crowded and well-lighted. If your station is deserted, wait and go on to the next one. If you are followed, go to the ticket booth. The attendant should offer help, or at least call the security guards for you. If you are attacked on the train, do not pull the emergency cord. Let the train get to the next station for help. If you can, bang on the motorman's door, and ask him to signal ahead for the police.

On Elevators

Before getting into an elevator, take a quick look and see who is inside. Be wary of an elevator containing one or more men, if you are the only woman. If you are already in an elevator and someone suspicious gets on, you should get off and wait for the next one. Once inside, stand next to the control panel by the door, not in the back of the elevator. Check the alarm button in your apartment building elevator regularly so that you know it works. If the man has a weapon or the building is deserted, do not push the emergency button or antagonize him in any way. Your only hope is to think of some way to attract attention or escape before he takes you to the basement or roof.

IF YOU ARE CONFRONTED BY A RAPIST

It is not easy for women to decide what tactics to use against the rapist. The subject of rape is entangled by myth and emotion. Authorities on rape prevention have not been able to agree on the best way for women to respond to a sexual assault. Some call for complete compliance with everything the rapist demands. Some feminist groups advocate direct physical combat the instant the assault begins. Authorities with more conservative views believe that psychological tricks, mechanical gadgets, body language, and other forms of communication are capable of deterring the rapist. Below we discuss various responses to the rapist and the best conditions for each one. Recent studies reveal the conditions under which violence can be anticipated and the consequences of the victim's resistance. Most of these studies support earlier conclusions about the rapist's personality. Familiarity between the victim and the attacker is an important condition. In *Against Rape* Medea and Thompson found that the *less* familiar the victim was with the attacker, the more violence was used. In their overall sample of rapes, violence occurred in 50 percent of the cases. When the rapist was a stranger, the chance of violence went up to 75 percent. If the rapist was an acquaintance of the victim, the chance of violence went down to 24 percent. The attitude of the rapist also seemed to affect the level of violence. There was a much greater chance that the rapist would use violence if he appeared "hostile" and "contemptuous," rather than "righteous" and "matter of fact."

Of utmost importance to women is the end result of resistance. Amir found that over half the victims displayed what he termed submissive behavior; many others screamed, kicked, or tried to escape, and others fought back by kicking, hitting, or throwing objects. Amir found that those women in the "brutally beaten" category had been the *least* likely to submit to the attacker.

Further evidence suggests that struggling and other physical resistance is not a good idea, at least at the early stage of the attack. In San Francisco, interviewers asked rapists a variety of questions about violence and resistance. Over half became angrier during the attack, and most of these offenders attributed this change in attitude to the victim's resistance at the beginning of the attack. A quarter of the men stated that they decided to hurt the victim when she started to resist either at the beginning of the attack or later. The offenders were asked what the victim could have done to stop the escalation of violence. Not quite half said that they would have liked their victims to comply and submit to their assault; but over a third of the rapists said that their victims should have resisted more, either verbally or physically, to deter the rape.

These studies run contrary to certain popular advice. Many women's groups advocate physical resistance from the first instant of attack. We feel that this advice is dangerous. Most self-defense suggestions, particularly those involving the martial arts, are extremely difficult for the uninitiated women to do effectively. The chief suggestions, such as chops and kicks to the vital areas, do not usually have much chance of working.

There are, however, some conditions under which we recommend the use of physical resistance. First, when safety is nearby. If you believe screaming will arouse attention and send someone to your rescue, then scream long and loud. If you think struggling will free you from the attacker and allow you to reach safety, then struggle with all your might. But if you are isolated from others, those tactics could make matters worse. Second, physical resistance is usually appropriate if you are attacked by an acquaintance. If the would-be rapist considers you an easy mark, your resistance might be enough to deter him. It would certainly dispel any ideas that you were merely playing ''hard to get.'' Physical resistance is even safer if he is not drunk. Third, we recommend physical resistance if you feel that you are in immediate danger of losing your life. If your attacker has a weapon and seems determined to kill you, you should resist in whatever manner you can. See the section on Self-Defense in this chapter (pages 136 – 138).

We do not advocate compliance. If you do not resist in some manner, you have very little chance of avoiding rape. Jerrold Offstein states in *Self-Defense for Women* that of all the women he studied who escaped successfully from their attacker, not one got away by total compliance. All of the women resisted in some manner. The question is: What form of resistance should you take?

The overriding principle to be followed is: Do not do anything that will put you in a worse position than you are already in. This principle calls for you to use your own good judgment, as well as follow these basic rules.

Do not antagonize the rapist. We are not contradicting ourselves. Rapists, particularly those who attack strangers, are emotionally unbalanced. If you physically resist or scream, this may trigger the rapist's hostility. Resistance does not always have to take the form of antagonizing the rapist. If you try to escape, you may be fulfilling his expectations that women cannot be trusted. He will feel justified to use force on you. If the rapist views you as being aggressive, he will likely reciprocate. If you introduce violence into the situation, there may be no turning back. Once violence starts, the winner is usually the one who is more violent. Unless you can escape, save your physical resistance until later.

Do not physically resist a man with a weapon. A weapon changes the situation from the possibility of rape to the possibility of murder. Remain calm. This may sound difficult under the circumstances, but you have to try. It is very difficult to predict the reactions of the rapist who carries a weapon.

The following rape case recently took place in the authors' hometown. A woman was watching television alone in her living room late one evening. She heard a noise in the bedroom and went to investigate. Upon entering the bedroom a man grabbed her from behind. She screamed and struggled, finally breaking his grip. The outside door was only fifteen feet away, but she never made it. The assailant caught her and threw her down hard on the fireplace. The fall broke her arm. The rapist proceeded to beat her severely. As he raped her, he taunted her with questions: "Who is the master of this house?" "Who is the boss?" An angry man, he had been looking for an excuse to beat up the victim and dominate her.

How far could you run before a rapist would be able to catch you? The victim made matters worse by struggling. It antagonized the attacker and gave him a reason to hurt her. There are better, less risky ways to attempt to get out of such situations with less chance of injury.

Struggling can also arouse the attacker sexually so that he will be filled with lust. Convicted rapists commonly state that they became more aroused when struggling with the victim. Struggling accelerates the rapist's heartbeat and tenses his muscles. Overcoming a struggling woman is often more enjoyable to a rapist than having sexual intercourse with a passive woman. This is part of the rapist's sexual need.

We have been telling you what *not* to do. How should you react if you are confronted by a rapist? The circumstances differ in each sexual assault, as do the offenders and the victims. Storaska noticed that women who successfully repel rapists exhibit common elements of behavior. Based on these common elements, the following rules are listed.

1. Keep yourself together. You need your wits about you to evaluate the situation and to plan a method of escape. Do not be afraid to show your fear. The rapist wants respect from you. He likes to know you are afraid. If you acknowledge, even nonverbally, that you are the weak person in this temporary relationship, the rapist may be psychologically satisfied.

2. Treat the rapist as a human being. People tend to live up to the way others act toward them. If you call the rapist a dirty pig, he is more likely to act like one. Try to be civil. You do not want the attacker's behavior to degenerate any further.

3. Gain his confidence. The rapist is usually just as frightened as the victim during the assault. You represent a serious threat to his security. He could be caught by the police at any moment. Unless you gain his confidence and ease his fears, you will be in danger throughout the attack.

4. Pretend to go along with him. If you are attacked, your first impulse may be to resist. Unless safety is near, that impulse could put your life in jeopardy. The rapist will interpret your resistance as aggression, and he will counter it in whatever way he can, usually by force. We are not suggesting that you give in to the rapist, but give the *impression* of going along with him. When his guard is down in anticipation of things to come, you can make your move. Escape to safety, use psychological tricks, or attempt physical self-defense tactics, which we will discuss later.

5. Use your imagination and judgment. Storaska found that most women who avoid rape did so by analyzing the rapist's personality and circumstances of the attack. They rarely resorted to any sort of combat techniques they learned in self-defense classes or in books. They used their imaginations, their wits, and their intuition to figure out what would work best in the present situation.

Psychological Tactics

Some tactics may repel the attacker, others may stall for time. Some are imaginative and require convincing acting, others are base and disgusting. These tactics work better if the attacker is an acquaintance rather than a stranger. They are more successful if the attacker is sober, rational, and matter of fact rather than hostile and angry.

1. Act crazy. You might babble and say irrational things. You could act manic and then depressive. The rapist may feel sorry for you and let you go. Or he may believe that raping a mentally disturbed person would not be fun. If you appear too disturbed to acknowledge the rapist's dominance, much of his pleasure is taken away.

2. Pretend you are ill. You might tell the rapist that you have cancer or a heart disease. Playing on his sympathy may cause him to stop the attack.

3. Tell the rapist you have VD. He may look for a purer woman. However, this tactic works better on men you know than on strangers. Many rapists already have VD and are not deterred if you are infected too.

4. Go limp or faint. The rapist probably does not want to carry over a hundred pounds of dead weight. It is also psychologically less rewarding for the rapist to have sexual intercourse with an unconscious person. The challenge is in the struggle.

5. Compliment the attacker. If you need to stall for time you can build up his ego by flattery. It may sound hypocritical to flatter a man who is attacking you, but it has worked for other women.

6. Turn the attacker off sexually. Certain vulgar behavior, such as urinating, defecating, passing wind, or sticking your finger down your throat and vomiting may cause the rapist to lose his desire. This may be disgusting, but you should not worry about social conventions when you are faced with the prospect of rape and bodily injury.

Even though most of these tactics appear neutral, they can be interpreted by the attacker as antagonistic if he believes you are faking. You must do a convincing act. It is important for you to choose a strategy suited to your personality and to the situation.

None of these tactics will work if you do not establish communication channels with the attacker. Communication does not have to be verbal. Facial gestures, a look of fright, and body language also get the rapist to pay attention so you can try to manipulate him.

Plan ahead. The panic that overcomes many women at the onset of an attack is largely a lack of mental preparation. Ask yourself how you would react to rape. You may be accosted by a stranger in the street, or you may be attacked by an acquaintance in your own home. Each rape situation calls for a different response. By rehearsing what to do, you have a better chance of reacting appropriately. Planning ahead has another benefit. A study of rape victims by the Rape Crisis Center in Palo Alto, California, found that women who had a defense strategy in mind before the rape recovered more quickly from its psychological aftereffects.

All of the recommended tactics are mutually supportive. It is important that you start out with a comfortable plan of action. If this strategy seems unsuitable, try something else. Do not give up.

Self-Defense

In some ways women are trained to be rape victims. Boys are taught to be aggressive, while girls are taught to be submissive and helpless. Boys learn to fight and defend themselves, but girls are discouraged from rough play. Although these values are being reexamined and criticized, they are part of our society and serve to make women victims.

All women should learn how to defend themselves against attack. In the previous chapter on Street Crime, we outlined some basic self-defense techniques, including the use of weapons (pages 107 – 114). A woman should follow these same general strategies when defending herself against the rapist. But because of the unique nature of rape, we have a few additional suggestions to make.

We recommended in the preceding chapter that you should not attempt any of the standard martial-arts kicks or hits unless you are an expert. The risks are simply too great. There are other ways to physically resist attack that do not require years of training. Frederic Storaska advocates two such tactics, both of which we endorse.

The first tactic involves hurting the attacker's eyes. Move your hands *slowly* to the man's face, as if you were going to caress his head. Place the palms of your hands on each side of his face, so that your fingers are touching his ears. Next, move your thumbs in front of his eyes. Now sharply push your thumbs into his eyes. If he is wearing eyeglasses, you can easily put your thumbs under them. With a moderate push lasting for a few seconds, he will go into a state of shock and pass out. If you press hard enough, his eyes can push against his brain and kill him. It may sound gruesome, but you have a right to use any means to protect yourself. The rapist is violating *you*. He may even kill you.

The second tactic also requires an attack on one of the rapist's vulnerable areas. Slowly reach down, as if to caress the attacker's testicles. The rapist may even request that you put your hand on his genitals. After you have access to his testicles, squeeze them. This will send the assailant into shock.

These two tactics have several advantages over the traditional kicks and chops of the martial arts. First, they can be used by all women. You do not need a black belt in karate to effectively hurt your attacker. Second, they do not signal your intentions. If you slowly move your hands to the attacker's face, he will not think you are being aggressive. Once you have your thumbs over the man's eyes or your hands on his testicles, it is almost impossible to make a mistake. Compare this tactic with an attempted karate chop to the throat. If you are not an expert, your chances of scoring a direct hit are very small.

For these two tactics to work, you have to get close to you attacker. Although your natural inclination may be to stand away, you are least effective in defending yourself from a distance. To neutralize the size and strength differences between you and the rapist, you should be as close as possible. He will be restricted from using long, hard striking blows and kicks, and you will be more able to attack his vital areas.

Against your best instincts, you are better off defensively while lying or sitting down. When we previously recommended going limp or fainting, you may have wondered what would have happened if the attacker simply let you fall. You would then be in a more advantageous position to carry out these two self-defense tactics.

Storaska mentions a few other self-defense tactics, but warns that they are not as effective because their chance of failure is greater. One involves hitting a pressure point on the side of the head. Gently place your hands on the sides of the man's head, as in the eye attack. Reach behind his ears with your index fingers. Slightly below his earlobes, where the skull and the jawbone meet, is a pressure point filled with nerve endings. This spot is very sensitive to pain. *Firmly* press your index fingers in these two openings for a couple of seconds and your attacker will go into shock. If you press this spot for more than six seconds, you will kill him.

The other method involves biting the rapist's upper lip. Bring your face slowly toward the attacker's, as if you were going to kiss him. Then bite his upper lip with all of your might. You have more strength in your jaws then you realize. The upper lip is very sensitive to pain. If you bite him in the right spot, he should go into shock and you can escape.

To employ any of these self-defense measures successfully, you must stay calm, gain the attacker's confidence, and wait until his guard is down. If you lash out blindly at your attacker from the very beginning of the encounter, he will not give you the opportunity to use our recommended self-defense tactics.

Although physical resistance is not recommended in the initial stages of an attack, there are exceptions. You should resist if people are near you or you think you can escape to safety. Physical resistance is also recommended if you personally know the attacker and believe he will not escalate the level of violence.

IF YOU ARE RAPED

For many women, what happens after a rape can be as traumatic as the rape itself. Crude police behavior, harsh hospital routines, and the apparent cruelty of the trial procedure make many women reluctant to report rape. Women also fear telling their husbands, relatives, or friends because of the shame and stigma attached to it. Men wonder if there was complicity, if she "asked for it"; friends silently wonder if she tried as hard as she could to resist and escape. These attitudes about rape are deplorable but real. Studies have shown that the divorce rate increases 15 percent after a wife has been raped. Until men better understand the rape situation, women must make their own choice in their own interests about reporting rape. But first, let us look at our changing times.

In response to the dreadful treatment of rape victims, women's groups have been instrumental in setting up rape crisis centers. Volunteers and professionals provide counseling and follow-up support from the police interrogation to the hospital examination to the court trial. Rape crisis centers not only give emotional support and guidance to the victim, but also educate the public about rape and rape prevention. Some give self-defense classes for women. They usually have an emergency phone number and a drop-in center where women can get immediate attention.

Because of the women's movement, other agencies and organizations involved with rape victims have improved. The police have also accepted a more understanding view of women's feelings and frequently assign women officers to interview rape victims. Hospital personnel have become more educated to the plight of rape victims, reflected in a less trying and more sympathetic medical examination for the victim. Finally, the court rules have slowly changed in favor of the rape victim; chastity is no longer an issue. Questions about previous sexual experiences are deemed irrelevant unless they have a direct bearing on the case at hand.

Although we understand the psychological and social barriers in reporting rape to the police, we urge all women to do so and we believe there is a compelling reason: Rapists should be apprehended and convicted. Even if you do not feel the need for revenge, think of other women. It is quite likely that the person who raped you will try to rape someone else in the future.

In reporting a rape you will be less filled with anxiety if you understand the procedure. We will present the usual sequence of events in the average rape where the victim is not severely injured.

Immediately After the Rape

First, call the police as soon after the incident as you can, especially if you have been raped by a stranger. Immediately calling the authorities significantly increases the chances of apprehending the assailant. A prompt call also increases the likelihood that the police will believe your story. By waiting several hours or days, the police and other authorities will be more skeptical of your complaint.

Next, call a good friend, preferably someone your own age and sex. That person will be more likely to understand and empathize. Try to predict the reactions of your husband or boyfriend. If you can count on him to be understanding, call him immediately. If he might be anything less, don't bother to call him right away. Whether or not friends or relatives are available, you should call the local rape crisis center. They will give you emergency advice over the telephone and possibly send someone to your residence. Your main consideration is to have some form of emotional support for the events that will take place in the next few hours.

If possible, try to remember as much as you can about the rapist — his appearance, manners, method of operation. Height and weight are important, but scars, tattoos, or other body markings are better aids for the police in identification. Do not bathe, douche, or change clothes after the rape. The police and the prosecutor need evidence of rape if they are going to apprehend and convict the offender.

The Police

One or two patrol officers will probably be dispatched to your residence soon after you call the police. They will drive you to the hospital. On the way, it will be necessary to ask you questions about the incident and the assailant. It is important for the police to work fast.

After the initial report and after you have been taken to the hospital, you will be interviewed by detectives from the sex crime unit of the police department. If the rape took place in your home, they will interview you there to observe any evidence. More likely, you will go to the police station and be asked to look through "mug shots" of suspects. In either case, you should have someone along for emotional support.

At the police station you may request a woman officer to interview you. The questions will be quite personal. The officers will ask, for example, if the rapist forced you to perform sex acts other than intercourse. Some rape victims have reported that police officers occasionally ask improper questions. One such question would be

"Did you have a climax?" Report such incidents to the proper supervisor.

After the interview you will be asked to sign a statement. Read this carefully and do not sign it unless it is correct. This report may be used in court. If you disagree with the report and the police will not change it, write your own version and attach it to the official police report.

If you decide that you cannot go through the ordeal of official proceedings, you can report the crime anonymously to the police. You will avoid the inconveniences, but you will still help the police. Your information about the rapist's operation and his description may be just the tip the police need to arrest the suspect.

At the Hospital

Needless to say, a rape victim is under great emotional stress at the hospital. This stress is heightened by overcrowded facilities, long waits, and the cold efficiency of a busy hospital.

In addition to a friend or person from a rape crisis center, you might consider asking your family doctor or gynecologist to accompany you to the hospital. Your personal doctor could assist at the medical examination. He will know your medical history and any allergic reactions. Hospital personnel will be more attentive if you have your own doctor with you.

Only if you are *sure* you do not want to prosecute, go directly to your family doctor. This has obvious appeal and obvious disadvantages. Your doctor may not collect the necessary evidence for you to have your day in court. Family doctors can offer beneficial emotional support, but they are probably not experts in the collection of evidence to prosecute a case of rape properly.

The reasons for having a medical examination are to determine the extent of your injuries and to gather evidence for prosecuting the case. The doctor will ask personal questions, many of which are standard medical procedure; others are directly related to the rape. The doctor will ask about your use of contraceptives, activity after the assault (bath, medication, etc.), and your medical history. Before the actual examination, you will be asked to sign a consent form for the examination, the collection of evidence, any photographs to be taken, and the voluntary release of information to the authorities.

The doctor will appear nonjudgmental and perhaps unsympathetic. The doctor has been trained to act this way, particularly since he or she may be called to testify in court and the medical records can be subpoenaed. The doctor will ask you to remove your clothes, which will probably be kept for evidence. It is a good idea, if you can remember, to bring along something to wear home. The physician will turn them over to the police in exchange for a detailed receipt. The crime lab will look for traces of blood, sperm, or male pubic hair.

Most hospitals follow a procedure recommended by the American College of Obstetricians and Gynecologists. The doctor will first examine the external genital area for trauma and then insert a nonlubricated, but water-moistened, speculum for an examination of your vagina and cervix. A vaginascope may also be used.

The doctor will take specimens from the vaginal pool and put them into test tubes for protection as evidence. Another swab may be taken from the vulva. The medical personnel will also comb your pubic hair, photograph bruises and lacerations, and check for sperm outside the vaginal canal. They may use a special lamp to locate dried semen on your body surfaces. The lab technicians are looking for the presence of acid phosphotase, a body chemical found in semen. The acid phosphotase test only indicates the possibility that the specimen is the male's discharge. It does not necessarily indicate that a rape took place. The technicians also determine if the sperm are alive or dead, confirming your version of the time of the attack.

As a result of the rape, you may have additional medical complications. There is the possibility of pregnancy or venereal disease. The doctor should inform you that other vaginal infections frequently occur at a later date.

To avoid pregnancy, you can take medication at the hospital. This is an immediate solution to the problem, but you may face certain medical risks by taking the medication. You can also wait to see if you get pregnant. If you do, then you have to deal with the pregnancy at that time. Part of your decision may rest on the chances of your becoming pregnant. In general, the chances of becoming pregnant from one random act of intercourse are only about 5 percent. Of course, the chances go up significantly between 10 and 18 days after the end of your last menstrual period.

One of the most commonly used methods to avoid pregnancy immediately after a rape is the so-called ''morning-after pill,'' which is properly called diethylstilbestrol, or DES. DES is an artificial estrogen that affects the lining of the uterus so that a fertilized egg cannot be implanted. DES is taken orally and treatment must begin soon after the rape. DES prevents you from becoming pregnant, but it does not abort an existing fetus. Since DES can harm a fetus, it is important that you find out if you were pregnant at the time of the rape. Do *not* take DES if you are pregnant.

DES is a known carcinogen, a cancer-causing agent. This drug has already been banned from beef and from use as an antimiscarriage drug in pregnant women. Its effects take years to determine. We know that an unusually high percentage of the daughters of women who took DES while pregnant have vaginal cancer, yet there is currently no proof that women who take this drug will get cancer themselves. You should not take DES if your mother took the drug when she was pregnant with you, if you are already pregnant (if you don't know, take a test), or if there is a family history of cancer, diabetes, or diseases of the liver, kidney, lungs, or heart.

Another morning-after pill has recently been developed. Called ethinylestradiol, it is supposed to be no more dangerous than a regular birth control pill. Thorough testing, however, has not been done. If you choose to take a morning-after pill, ask the doctor about this new drug.

We recommend that you think carefully before you take any synthetic hormones. They may be dangerous. You should know that there are alternatives to the morning-after pill. You can ask for a dilation and curettage, or D & C. In this procedure, the doctor scrapes away the uterine lining, preventing the growth of a fertilized egg. If it is conducted soon after intercourse, it is not necessarily considered an abortion. It can be conducted as soon as two weeks after the rape or as late as two weeks after the menstrual period is due.

Another alternative is menstrual extraction, removing the lining of the uterus by suction through a narrow tube inserted through the cervix. In many cases, the tube can be inserted without anesthesia or dilating the cervix. Many people consider menstrual extraction superior to a D & C because it is faster, less complicated, and has less risk of uterine perforation. Menstrual extraction can be performed a week or two after the rape or up to ten days after menstruation is due. This procedure is similar to an abortion, except that there need not be positive knowledge of pregnancy.

If you have a pregnancy test and determine that you are pregnant, legal abortions are available for rape victims. In some states these abortions are free, in some a small fee is charged. Check with local law enforcement agencies for details.

Some hospitals routinely test rape victims for venereal disease (VD). But the VD test will only determine if you already have VD, not if you contracted it from the rapist. Therefore, it becomes your decision whether you want to be tested at this time or wait until some later date.

It is essential, however, that you get diagnostic tests for VD at some time after the rape. The gonorrhea culture can be taken from one week to three months after contact and the syphilis blood test can be taken as soon as three weeks after contact. Therefore, we recommend that you take the tests from four to six weeks after the rape. Keep in mind that a negative result of your VD test six weeks after the rape does not mean that future tests will not be positive. VD testing every six months for two years is advisable.

Even though you will not know if you have contracted VD from the rapist, most doctors will routine recommend prophlyactic antibiotic therapy — injections of penicillin. You may be given one gram of probenecid taken orally thirty minutes before the injections to retain the penicillin in the bloodstream for the longest possible time.

You can also receive an oral form of penicillin for the treatment of VD called ampicillin. It is usually given with probenecid and should be taken on an empty stomach. Avoid eating for an hour after. This is necessary because food in the stomach, especially milk products, greatly decreases the absorption of this medication. If you are allergic to penicillin, you will probably be given tetracycline. Be sure to let the doctor know of any allergic reactions you have had in the past.

Court Procedure
If the attacker is known to you or has been caught, you will want to know if he is out on bail and when he comes to trial. Many victims

complain because the police and the district attorney do not keep them informed. If the police do not call you, you should call them to learn of the progress of the investigation.

If the police and district attorney decide you have a good case, they will proceed with the prosecution. To gain a conviction, they need your cooperation. If you do not want to appear in court, the case will be dropped. If you press charges and the case proceeds to trial, it is much harder for you to get the case dropped. Many victims decide not to testify in court and find themselves subpoenaed by the district attorney to appear as witnesses in their own case.

When charges are pressed and sufficient evidence against the defendant is gathered, the case can be brought to trial. More likely a plea bargain will be struck. The defendant's lawyer and the state agree that the defendant will plead guilty to a lesser offense.

If the case is prosecuted, you cannot choose the deputy district attorney you want to handle the case. If you can afford it, you should hire your *own* attorney to help you throughout the proceedings. Your lawyer will act as your advocate and will also advise you of the chances of conviction, given the amount of evidence in the case.

A court of law is a public forum. You have to expect strangers, reporters, and friends of the defendant to be in the gallery. The courtroom can be closed to the public only if both sides agree. You can have the district attorney ask, but the rapist's defense attorney is unlikely to agree to this request. You can also request that your address not be read aloud in open court, but the judge may or may not grant it. If your address is on the public record or mentioned in court, you could be subjected to harrassment from the defendant or his friends.

Cross-examination can be a grueling and painful experience for many rape victims. Although the rules of evidence are changing for the benefit of the victim, the attorney will still try to insinuate that you are mistaken about the assailant's identity or that you consented to have sexual relations. The defense attorney might also try to show that you are promiscuous and that you did not resist sufficiently for a rape to have taken place. The defense attorney's goal, of course, is to convince the jury that there is reasonable doubt that the rape occurred. If the jury finds reasonable doubt, the defendant will be found not guilty and set free.

CONCLUSION

Women fear rape. Yet most women know little about it. We attempt to make clear in this chapter that any woman can be the rapist's target, but by knowing the facts, you can lower the odds of being victimized. If you are confronted by a rapist, you do not have to resort to passive submission or physical resistance. We urge our readers to choose from our recommended rape prevention techniques.

If you are raped, understanding legal procedures will reduce the trauma of official actions. Remember, there are alternatives that you can choose.

Finally, the subject of rape prevention is not just for you. You should discuss with family and friends what you would do in the event of a sexual assault. Rape and rape prevention must be discussed openly and frankly if harmful attitudes and prejudices are going to be changed.

Chapter 6

Physical and Sexual Abuse of Children

Every year thousands of children suffer severe mistreatment, ranging from neglect and deprivation to physical and sexual abuse.

The nature of child mistreatment is frequently misunderstood. When most people think of crimes against children, they envision a dirty old man lurking in the park waiting to sexually molest an unsuspecting child. Or they think of something worse — the kidnapping and murder of a defenseless youngster. Although these tragic crimes do occur, most abuse of children is committed by the children's *own* parents or guardians.

In this chapter we divide child mistreatment into two categories: the physical and the sexual abuse of children. We discuss the physical and sexual abuse of children separately because normally they are quite unrelated.

In both types of abuse distinct behavior patterns on the part of the offender can be seen. Physical abuse, often called child abuse, is the intentional and repeated use of physical force by a parent or guardian aimed at harming the child. Child abuse is frequently linked to excessive physical punishment. It typically involves beating, hitting, burning, or other forms of physical punishment; sexual assaults are ordinarily absent.

The sexual abuse of children, also called sexual molestation, consists of a wide range of sexual activity between adult and child. The offender exploits the child. The sexual organs of the adult or child are in some way involved in the offense, from the fondling of genitals to forcible rape, although usually the child is not seriously injured.

147

Statistically, sexual abuse of children is much less prevalent than physical abuse.

The offenders' motivations in each form of abuse are also distinct. The child abuser seems primarily intent upon hurting the child, whereas the child molester seeks sexual gratification. Child abuse is usually spontaneous; sexual molestation is calculated.

Solutions, too, usually differ for each type of offense. Because the motivations of the offenders differ, so must the preventive measures taken by parents, and the therapeutic strategies used by local agencies.

In the following pages we discuss each of these two types of child abuse in depth; we refer to studies and statistics to create a clearer picture of the nature and extent of the abuse and suggest what to do in the event of child mistreatment. Most people do not know where to turn for help. As people learn about available programs, they will be more willing to report this hidden social problem or to seek help for themselves and their family members.

PHYSICAL ABUSE OF CHILDREN

Some of the cruelest acts imaginable have been perpetrated against children. The list of tortures suggests a Nazi concentration camp. Yet these brutalities happen every day in the United States, and they are usually committed by the children's own parents or caretakers. Child abuse is a major social problem; its enormous dimensions are only beginning to be realized.

Child abuse can have disastrous consequences. Abused children have a higher mortality rate. Death is sometimes the direct result of injuries inflicted by parents; but abused and neglected children, even if given the minimum requirements of food and shelter, also tend to die sooner than children whose families provide abundant love and attention.

Abused children suffer a loss of self-esteem. If their parents treat them as undeserving of love, children begin to look down on themselves and believe they are unworthy of parental affection. Loss of self-esteem and feelings of rejection can lead to behavior problems in later life. Abused children frequently turn into juvenile delinquents, commit suicide, or repeat child abuse patterns on their own children.

Children who suffer abuse often develop characteristics that make them more unlovable. They exhibit such traits as fear of being alone, continued whimpering, shyness, depression, hyperactivity, and destructiveness. These undesirable features often cause parents to become even more abusive.

Recent Interest in Child Abuse

Historically, child abuse has been a hidden crime, given insufficient attention by scholars, doctors, or criminal justice officials. Child abuse began to attract serious professional consideration in 1962 when C. Henry Kempe, a pediatrician at the University of Colorado School of Medicine, and several of his colleagues published an article in which they coined the term the "battered child syndrome." The authors presented findings of a study of 749 child abuse cases reported by seventy-one hospitals and seventy-seven district attorneys throughout the country. Many of the children had died or been seriously injured. The authors concluded that child abuse was a major cause of death and trauma in children.

Dr. Kempe and his associates recommended that physicians notify the authorities of suspected cases of child abuse, and this recommendation was endorsed by the *Journal of the American Medical Association*. By June of 1967 every state in the Union had adopted laws that required physicians and other specified professionals to report all suspected cases of child abuse to local law enforcement or welfare agencies. Most new laws also exempted from civil and criminal liability those people who reported in good faith suspected cases of child abuse.

As additional scientific research about child abuse has been published since 1962, government officials have realized the need for special legislation to protect children. Congress passed in 1971 the Child Protection Services Act which required each of the fifty states to set up programs or agencies for abused or neglected children. In 1974 President Nixon signed into law the Child Abuse Prevention and Treatment Act, which founded the National Center for Child Abuse and Neglect in Washington, D.C. During the 1970s, a variety of demonstration and prevention programs emerged throughout the United States. As a result, professionals have learned a great deal about the causes and treatment of child abuse.

What is Child Abuse?

Child abuse has never been clearly defined. For some experts, the definition of abuse rests solely on the physical injury inflicted on the child, rather than on the intention or motivation of the abuser. This definition is highly ambiguous. Consider two examples. In the first, a parent wants to punish his child, so he slaps her firmly on the side of the face. The slap causes a bruise, but there is no lasting blemish or injury. In the second incident, the parent again strikes the child on the side of the face. But this time the child is standing off balance, falls, down, and cracks her head on the fireplace. The child loses consciousness, has a fractured skull, and must be hospitalized. What is the difference between these two incidents? Was the parent abusing the child in the second example, but not in the first?

The dividing line between stern, yet acceptable punishment and child abuse is blurry, particularly in our society, where corporal punishment is so often regarded as a necessary and sometimes desirable disciplinary measure. Surveys reveal that more than nine out of ten American parents physically punish their children.

Many parents get carried away when correcting their children and occasionally inflict unintended injury. In this book we do not consider isolated incidents of unintentionally excessive punishment to be child abuse unless the child is severely assaulted. Our definition of child abuse contains two key elements. First, the parent must *intend* to harm or injure the child. Intention may be a temporary state. The parent may regret his actions and be remorseful the next day, but at the time of the incident the parent wanted to hurt the child. There must also be a *pattern* of mistreatment. A single act is not sufficient; repeated injury is required. Recognizing a pattern of abuse is also important because prevention is one of the purposes of this book. One incident cannot be prevented; repeated abuse can.

The Extent of Child Abuse

No one currently knows the full scope of child abuse. In fact, less is known about the extent of child abuse than about most other crimes. Child abuse is rarely reported. Parents do not report the abuses they inflict on their children; family members too often view child abuse as a family problem, hiding it from outsiders; many doctors view child abuse as a medical problem, and frequently do not report possible mistreatment. Only the most serious cases are reported, after a child must be taken to the hospital.

Estimates of the incidence of child abuse range from 60,000 to 2 million cases per year. There are two principal sources of data: official agency reports and national surveys. The low estimates of child abuse come from the records of hospitals and community child protection agencies. Agency contacts represent only a fraction of all child abuse cases; the rest go unreported. Higher estimates come from national surveys. Interviews with parents across the country and questionnaires sent to doctors reveal thousands of cases of child abuse that are never reported to the appropriate agencies.

The most recent estimates of child abuse come from Richard J. Gelles, a sociologist at the University of Rhode Island. Appearing before Congress in 1978, he testified that between one and two million parents have attempted or succeeded in stabbing or shooting their children; between three and four million children have been kicked, bitten, or punched by their parents; and as many as two million children are abused in some manner *each year* in the United States. Additionally, Gelles' research concluded that mothers are more likely than fathers to abuse their children, and sons are more likely than daughters to be victims of abuse.

Child abuse appears to be on the increase — at least based on an increased need for protective services of abused children. In California, for example, there were 43,113 referrals for protective custody to county welfare departments in 1972. By 1976, the number of such referrals had jumped to 62,725, an increase of 45 percent in just four years. It is not clear, however, whether the annual rise in reported cases is due to an actual increase in the rate of abuse or simply to the greater willingness of citizens to step forward.

Reasons for Child Abuse

Each academic discipline has its own explanation for child abuse. Psychiatrists emphasize the psychological abnormalities of the offenders. Mental illness, it is asserted, causes parents to abuse their children. Sociologists claim, however, that most parents who engage in child abuse are not mentally ill. They focus instead on stressful environmental factors that push normal parents over the line of acceptable disciplinary practices. Economic pressures put great stress on many families, as do temporary unhappy situations like family illness, marital problems, and sexual frustrations. Many socially oriented professionals examine how a child may alter or disrupt the social, sexual, and economic stability of the parents.

Many stressful and frustrating situations, particlarly economic, are found in the lower classes. But current data do not indicate a strong relationship between child abuse and poverty. Many middle- and upper-class parents also abuse their children, though their abuse does not as readily come to the attention of official agencies.

Some experts claim that a key to understanding the physical abuse of children rests in our culture's attitudes toward punishment. American society permits, and in some cases encourages as necessary, the use of physical force by parents and others to modify children's basic antisocial tendencies.

Physical punishment often has unintended consequences. Studies reveal that parents' uncontrolled disciplinary outbursts frequently cause their children physical injury. Furthermore, abuse breeds abuse. A major cause of child abuse is the parents' repetition of the pattern of abuse to which they were subjected as children. The psychological and sociological factors that contribute to child abuse must be measured against our culture's permissive attitude toward the use of physical force on children.

A factor frequently overlooked as a cause of child abuse is the child's own behavior. Some children cry endlessly, others engage in obnoxious or delinquent behavior. When parents are under unusual stress, such undesirable behavior often precipitates abuse.

We must conclude that there is no single cause of child abuse. Neither psychiatry nor sociology can provide complete explanations for this multifaceted problem.

Possible Signs of Child Abuse

Child abuse is sometimes obvious. Occasionally a child will be severely beaten and willing to identify his parent as the person who hurt him. Most of the time, however, evidence of child abuse is less apparent than we would like. If the parent will not admit his abuses and if the child will not complain, you have to look for other indicators. To spot child abuse, you must know what to look for.

Dr. Vincent Fontana, a foremost authority on child abuse, has provided a list of clues to help nonphysicians recognize possible causes of abuse and negligence. Abuse or neglect *may* be present if:

1. The child shows evidence of repeated skin or other injuries.

2. The injuries are inappropriately treated in terms of bandages and medication.

3. The parents blame a sibling or other third party for the child's injuries.

4. The parents delay in seeking medical care for their sick or injured children.

5. The child seems unduly afraid of his parents.

6. The child cries often for no apparent reason.

7. The child is unusually fearful.

8. The child is described as "different" or "bad" by his parents.

9. The child is notably destructive or aggressive.

10. The parent appears to be misusing drugs or alcohol.

11. The parents ignore the child's crying or react with extreme impatience.

12. The parents have unrealistic expectations of the child — that it should be mature beyond its years.

Naturally, none of these factors necessarily indicates child abuse; a perfectly normal and loving family may exhibit several of them. But medical experience has shown that many of these indicators are likely to be present in most child abuse situations. If you observe any of them, watch carefully for further signs of child abuse.

Reporting Child Abuse

People outside the immediate family are largely responsible for protecting children from abusive parents. Professionals in some occupations have a legal responsibility to report suspected cases of child abuse. The list of professions varies somewhat from state to state, but usually includes doctors, dentists, nurses, teachers, school counselors, and, of course, the police.

The average citizen has a moral responsibility to report suspected child abuse. By informing the police or local child abuse agency that you suspect a child is being mistreated by his parents, you may well be saving a life, preventing permanent physical damage, or protecting the child from future emotional trauma.

Do not be afraid to get involved. Make sure you know the facts, and then act. You cannot be prosecuted or sued for reporting child abuse in good faith. If you wish, you can remain anonymous. Just a tip to the police or any social welfare agency could save a child from untold suffering.

Public involvement in serious child abuse is quite common. In one nationwide survey, nine out of ten of the respondents said they would try somehow to protect a child from severe parental abuse. Yet in less serious cases, a majority of respondents indicated a tolerant attitude toward abusive parents — an attitude that reflects our culture's acceptance of a certain measure of physical punishment.

The actions you take if you suspect or witness child abuse will depend in part on the severity of the abuse and on your relationship with the abuser. If the abuser is a stranger, you will naturally follow a different course of action from that if the offender is your spouse. If you witness child abuse in public and you do not know the abuser, treat the situation as you would any other crime. If the abuse is severe, try to stop it on the spot. If the abuse does not pose an immediate threat to the child, get the facts and report the incident to the police. They are trained to handle such matters.

Most likely you will not witness child abuse in public, since it usually takes place behind closed doors. You will probably hear about the abuse as a neighbor, friend, or relative of the offender. You may also learn about the abuse from seeing the child's bruised and battered body. If you know the abuser, you should first be a friend. An abusive parent often needs someone to talk to for advice and support. Do your best to offer a sympathetic ear and suggest some sort of social or medical services that can provide help. (Child abuse programs and services will be described later in this chapter.)

If your spouse is abusing your child, first try reason with him. Try to convince him to get outside help. Be understanding and sympathetic, yet firm. You cannot permit your spouse to ruin your child's life. If you are not sure that your spouse's behavior constitutes child abuse, call the child protective services agency in your area. Specialists can give you sound advice.

If your spouse refuses to cooperate and continues his abusive patterns, you should report the matter to someone outside the home. In reporting child abuse, we suggest you use only the amount of official coercion necessary to stop the abuse. The less you involve government agencies, the better for everyone. If you can convince your spouse to change his ways by talking to your local minister or a family friend, there is no need to go further. When abusive patterns persist, it may be necessary to go to your county welfare agency or directly to the police. Do not let child abuse patterns drag on. Reporting your spouse will obviously put a strain on your marriage, but it must be done for the sake of your child.

Do not expect your involvement with a child abuser to go smoothly. Getting someone to admit he has a problem is usually a difficult matter, and persuading him to do something about it is even harder. Often the child abuser feels justified in his abuse. The parent may state the punishment is only situational, that there is no pattern of abuse. He will point out that the child has done something to deserve punishment. Most parents who abuse their children do care very much about them, yet an abusive parent may be misguided in his violence. He may have been physically punished when he was a child, and he believes he has the right to bring up his children the same way. The abuser feels that his methods of disciplining his children are his business, not yours. He will be hostile to what he considers an unwarranted intrusion into his rights as a parent.

The child abuser will also resist help because of his personality. He may feel that the environment is hostile toward him in general, and your intrusion only confirms his suspicions. He will resist because he does not want to become involved with local agencies that will substantially alter his style of life.

If you think *you* may be an abusive parent, many programs and services, both government run and private, are available to help you. Your problem may be only situational. If so, social agencies can assist you in finding a job, provide marriage counseling, or help solve it. If you abuse your children, the chances are that the problem won't go away by itself. Recognizing that you have a problem is half the battle.

Resistance to help by abusive parents is to be expected. Resistance by the children is surprising — but real. Contrary to common sense, most abused children do not feel victimized. Children often feel worse about making problems for their parents than they do about being abused. Professionals who deal with child abuse cases know that many children try to make excuses for their parents' behavior. The children feel guilty because they require medical treatment. Sitting back and waiting for the child to complain about the abuse, therefore, is not a good idea. The complaint may never come.

Where to Report Child Abuse
The usual places to report child abuse, witnessed or suspected, are the police or a child welfare or protective agency. We recommend you call a child protective services agency (listed in your phone directory) under the following conditions: 1) if the abuse is not too severe, that is, if the child is not in immediate physical danger; 2) if the parent expresses a strong motivation to stop the abuse; and 3) if the abuser agrees to participate in a therapeutic program. You should call social welfare or child protective services under these conditions because specialists at these agencies handle such cases every day and know what action to take. Calling the police may put unnecessary strain on your family, and in cases where the child is not in immediate danger, the police will refer the case to a social services agency anyway.

We recommend that you call the police directly under the following circumstances: 1) if severe physical abuse has already taken place; 2) if it is likely the child is in imminent physical danger; 3) if the abuser refuses to cooperate with any form of social intervention; and 4) if the abuse is perpetrated against a child under four years of age. Although studies show the average age of abused children is between seven and eleven, the child in greatest danger is below the age of four. With no defenses and a fragile body, the very young child is in special danger of death or serious physical injury.

Calling the police has several advantages. The police are good in emergency situations. They are on call twenty-four hours a day in every city in the country, unlike social agencies, which, particularly in small communities, do not have services available around the clock. The police are also better from a legal perspective: They can more easily secure a warrant to enter a home on probable cause that child abuse is taking place; they are more familiar with legal concepts of search and seizure; they are better trained in the investigation of crimes and gathering evidence; and they are better able to determine if a criminal action is justified.

Child Abuse Programs

The recognition of child abuse as a major social and medical problem has spawned the development of numerous community programs and services aimed at helping abusive parents. Child abuse programs may be government run or privately operated. These programs vary greatly in their goals, philosophies, methods, and effectiveness. Short-term programs, with limited goals and resources, are designed primarily to prevent abuse in potentially explosive situations. Other programs have comprehensive services to provide long-term therapy such as the modification of the parent's personality, values, or social situation. Child abuse programs may be highly structured, almost coercive, or loosely structured and supportive. Some programs focus exclusively on the behavior and problems of the offenders. Other programs attempt to modify the child's behavior, because the child, through undesirable behavior, is often partially responsible for the parents' abusive behavior. Still other programs attempt to deal with the complete family unit, treating all family members as integral parts of the child abuse syndrome. No single program can help all offenders, but with many types of programs to choose from, every child abuser, no matter what the cause of his abusive behavior, can find some help.

The following section discusses the child abuse programs available in most communities. The list does not include police or county' welfare departments, which are available in every county in the United States.

Child abuse hot lines. Emergency telephone lines for the prevention of child abuse now exist in most metropolitan areas. Child abuse hot lines are modeled after similar emergency telephone services for the prevention of suicide; they function as crisis intervention programs that provide services to distressed, potentially abusive parents. Whenever a parent feels the urge to beat his child, the parent calls the hot line number and is counseled over the telephone. In serious cases, someone from a child protective services agency may come and remove the child from the home until the crisis has passed.

Hot lines have proved valuable. The rate of self-referral to hot lines is higher than it is to regular state social service agencies. Parents are more willing to call someone anonymously on the phone than to drive downtown to a welfare office. Hot lines are also helpful to the friends, relatives, and neighbors of child abusers, and information or anonymous tips about suspected cases of child abuse are indispensable to the authorities.

Government-sponsored home support aides. Upon personal request or court order, representatives from official government agencies will provide abusive parents with special services, which vary in name and content. For example, some communities have ''health visitors'' who drop by the home and evaluate the parent-child relationship, give advice on common family problems, and check for abnormalities in the child's development. The health visitor also provides a link between governmental and nongovernmental health care agencies in the community.

Voluntary home support aides. Voluntary nongovernmental aides can sometimes help abusive parents control their behavior. The voluntary aide usually works right in the abusive parent's own home. One of the best-known home support groups is Parent Aides. The aides, lay therapists responsible for only one or two families at a time, give advice and counseling to help solve problems between parent and child. Emergency services are usually available twenty-four hours daily.

Group Mother programs are designed to strengthen the mothering capabilities of abusive women. Group mothers provide role models for abusive women, teaching them how to care for their children, handle children's tantrums, and cope with the stresses of family life.

Another program is called Foster Grandparents. Volunteers over sixty-five years of age act as stand-in grandparents, particularly for hospitalized children. Children separated from their parents, either in the hospital or in a protective home, benefit from the care and attention given by the older members of the community.

Self-help groups. Voluntary self-help programs aim at getting the abusive parents to help themselves. The largest self-help group is Parents Anonymous, founded in Los Angeles in the early 1970s. Modeled after Alcoholics Anonymous, its premise is that people with common problems can work together to help themselves and their children. Parents Anonymous does not give lessons on how to parent. Instead, it seeks to change parents' abusive patterns — to teach parents how to handle their negative feelings and to ward off or rechannel their destructive actions. But before change can take place, parents must acknowledge their problems. At meetings, parents vent their frustrations and get support from fellow members. Parents Anonymous members also take telephone calls from parents in crisis.

Parents Anonymous is a good organization for people who do not want to become involved with official government welfare programs, yet still desire to change their abusive patterns. It can often provide better services and more immediate attention than many overworked and understaffed local welfare agencies.

Day-care centers and nurseries. If a parent is under stress and feels he may abuse his child, he can temporarily leave the child at a local day-care center or nursery. Day-care centers provide time for parents to cool off, and some also furnish training in child rearing and anger control. Many are open twenty-four hours a day, offering the parent and child some distance from each other without long-term separation.

Educational programs. Many child abusers share common misunderstandings about child rearing, and often have unrealistic expectations of how a child is supposed to behave. In many localities, therefore, parents can take classes that teach them skills in handling children and give them a realistic look at normal childhood behavior and development. As parents become more realistic and understanding about their children's behavior, they will become less abusive. Classes on child rearing are available at community colleges, continuation schools, and adult high schools. Infant care classes are available to new mothers at many institutions, including public hospitals, the Red Cross, and some welfare agencies. Parent Effectiveness Training

(P.E.T.) programs have also recently spread throughout the country. Call your local welfare agency for information about child rearing education.

Public education about child abuse also aims at making the general public more aware of the nature and extent of this serious social problem. As citizens learn more about child abuse and what to do about it, they will be more likely to report it to the proper authorities.

Techniques to Reduce Child Abuse

Techniques used in the programs just listed vary. Some of the current techniques for reducing child abuse are as follows:

Anger control. Anger control techniques are taught to parents who lose their tempers easily and abuse their children in a fit of rage. Anger control involves training the parent to be calmer in anger-producing situations through role-playing and modeling of non-angry reactions.

Time out. "Time out," a technique used for both parent and child, is the temporary removal of the child from the friction causing situation. For the parent this new disciplinary measure is a means of controlling his child without resorting to physical punishment. Studies show that time out also helps improve the child's behavior.

Extinction. This technique is the nonreinforcement of a child's undesirable behavior. Adults ignore their children's aggressive behavior and reward cooperative behavior, thereby reducing the former and increasing the latter.

Behavior modification. Wide in variety, behavior modification techniques attempt to change the behavior patterns of abusive parents through role-modeling, where parents copy the behavior of nonabusive parents, or by rewarding desirable behavior and discouraging unwanted behavior.

Reasoning and education. Some techniques appeal to the parents' reason by making them aware of the harmful effects of their abusive behavior. Many parents tend to minimize what they have done. With a realistic assessment of their behavior from outside sources, parents become more attuned to the actual and potential damages of abusive behavior to their children.

Summary

Child abuse is a serious social and medical problem, long hidden from public view. Many child abuse programs and services have become available in the past decade, bringing isolated child abusers into closer contact with the community and enabling them to get help. Experts claim that from 50 to 80 percent of child abusers can be rehabilitated, at least to the extent that they no longer pose a physical threat to their children. But child abusers must be identified before they can be helped. It is up to the citizens of every community to become more aware of this serious problem and report it to the proper authorities.

SEXUAL ABUSE OF CHILDREN

Sexual offenses against children arouse greater public horror than any other crime. The person who seeks sexual gratification from a child is viewed by the average person with disgust. His crime is seen as contrary to nature, and therefore he is looked on as perverted.

Some sex offenses against children are extremely devastating. Rape is especially traumatic and can happen to females of all ages. No child, however young, is immune from sexual attack. In July 1974, a man from New York State was accused of raping a twenty-two month-old baby. Fortunately such horrible crimes are relatively rare.

As a result of a few sensational cases, the popular media characterizes the child molester as a mentally deranged, oversexed fiend who has a driving compulsion to attack little children. This portrayal is largely mythical. Contrary to common belief, the average child molester is not particularly dangerous. Typically, a relative, neighbor, or friend of the family — someone the child knows — will fondle the child's genitals. The adult may also expose himself to the child or bribe the child to touch his own or the adult's sexual organs.

In some instances the line between bad judgment and psychological abnormality runs thin. Is it abusive for parents to walk around the house nude in front of children? Is dirty talk to a child sexual abuse? Is it sexual abuse for men to make advances toward underaged, but physically mature teenage girls? There are no definite answers to these questions. But in this chapter our sights are more limited. When we discuss child molesters, we are referring to people who seek sexual gratification from biologically immature boys and girls. Technically, these people are called pedophiles — lovers of children.

Extent of Abuse
Official statistics on the extent of sex crimes against young children are sorely lacking. A substantial percentage of these crimes go unreported. When sexual abuse is discovered in the family, it often becomes a family secret, never mentioned to outsiders.

Our present information about the extent of sexual molestation is limited to isolated statistics, fragmented studies, and educated guesses by experts. One thing seems clear: Severe sexual abuse of children is relatively rare compared to physical abuse. Data on referrals of children to public agencies support this assertion. The Assistant Commissioner of Special Services for Children in New York City, for example, reports that of a total of 26,500 children referred to the Special Registry in 1975 for suspected maltreatment, only 540 were found to be victims of sexual abuse.

Much of our knowledge about sexual molestation comes from interviews with adults who reveal their childhood experiences. Using this method in his famous book, *The Sexual Behavior of the Human Female,* Alfred Kinsey found that one woman out of every four interviewed, or 25 percent, reported an unwanted preadolescent sex experience of some sort with an adult male. Eighty percent of the women said that they had been frightened sexually by an adult.

In a similar study conducted at a coed college, 21 percent of the males and females said that in their childhood they had received verbal signals of a sexual nature from an adult. Seventeen percent reported some type of physical sexual advance. According to the participants of the study, the vast majority of these verbal and physical overtures came from relatives, neighbors, or friends of the family.

Studies of the victims of reported crimes also provide information about the extent of sexual abuse against children, showing, for example, that a significant percentage of rapes are committed against young girls and teenagers. A Washington, D.C., study found that 12 percent of the rape victims were twelve years old or younger. Brenda Brown's study of rapes reported to the Memphis Police Department revealed that 6 percent of all victims were twelve years old or under. Menachem Amir's study of rape in Philadelphia found that 8 percent of all victims were ten years old or younger, and 28 percent were age fourteen or below. More than 50 percent of the rape victims in Amir's study were between ten and nineteen years of age.

In sum, sexual advances toward children are not uncommon. This may be an expected result of the preoccupation Americans have with sex. But the chances of a small child being severely abused sexually by a stranger are quite small. The sensational cases that make newspaper headlines are rare indeed. Time and again, studies prove that child molesters, as a group, are not physically dangerous.

What Type of Person Would Sexually Abuse a Child?

True pedophiles are generally middle-aged men, often married and leading conventional lives. Only 3 percent of all reported child molesters are women. Child molesters tend to restrict their criminal activity to that one offense. They do not have the extensive criminal background of other street criminals, nor are they as aggressive as the average rapist.

Pedophilia is commonly explained by a fear of adult women. Some men prefer little girls, it is claimed, because girls are helpless, easily controlled, and less capable of rejecting advances. The child molester often has a low opinion of himself. He is too insecure and frightened to seek sexual gratification with mature women. Yet there is often more to the pedophile's personality than an aversion to adult women; many child molesters simply prefer children to adults.

Some psychiatrists focus on the child molester's seeming mental disorder, claiming that the child molester is unbalanced, oversexed, and suffering from a psychiatric illness. But seeking bizarre psychological causes of pedophilia has not been fruitful. Aside from their interest in children, pedophiles possess few if any psychological abnormalities. As cited in *Sex Offenders*, one of the most extensive studies of the subject ever conducted, Paul Gebhard and his associates at Indiana University found that most child molesters are "conservative, moralistic, restrained and religiously devout." Other studies reveal that sexual molesters are, if anything, undersexed rather than oversexed. They have often had limited sexual experiences before and during marriage.

The terminology used to describe child molesters has changed. The once fashionable term "sexual psychopath," which evoked strong emotional reaction, was abolished by the American Psychiatric Association in 1952. Most psychiatrists now realize that the term is meaningless and that no single psychological problem is common to all child molesters.

Homosexual child molesters have aroused public interest lately due to the controversy surrounding gay rights. There is heated debate over whether homosexuals should be allowed to work where they come in close contact with children, such as in public schools, recreation programs, and the like. We should point out that homosexual child molesters are relatively rare. A young girl is ten times more likely to be molested by a heterosexual male than a young boy is by a homosexual male.

Homosexual child molesters seem to have many of the same personality characteristics as heterosexual pedophiles, but science really cannot explain why men are attracted to little boys or little girls. In research conducted by one of the authors of this book, it appeared that many child molesters did not care what sex their victims were. Often child molesters have problems with alcohol and are so intoxicated they do not differentiate between boys and girls.

As with most crimes against the person, the victim of child molestation is likely to know the offender. The 1969 results of Vincent DeFrancis's comprehensive Brooklyn-Bronx study revealed, for example, that in 75 percent of the cases of child molestation the child or her family knew the offender. Frequently, the sexual abuse of children occurs in the family setting. One study showed that the child's natural father was guilty in 13 percent of the cases and the child's stepfather or the man with whom the child's mother was living was responsible for another 14 percent. In that study, therefore, over one-fourth of the child molestation took place in the immediate family.

Most cases involving family sexual molestation are not isolated incidents. The Brooklyn-Bronx study found that in 40 percent of the cases, the molestation occurred over a period ranging from weeks to several years. In the typical family case, the father or stepfather engages in playful bantering with his daughter or stepdaughter. Slowly, the play takes on sexual overtones. Eventually, the man may fondle the girl's genitals; he may attempt or succeed at sexual intercourse. Although the child is not completely willing to participate in the sexual activity, there is usually some complicity. Rarely does a family member sexually attack a young girl outright against her will.

No single valid theory currently explains why some people molest children. There are many reasons for abuse, just as there are many types of child molesters. We must await further research to understand fully the nature of sexual abuse of children.

Prevention of Sexual Abuse

The best way to protect your children from sexual molestation, particularly from strangers, is through education. You should teach your children safety consciousness and crime prevention from the time they are old enough to understand. As your child grows older and you continue to teach him or her about the values of safety and protection, these values will remain. Teaching safety and crime prevention is as important as teaching hygiene and preventive medicine.

Try to instill all of the traditional safety rules in your children. Although you may be familiar with most of these rules, a brief review should prove useful. The following list of safety rules for children was drafted by the Child Safety Council:

• Never enter a stranger's house.
• Never play alone in vacant buildings or alleys.
• Never let a stranger touch you or join in your play.
• Never accept anything from a person you do not know.
• Never get into a car with any stranger or go anyplace with him.
• Never go to playgrounds, movies, or other public places alone. Stay with your friends.
• Always report any stranger who bothers you to your parents, teacher, law enforcement officer, bus driver, or an adult you know and can trust.
• Always try to remember what the stranger looks like and how he is dressed.

• Always get the license number of his car. Write it on a paper or on the sidewalk with a stone, or scratch it in the dirt with a stick.
• Never go with any stranger who asks you for directions.
• If you see a playmate get into a stranger's car, copy the license number and notify your parents, teacher, or law enforcement officer at once.

How to Teach Your Child
It is obvious to most parents that they should teach their children lessons in personal safety. What is less obvious is *how* to ingrain crime prevention techniques in their children. What, specifically, are parents supposed to tell their children about sexual molestation or kidnapping? How can parents convey this information without doing more damage than the crime itself?

You can teach your children about protecting themselves from sexual abuse in a variety of ways. Whichever way you choose, you should follow a general rule: Do only what is necessary to train your children to comply with the recommended safety precautions. Do not scare your child into compliance unless absolutely necessary. This general rule should be followed despite the age and personality makeup of your child.

Many parents are so fearful of strangers making sexual advances toward their children that they exaggerate the danger. Badgering children to be suspicious of strangers often makes children fearful of all adults, and this fear can last a lifetime.

We recommend a matter-of-fact approach geared to the child's age and level of understanding. For example, tell a small child (ages four to six) that if she (or he) gets into a car with a stranger, the stranger may take her away and she will never again see her mommy or daddy or any of her favorite dolls. The thought of separation from parents and cherished toys will make most children comply with your rules.

There is no need to tell the child about possible death, sexual abuse, assault, ransom, and so forth. On the other hand, do not simply tell the child to "stay away from strangers" and leave it at that. The child will not know what to think of strangers and will have no idea why she is supposed to obey the rules.

As the child gets older (ages seven through ten), she will be interested in the possible motivations of strangers. The child will wonder why it is necessary to be leery of strangers. Discussing sexual perversions in graphic detail is inadvisable. An easier explanation for you and for the child to understand is that some men are "sick" and that they may want to touch her all over her body. You want to convey to the child the idea that some people have mental problems that they cannot help, in much the same sense that people suffer involuntarily from physical diseases.

Most children can understand the notion of sick people doing things they do not really intend. With this method you avoid a lofty discussion of the moral implications of sexual activity with children who are too young to understand. Describing sexual abusers as sick people is also better for the child who has been molested by someone he or she knows. It is easier for the child to comprehend illness than evil or sin.

Avoiding the moral interpretations of sexual behavior with young children has other advantages. The more you take a matter-of-fact approach, the more likely your child is to report any sexual abuse if it occurs. The more you discuss the moral implications of sex — guilt and sin — the more likely the child is to feel guilty if he or she is sexually molested, and the less likely the child is to inform you or anyone else about the molestation.

If Your Child Is Sexually Abused

Child molestation itself rarely has long-lasting effects, unless the abuse is especially hostile or aggressive. The child, particularly the young child, does not know how to interpret the situation. As with other events in the child's life, he or she will look to the parents for the significance of the incident. Your child will learn from your reactions.

Usually, parents react in horror, disgust, guilt, and anger to a sexual molestation. These reactions are unintentionally transferred to the child. What happens after the molestation is often worse for the child than the incident itself. Most psychological damage comes not from the abuse, but from the interpretation and handling of the situation by parents, medical personnel, law enforcement officials, and social workers.

What you should do if your child is sexually molested, particularly by a stranger, depends in large part on the age of the child. If the offense was not serious, such as exhibitionism or minor fondling of the genitals, most young children will not know anything wrong has taken place. Nor can a young child distinguish between severe sexual molestation and any other form of physical abuse. Young children do not understand the social and moral implications of sex in our society.

As the child grows older and knows more about social taboos in our society, she may experience some guilt over being molested or raped. The child may feel that her parents or others close to her are ashamed of or angry with her over what has happened. This is particularly true if you have drummed into your child's head the rule about staying away from strangers. Your child may not even want to tell you about the incident if she has violated one of the safety rules.

Older children are also afraid of what might happen to them or their parents if they report the crime. The child molester may take advantage of the child's fear, for example, telling the child that he will kill the child's parents if the child says anything about the offense. Such a threat can be devastating to a ten-year-old child.

If your child is molested by a stranger or anyone outside the family, you must try to leave your anger behind and deal with the situation as reasonably as you can under the circumstances. Becoming enraged only makes matters worse. When you talk to the child, be calm and gentle. Talk in a language she can understand. If you have to go to the police or hospital, talk to the child in a direct and sympathetic manner. Calmly explain what will happen, trying not to alarm or shock her.

You may feel guilty about what has happened because you did not do as much as you could have to prevent the crime, but you should avoid expressing guilt or remorse. Your child will internalize the guilt and will have a hard time handling these feelings in the years to come. The healthiest thing you can do is to direct your anger and frustration toward seeing that the offender is brought to justice. Try to get the family back to its normal routine as soon as possible after the incident. It is comforting to the child to do what is familiar. Changing your child's routine any more than necessary only causes more trauma.

If the sexual abuse is taking place in your home, the first order of business is to stop it. Talk to the abusing party and try to get him to seek professional help. A good temporary deterrent to further abuse is to air the complaint in front of the entire family. Everyone will then know what is going on. Inform everyone that any further incidents will result in action by official agencies. This might mean prosecuting the abusing party or temporarily removing the child from the home. Often the parent will deny any wrongdoing, and he may say that the child made up the story. You must convince the person that most children do not invent stories about being molested by relatives. At the least, such stories indicate a strain in family relationships.

If the offense is serious, or if the person refuses to participate in professional counseling, report the incident to the authorities. This tactic may sound antitherapeutic, but we believe this step is necessary to end the pattern of abuse. It brings everything out into the open and stops the abuse so the family can begin to work out its problems, with or without the aid of professionals.

CONCLUSION

The facts we have presented in this chapter may sound shocking, but they are true. The physical abuse of children occurs much more often than official statistics suggest, although serious sexual molestation is less common than newspapers and television would have us believe. By following our advice, you can significantly lower the chances that your child will fall victim to these devastating crimes.

Chapter 7

Watchdogs

Mounting evidence indicates that the presence of a dog decreases the chances of burglary or unwanted entry in both residences and businesses. A 1972 government-sponsored study titled *Patterns of Burglary* analyzed residential burglary in Fairfax County, Virginia; Washington, D.C.; and Prince George's County, Maryland. The study found that "more nonvictims had dogs than did victims at the time of the burglary."

One of the authors of this book has found this conclusion true. In one instance, a local business for repairing rental trucks had its equipment repeatedly vandalized and stolen. The company's main building had steel bars on the windows, was wired with a burglar alarm, and was surrounded by a high wire fence with double-strand barbed wire on top. None of these protective devices stopped the criminals. Finally, a company employee brought in two large German shepherds that had been raised on a ranch and disliked strangers. The dogs were left in the enclosed yard every night and on weekends and the vandalism and thefts ended soon thereafter. This success pleased the owner of the company so much that he built a dog kennel on the premises and started paying for the dogs' upkeep.

Even a dog's bark is valuable. A family pet that barks loudly and fiercely when he hears a potential intruder serves the same funciton as a burglar alarm. Loud barking warns you of possible danger and acts as a deterrent to burglars. Burglars don't like to attract attention; they don't want unnecessary hassles. If a burglar hears a barking dog inside your house or yard, he is likely to seek out a home that poses less threat.

Because dogs have proved to be such valuable allies in fighting

170

burglary and other crimes, guard dog agencies are springing up all over the country. They are experiencing a thriving trade from business and home owners alike. Many families, particularly the wealthy, are using fully trained guard dogs to protect themselves, their loved ones, and their property.

If you are considering a dog for protection, you will have many questions. What kind of protection do I want? What breed of dog should I get? Should I buy a puppy and raise it, or should I get a full-grown dog? How much will it cost? Should I train the dog myself, or should I hire a professional trainer? These and other questions will be answered in the remainder of this chapter.

SELECTING A DOG

Almost any dog, large or small, can aid you in protecting your home. But before you select a dog, you must decide what function you want the dog to serve. Do you simply want a family pet that also barks when strangers come near your residence? Do you want a more aggressive dog to guard your yard or property? Do you want a highly trained dog that will protect you by attacking others on command? The type of dog you select will depend on your personal needs.

If you are part of a typical family, you probably don't need or want a fully trained guard or attack dog. You want a barking house dog to ward off strangers and let you know when someone is on your property, a living burglar alarm. Fortunately, such dogs can also be great pets for the family.

Just about any kind or size of dog will make an adequate four-legged alarm. Do not fall for a dog seller's pitch that you must have a special breed of dog, or one that has undergone extensive training. You can buy an excellent mongrel or crossbreed dog at your local pet store, or you can get one free at your nearest animal shelter, SPCA, or animal protection society. Mongrel dogs cost less and can bark just as well as purebred dogs. Many dog training books are available at libraries and pet stores to help you train the dog yourself.

Guard dogs, by contrast, are trained to patrol a certain area and attack anyone but the owner who crosses the boundaries. Guard dogs are most effective protecting large, private estates. Small businesses in high crime areas also profit from guard dogs stationed near cash registers at night. Since these dogs can also be trained to protect people as well as places, the elderly, the disabled, or others needing extra personal security would be better off owning a guard dog.

When selecting a guard dog, you should look for the following qualities: good temperament, stability, intelligence, loyalty, aggressiveness and courage. Many dogs have these qualities, but we recommend the two most commonly used breeds — the German shepherd, sometimes called a "police dog," and the Doberman pinscher, known by some as "devil dog."

Other large breeds that make good guard dogs are the Dalmatian, boxer, Rottweiler, Weimeraner, Airedale, and Great Dane. Not all large dogs, however, can be easily trained as guard dogs. The collie and Labrador retriever, for example, are not aggressive enough for guard duty. But just having a large dog around the house may deter a burglar; the imposing size of a Great Dane in itself offers protection.

Smaller dogs can also be trained for guard duty. In the terrier breed the Scottish, Welsh, Kerry blue, and wire-haired fox terrier are commonly used. Still smaller dogs that may serve your needs are the beagle, poodle, and dachshund.

An attack dog will provide you with the ultimate protection. Attack dogs are highly trained and dangerous weapons, most effective when following the commands of a handler. On command these dogs will chase, fight, hold, and release. They are most frequently used by the police to seek out and subdue suspected or known criminals. Since attack dogs successfully foil the plans of sophisticated kidnappers and robbers, they are also used by security agencies to protect large businesses and estates for the rich and famous. Attack dogs, however, are unsuitable for the average family. They should not be allowed to roam around a home where children are present, or where people come and go freely.

The best choice for an attack dog is either the German shepherd or the Doberman pinscher. The German shepherd generally matures earlier than the Doberman pinscher, and the Doberman is considered a rather fierce and unpredictable dog. With proper training, however, the Doberman pinscher can also become loyal to its master without losing its fierceness. Both breeds possess essentially the same qualities, so the choice is really a matter of preference.

Many people believe that protection dogs should be purebred. The main advantage to buying a purebred dog is that you know better what you are paying for in terms of temperament and, in the case of a puppy, of its full-grown size. But it is not necessary to buy a purebred dog. If you only want a noisy dog around the house, a mongrel can be just as effective and a lot cheaper. It is difficult to predict a mongrel puppy's future size and temperament, however, so a mongrel should be purchased full-grown.

You must also choose between a male and female dog. Although both sexes make good watchdogs, many trainers believe that the female is the better choice because of her greater tendency to become possessive of her master, family, and surroundings. Even without training, the female dog will become more of a natural watchdog than the male. Moreover, females won't be distracted by other female dogs in heat.

Before you buy a dog, there are several other things you should consider. Although dogs can adapt to almost any home environment, you should have a special place to keep the animal, particularly if you have company and you don't want it underfoot. Consider who will feed the dog and care for it. Some families decide that only one person will take care of the dog. However, since care and feeding is a daily routine, it can become tiresome. Also, other commitments will sometimes disrupt the routine and another family member will have to fill in; the dog should be used to such changes. We advise sharing the responsibilty for the dog with the entire family. Whatever method you choose, it is best to work out the details before you buy the dog.

PURCHASING A DOG

Prices for a purebred, unhousebroken puppy usually start about $100 and go up to $250. Some of the rarer purebreds cost as much as $500. If you want to buy a guard or attack dog, look in the Yellow Pages of your telephone directory under "Dog Trainers." For a fully grown and professionally trained guard dog, you can expect to pay approximately $1500, and some highly trained attack dogs can run as high as $5000. Once you buy a dog, care and feeding will average an extra $50 per month.

If you purchase a purebred dog, make sure the kennel you buy it from gives you a written guarantee. This guarantee should include a "get acquainted time" — a period of time from two weeks to one month to make sure that the animal accepts your family and your family accepts it.

Remember that the ideal time for training a dog is between six and ten months old. Some trainers like to start training earlier than others. If you purchase a puppy for training, you should discuss the matter with the trainer first.

If you decide on a fully trained attack dog, here are some things to look for:

• The dog should not attack unless you tell it to.
• The dog should not attack unless you are attacked (master protection).
• The dog should not attack unless someone breaks into its domain — house or car.
• The dog should bite and hold, not rip and tear.
• The dog should come off and stop when you tell it to.
• The dog should never show aggression toward small children.

Never buy someone else's guard or attack dog without immediately retraining it or having it retrained. If you don't, the dog may prove uncontrollable and pose a serious safety hazard.

TRAINING YOUR DOG

The training you give a dog will depend in large part on the kind of dog you want. It's best to hire a professional trainer if you want a guard or attack dog. If you want a barking dog around the house, you can train it yourself just as well and for a lot less money.

Pick a professional trainer with care. First, check the Yellow Pages to find a list of all available animal trainers in your area. Then check with your local Better Business Bureau to find out whether any complaints are on file against the trainers you are considering. Law enforcement agencies are not supposed to recommend private professional services to the public, however, your police canine officer might provide you with the information you need to find a good trainer.

A dog can be put through four levels of training. The level you choose will depend on your needs, as well as on the trainer's fee, which can range from $25 up to $1500. For a hundred dollars or so, you can get the lowest level of *protective* training, which includes basic obedience and minimal protective training. If you just want a family pet and you don't want to train it yourself, we recommend you put your dog through this type of training.

A second type of training, called security patrol, consists of basic obedience and protective training, plus searching techniques. A dog with this level of training can seek out and capture suspected criminals hiding in buildings and fields. Obviously, such training is not necessary for the average citizen's dog.

Area attack training is the third level of training. Dogs trained at this level are locked inside an enclosed area such as a fenced yard or warehouse. They are very aggressive and will attack anyone but the owner who comes within the confines of the protected area. The trainer should be sure to teach the dog not to accept food from strangers; drugged meat is a common tactic to silence barking dogs.

Attack dog training is the fourth and highest level of training. An attack dog is trained to attack and come off the attack on the command of its master. But if the dog's master is assaulted, the dog will attack the assailant without a command. We recommend attack dog training only for owners of large estates or for people who are particularly fearful of personal attack.

A reputable trainer will require that you go though a training period with the dog. This applies to all levels of training. The dog has to be taught how to take commands and you have to be taught how to give them. Having a well-trained dog also means periodic in-service training, since your dog is likely to forget what it has been taught. Unless you are committed to giving the time for continued training, you are wasting your money on the initial training.

If you train your dog yourself, or do at least part of the training, you naturally cut down on expenses. Once your dog has had basic obedience training, there are several ways you can train it to be a better guard dog. First, allow your dog to be around children at every opportunity. A guard dog that lives in a family atmosphere learns tolerance. This assists in its training because it helps the dog learn not to attack until it is told to do so. If you don't have children around the house, walk your dog frequently in parks, playgrounds, and schools.

Second, always isolate your dog when adult guests come to visit. By so doing, your dog will not become a lovable lap dog for everyone it sees and, eventually, your dog will become possessive of its family and home. It will probably bark and become aggressive around adult strangers.

If you undertake this training procedure, you must be careful when you take your dog away from your residence, and you must be cautious not to let people accidentally walk into the room or area where the dog is kept. Since the dog is not used to strange adults, it may bite without provocation if surprised.

You can train your dog in any language, or any combination of languages. A dog will respond to any word and the given function you show it. It may be valuable to train your dog in a foreign langauage if you speak one. Police canine officers often use this trick because it is a big psychological advantage not to have anyone know what you are telling the dog to do.

FINAL HINTS

Dogs cannot replace good locks. Nor are untrained dogs as reliable as electric burglar alarms. A nice steak or doggie treat may make your dog friendly with an intruder. To train a dog not to accept food from a stranger is very difficult, and not always successful; some dogs can never learn to resist temptation. Dogs should therefore be used only to supplement other crime prevention measures — not as a substitute for them.

A ''Beware of Dog'' sign on your fence is also a deterrent to many potential burglars. But don't rely on this trick alone. Eventually, burglars, particularly juveniles who live in your neighborhood, will realize you are only bluffing.

Remember that you are responsible for the actions of your dog. Your homeowner's insurance probably covers most liability problems, but be sure to check with your insurance agent to see if it covers injuries inflicted by your dog. If someone breaks into your home or physically attacks you and your dog bites that person, you are not liable for the damages incurred. But if you allow your dog to bite someone with no justification, you will find yourself not only civilly liable for damages, but you may also be held criminally liable on assault charges. Merely posting signs about your residence reading "Guard Dog on Duty" will probably not relieve you of liability if an innocent person is bitten.

Because dogs are becoming more valued possessions, dognapping is on the rise. One useful tip to help recover a missing dog is to have it registered with its own identification number. A new agency has been created to help return stolen or lost dogs to their rightful owner. For a $5 registration fee, the Canine Bureau of Identification will send you a special identification number and dog tag. Write to 17 Battery Place, New York, New York 10004. If a dog is found, the identification tag instructs the finder to send the Canine Bureau of Identification a collect telegram. The bureau will then notify you so you can retrieve your pet.

To make sure the identification number will never get lost or removed, you should have it tattooed on your dog. A nearby veterinarian or humane shelter will tattoo the ID number on your pet's right thigh or ear at minimal expense. The identification tag and tattooed number warn the potential dognappers that your dog is registered.

CONCLUSION

Having a dog around the house will give you added security, whether you live in a modest bungalow or an elegant mansion. You can choose from a wide variety of breeds to suit your needs and taste. Most people do not need a fully trained attack dog to protect their home; any noisy house dog is sufficient to deter all but the professional burglar.

Owning a dog is a big responsibility; proper care and feeding are expensive and time-consuming. With the exception of those people with large homes and valuable possessions, we believe you should not purchase a dog for protection unless you also want one for a pet. In most cases, the expense of dog ownership will not offset the possible losses if your home is burglarized.

Chapter 8

Consumer Fraud

Over the next ten or twenty years, the chances are good that criminals will steal a sizable portion of your hard-earned money. We do not mean the criminals you probably imagine. Contrary to public belief, you are most likely to lose your money to a fast talking swindler than to a thug on the street. Year after year, Americans lose more money in fraudulent schemes than in robbery, burglary, and theft combined.

Swindlers have devised an infinite variety of schemes to cheat unsuspecting people. A retail business person may defraud a customer; a ''confidence man'' may trick a greedy and naïve person out of his life savings. The line dividing different types of fraud is difficult to draw, but for the purpose of this book we group all frauds in two categories. In this chapter we discuss consumer fraud, by which we mean the distortion or suppression of the truth to exploit a person buying goods, services, or credit. We devote the following chapter to con games and bunco schemes.

The exact amount of money lost to consumer fraud is difficult to determine. As with most other crimes, consumer fraud is vastly underreported. At least nine out of ten victims never complain to the authorities or to anyone. Some customers do not know that they have been defrauded; others are embarrassed to admit their gullibility.

Estimates of losses from fraud and white collar crime have been made, however. Experts believe outright frauds, such as fraudulent home improvement schemes, real estate developments, and auto repairs, cost Americans about $5 billion per year. The Food and Drug Administration estimated that more than half a billion dollars is spent each year on worthless or misrepresented drugs alone. And recently, the federal General Accounting Office reported that fraud against the government may run as high as $25 billion a year.

When the wider scope of white collar crime is considered, the figures are staggering. Some experts put white collar fraud conservatively as high as $40 billion a year — or *ten times* the value lost through traditional street crime. This figure does not include antitrust violations, which amount to more than $150 billion per year.

Although consumer fraud is disproportionately high among poor and uneducated people, swindles are common in the middle and upper classes, too. Otherwise, the consumer movement wouldn't be as strong as it is today. It is important for *all* consumers to learn how to protect themselves against fraudulent schemes and deceptive business practices.

Only a few years ago criminal justice agencies were unsympathetic to consumers. The police and district attorneys felt that consumer fraud was a civil problem — that a person who had been defrauded should contact his own lawyer, not a law enforcement agency. Recently however, this attitude has changed. With the rise of the consumer movement, many states have passed consumer protection laws that are enforced by state consumer fraud bureaus. These laws enable government officials to take action against businesses engaged in various fraudulent practices. Consumer fraud units have also been established in local district attorneys' offices.

The Better Business Bureau (BBB) has a slogan: "Being Forewarned Is Being Forearmed." In other words, an informed buying public is one consumer weapon swindlers cannot defeat. We agree that knowledge is your best protection. The information in this chapter will help you lower your chances of being victimized by the ever-present gypster. We cannot hope to detail every type of swindle; consumer fraud is too varied, permeating all fields of business. But we will present general rules for avoiding the most common swindles, and these rules can be applied to other, less common types of consumer fraud.

RETAIL SWINDLES

Greed sets consumers up to be swindled; ignorance allows it to happen. And happen it does. Over half the complaints received at consumer protection agencies come from gullible consumers who thought they were going to get fantastic bargains, but who instead got less than they paid for.

Whenever a bargain sounds unbelievably good, check it out carefully before you buy. Legitimate businesses welcome investigation; swindlers will disappear when you say you want some time to think about the deal. The Better Business Bureau advises: "If an item for sale sounds too good to be true, it probably is ."

Most frauds start with a promise. The promise may be to sell a product at a fraction of the normal cost or to perform a service that legitimate businesses won't. Whenever you hear a promise that sounds exceptionally good, watch out. In a country where money is king, don't expect a stranger to do you a favor. There's usually a catch.

You should follow two sound principles in all business transactions. First, the less you know about a product, the more important it is to deal with an established, reputable dealer. If you are knowledgeable about an area of business, it may be safe to cut corners and buy from an unknown firm. But ignorance makes consumer fraud possible. It is extremely difficult to be familiar with all products, particularly specialty items such as antiques or jewelry. So if you are not sure what you are buying, play it safe and go to an established firm.

Second, never make a major purchase without first comparing prices at a few other businesses. Of course, the extent of the comparison shopping will depend on the amount of money involved. It would not be economically sound to drive all over town in an attempt to save five cents on a carton of milk. Comparison shopping serves two purposes. It can save you a lot of money. You can often find a 20 to 30 percent difference between what two businesses charge for the same product or service. One store may ask the full list price while another store is holding a special sale. You can find such bargains only if you shop around. It is important to realize, however, that legitimate bargains where you save 50 percent or more are few and far between. Legitimate businesses don't sell merchandise for more than 50 percent off because they would be selling the product for less than they paid for it. If prices are slashed, the goods are likely outdated or defective. And if you buy an item at less than half price on the street, it is probably stolen.

Shopping around also helps prevent one of the worst consumer traps — buying on impulse. Few, if any, bargains must be snapped up immediately. Comparison shopping gives you the chance to think objectively about the purchase. It gets away from overbearing sales-people who encourage you to make your decision on the spot. Whenever a salesperson tells you to decide immediately or lose out on a bargain, the chances are that you are about to be gypped, or at least talked into an unwise purchase. Consumer fraud could be drastically reduced if everyone contemplating a large purchase took the time to comparison shop.

Here are some other tips to keep in mind:

1. Always investigate a company before buying a product or con-tracting services. Ask for references and follow up on them. If you have any doubts, call your local BBB or chamber of commerce to see if complaints have been lodged against the business in question.

2. Your best defenses against fraud are a suspicious nature and time to consider the deal. Be skeptical of everything, even your own judgment. If an offer sounds really good, sleep on it and see if it still seems as attractive the next day.

3. Don't be taken in by slick advertising. The average consumer is bombarded by over fifteen hundred advertising appeals each day, some of which contain misleading statements, if not outright lies.

4. Don't rely on the store's estimate of your savings on sale-priced items. Businesses sometimes practice fictitious pricing. Find out what other stores are charging for the same or similiar merchandise.

5. Before you buy, check the retailer's policy on exchange privileges.

6. Always save your receipts in case the product is defective and you want to take it back.

7. Before you put down a cash deposit for a lay-away plan, be sure you can afford the item and that you really want it. If you fail to make payments, you may forfeit your down payment.

Bait Advertising

Because people want to get something for nothing, some merchants use "bait and switch" tactics to lure unsuspecting customers into stores. Bait and switch, a selling scheme practiced by some of the country's largest retail stores, is an attempt to entice consumers by misrepresenting what is being sold. The bait in the scheme is merchandise advertised at an exceptionally low price that the store has no intention of selling, or has in short supply only. Once the customer is inside, the merchant switches him to the higher-priced merchandise the company is actually trying to peddle.

To switch you to the higher-priced goods, the sales person will criticize the advertised product: The warranty is deficient or the manufacturer has gone out of business and replacement parts are hard to get. Skilled sales personnel can make switches so subtle you won't know you've been cheated. You may even be impressed by the salesperson's "honesty" about the deficiencies of the advertised product.

If you respond to an advertisement and are told that the advertised product is sold out or no good, the chances are that you are being baited for the switch (unless you are offered a raincheck for the product at the advertised price). Do not let a salesperson switch you to a different product, especially if it costs more. Shop in other stores for a genuine sale. If you allow yourself to be switched, you are encouraging fraudulent advertising. You are also hurting businesses that use honest advertising practices.

Bait and switch should not be confused with "loss leader" advertising. The loss leader is also a product offered at an exceptionally low price to lure people into the store. But the loss leader is a genuine bargain because the merchant intends to sell the product. He is simply gambling that the customer who visits the store to buy the leader will also purchase other items at the normal price. For example, a sporting goods store may offer a can of tennis balls at half price. If the tennis balls are brand name and sealed the store is offering an excellent bargain; the manager simply wants to get you into the store, hoping you will buy other sporting equipment at the same time.

There are two keys to detecting bait advertising. The bait is usually a relatively expensive item (loss leaders are always inexpensive), and the salesperson will actively attempt to discourage purchase of the advertised product.

The Federal Trade Commission lists additional indications that a business may be guilty of bait and switch selling.

• If the salesperson refused to show or demonstrate the advertised product
• If the salesperson criticizes any of the conditions of the sale (for example, the guarantee, the credit terms, the ability to get service or replacement parts)
• If the business does not have enough items of the advertised product to meet a reasonable demand (unless the offer originally stated that the supply would be limited)
• If the salesperson will not take orders for the advertised product to be delivered within a reasonable time
• If the salesperson shows merchandise that is defective or unsuited for the purposes represented
• If the salesperson accepts a deposit for one product, but then tries to switch the customer to more expensive merchandise

CONTRACTS

Whenever a fraud is designed to get more than a few dollars, a contract is usually involved. Not understanding what they are doing, many unsuspecting people sign contracts that place them under impossible financial burdens and by which they forfeit their legal rights. At the same time, the fine print of the contract often puts the unscrupulous business person in an advantageous position.

A contract is an agreement that describes the responsibilities and obligations two or more people, or parties, have toward one another. Many people imagine a contract to be an official-looking written document. Indeed, this is the most common type of contract — and usually the most important. A written contract is also referred to as an "instrument," "agreement," or "document." But a contract does not have to be in writing or signed. A contract can also be a discount coupon from your local newspaper, a receipt you sign for merchandise received through the mail, a wave of the hand at an auction, or even a friend's handshake when he agrees to sell you his used bicycle.

You are likely to sign a contract under varied circumstances: when buying anything on time, borrowing money, renting or buying a car, or having your home remodeled. A contract obligates you to do certain things — usually pay money in exchange for goods or services.

Generally speaking, any contract you sign should include: 1) the price to be paid for the product or services; 2) the manner of payment (for example, cash on delivery or installment payments); 3) a description of the product or service sold; 4) any terms of credit; and 5) a description of the warranty.

Occasionally, contracts contain clauses that can be extremely disadvantageous to the consumer. Keep your eyes open for the following terms or phases.

Waiver. A waiver means giving up one or more of your rights under law. Whenever you see the word *waive* or *waiver,* be on guard. Check with a lawyer to make sure you aren't giving up rights you should keep.

Acceleration of payments. An acceleration of payments clause deals with the collection of delinquent payments. If you fail to make a payment, the lender can demand that you pay off the entire loan. An acceleration of payments clause may also require you to pay the costs of collecting the money, and collection fees are often as high as one-third of the entire loan.

Holder-in-due-course-clause. Some contracts contain the following clause: ''No transfer, renewal, or assignment of this contract, or any loss, damage to, or destruction of said property shall release Buyer from his obligations hereunder.'' This is known as holder-in-due-course clause. Do not enter into any contract containing this provision. If you do, the business can sell your contract to a third party (such as a collection agency) and you may still be required to make your payments even if the merchandise is defective. Once your loan contract is in the hands of a collection agency, the original business is less likely to care about your problems or to repair or replace a defective product.

Observe the following rules before entering into a contract:

1. At the very minimum, you must thoroughly read and understand the contract before you sign it. Salespersons sometimes try to discourage customers from studying contracts. Don't be swayed if the salesperson says, ''Don't bother to read the contract. It just contains the details.'' Read every clause. The important provisions may be in the fine print, and failure to read and understand them will not excuse you from your obligations once you have signed your name.

2. Don't act hastily, particularly if the salesperson is insistent that you sign immediately. The more insistent the salesperson is, the more suspicious and careful you should be. Honest business people don't mind if their contracts are carefully scrutinized.

3. Insist that all oral promises be written into any contract involving a significant amount of money. Even though the salesperson's oral promises may be legally binding, you will find it nearly impossible to have them enforced in court unless you have witnesses who will testify that the promises were made. It is perfectly legal for the salesperson to alter a standard-form contract and add oral promises in handwriting. Just make sure that you and the salesperson both initial the handwritten changes.

4. Do not sign any contract that contains blank spaces. If blanks appear, draw a circle with a line through it in each of the blank spaces before you sign. Otherwise the blank spaces can be filled in without your approval at a later time.

5. If the business transaction involves a great deal of money, or if the contract contains any particularly complex clauses, you should consult an attorney. In the long run it may be cheaper to pay an attorney's fee than lose hundreds or thousands of dollars because you signed a contract that was to your disadvantage.

6. If you do not like a certain provision in the contract, you can ask the merchant to take it out and add words that you find more suitable. If the merchant really wants to close the deal, he may consent to your request. The merchant may also reject your proposal and decide not to close the deal, or to negotiate the matter still further, but it doesn't hurt to ask. You can be sure the merchant will never change the contract on his own initiative.

7. Make certain all of the terms of the contract are contained in a single document, and that both parties sign it. Get an exact copy of the contract at the time you sign it. If it is not a carbon copy, have the copy signed by the person who made it out and have him acknowledge in writing that it is an exact copy.

8. Note all extra charges in your contract. Do you have to pay extra for delivery or installation? If the contract does mention extra charges, request a provision specifically stating there will be no extra charges.

9. Make sure that the conditions of the warranty are spelled out in detail. For example, what is the exact duration of the warranty? Are you entitled to a cash refund or a replacement if the product is defective? Unless you know exactly what the seller is guaranteeing, you have nothing to hold him to. (More about warranties later in this chapter.)

10. The contract should state what will happen if either party breaks his part of the bargain. Don't sign a contract that gives the other party more rights than you if either of you defaults. Don't allow yourself to be penalized beyond reason if you break the contract.

11. Make sure you are signing a contract for a product or service you really want. Never sign a contract just to get rid of a salesperson.

CREDIT

Credit is an important, sometimes indispensable, element of many business transactions. Americans routinely use credit for major purchases; most of us simply don't have the cash to buy a house or a new car. But by using credit extensively and unwisely on smaller purchases, Americans waste billions of dollars each year. Some consumer experts believe that high interest rates cost consumers more money each year than any other consumer swindle.

You can lower your chances of being taken by following one general rule: Calculate the total cost of any product or service you are considering. The total cost of an item or service is made up of the following components:

Cash price. The cash price is the cost of the goods or service if you make the purchase in cash. For example, the cash price of a $75,000 house is $75,000.

Finance charge. The finance charge is the amount you pay for credit. The way to judge the finance charge of different companies is by comparing the annual percentage rate, which is the cost of credit expressed in a percentage. By comparing the annual percentage rate in proposed installment contracts, you will be able to determine which company offers the lowest finance charges. You will know the annual percentage rate because the truth-in-lending laws require lenders to state the interest rate on all loan contracts. Some states have maximum limitations on finance charges. Check with your local BBB or consumer protection agency if the finance charges proposed to you seem excessively high.

Insurance costs. Some businesses require their customers to take out life or disability insurance with the purchase of any expensive merchandise. This assures the company that it will be paid in case the buyer dies or becomes disabled. You may decide that you want this type of insurance. But you should be aware that you are paying for it, and that the rates are usually high for the protection given.

When the total cost (cash price, finance charges, insurance costs) of an item is calculated, you will find that stores with the lowest cash prices do not always offer consumers the best deals. Store A may have a lower cash price than Store B for the same item. However, Store A may have higher finance charges and insurance costs, making the total cost of its products higher.

Credit Contracts

If you buy an item on time, you will probably sign a credit (or loan) contract. Before you sign such a contract, you should be familiar with the following terms and phrases:

Balloon payment. Normally all payments are of an equal amount over the duration of a loan. Some companies, however, offer relatively low payments at first (to entice the buyer) and then require large "balloon" payments at the end. This may mean that you will pay a larger interest charge than if your payments had been evenly divided. Moreover, if you cannot meet the balloon payment later on, you may be forced to sell the item or refinance the loan at an even higher interest rate.

Wage assignment. If you do not make payments on time, wage assignment gives the creditor the right to collect a certain sum each month from your salary. Always try to avoid putting yourself in a position where a creditor can take part of your earnings.

Default payment. If you don't make your regular payments on time, you may be required to pay an extra charge (sometimes called a *late charge*). Default payments are simply a waste of money for the consumer.

Contingent obligor. A person who agrees to furnish the entire unpaid balance of a loan in case the payments aren't made is called a contingent obligor, commonly known as a cosigner. Think twice before cosigning any loan; being held responsible for the entire balance of a loan can obviously be a terrible financial burden.

Holder-in-due-course clause. As was mentioned in the previous section, a holder-in-due-course clause allows the business from which you bought the product to sell your loan contract to a third party, such as a collection agency. You must then make your payments to the collection agency, not the business. Bear in mind, however, that in many states and under federal law you are not legally obligated to pay the third party if you were defrauded or if the product was defective. Check with your local district attorney for the law in your area.

We state in the first section of this chapter that you should compare retail prices before making your purchase. You should just as diligently shop around for the cheapest finance charges. Normally, independent lending agencies will have lower rates than a small business, particularly an unreputable business. But there is one major disadvantage to borrowing money independently from a loan company. If the product you buy is defective (or if you are defrauded), your complaints to the loan company will fall on deaf ears. If you take credit from the business where you buy the product, you can at least stop payment if you have been cheated.

LOAN SHARKS

No matter how desperate you are, never borrow money from a loan shark. Loan sharks make you repay on their terms, or else they may harm you or your family. Nobody needs money that badly.

Loan sharks charge exorbitant fees. The interest rate for small sums is usually about 20 percent per week. Thus, after a mere five weeks, you owe twice as much as you borrowed. The loan shark also adds financial penalties if you can't make your payments. Assume you borrow $500 and you keep up the weekly payments until you have paid back $400 of the original loan plus interest. Then, through no fault of your own, you miss a payment. The loan shark may make you pay twice your remaining obligation. It is not uncommon for a person to pay back $1000 or more of the original $500 borrowed.

Many borrowers feel that when a lender advances them money, he is doing them a favor. These borrowers unfortunately do not look closely enough into the conditions of the loan or the reputation of the lender. Don't make this mistake. Don't do business with any lender who does not show his state license when asked, who dates the loan prior to the time the money is advanced, or who asks you to sign the papers before the figures are filled in.

WARRANTIES

The main purpose of a warranty is to spell out the company's (warrantor's) obligations if the item you purchase doesn't work properly. Warranties vary greatly in the extent of protection they offer the consumer. A warranty may provide complete refund of all money spent, or it may provide limited service to certain parts of the product.

The seller is supposed to show you a copy of the written warranty prior to the sale. Therefore, the time to read the warranty is *before* you buy a product. Read the warranty carefully. Learn what protection you have against defective parts or faulty workmanship. Find out what portion of the labor costs will be covered if the product must be repaired.

Warranties must be written in plain, understandable language and must not mislead the consumer about what protections are provided. Moreover, the Magnuson-Moss Consumer Warranty Act requires the warrantor to state plainly all information of importance to the consumer.

Despite this law, some warranties are better than others. As with other factors in your purchase decision, you should shop around and carefully compare the contents of written warranties.

A written warranty can be of two basic types: a *full warranty* or a *limited warranty*. A full warranty provides complete replacement or refund if the product or its parts are defective. The full warranty may include the cost of removing or reinstalling the item, for example, a new kitchen sink. The warrantor may offer you a refund instead of a replacement. You don't have to accept the refund unless repair or replacement is not feasible or cannot be completed within a reasonable time. Contrastingly, a full warranty does not necessarily give the consumer the right to demand a refund, if the warrantor is able to supply a perfectly good replacement within a reasonable period. A full warranty must also state the period covered, such as a ''full one year warranty.''

As the name implies, a limited warranty does not offer full coverage of the product or its parts. The limitations apply to certain parts or to the length of the warranty period.

Warranties can be further divided into *express* and *implied* warranties. Express warranties are advertisements, sales brochures, instruction manuals, or verbal or written statements made at the time of the sale. A bona fide express warranty must pertain to the particular sale.

An implied warranty, which exists in many states, is a promise implied by law that the product is fit for its intended function. An implied warranty covers the entire product for a reasonable period and can often fill the gaps in an express warranty that may be limited to certain parts or to a short duration. If the product is sold without an express warranty, the implied warranty usually lasts one year. If the express warranty comes with the sale, the implied warranty applies as long as the express warranty, although it cannot be for less than sixty days nor for more than one year. Ask you local BBB about the law in you state.

Some warranties are nothing but advertising gimmicks, offering the consumer little protection. The language in warranties sometimes sounds good, but is often next to meaningless. Consider the phrase''guarantees your satisfaction.'' If there are no details defining how your satisfaction is to be guaranteed, you will probably be unable to enforce the warranty.

Many warranties are deceptively written, despite the requirement that they be clear. For example, one "ten-year warranty" implied that the entire appliance was protected for the period specified. But the customer learned, upon examining the fine print, that the ten-year period pertained to only a few inexpensive parts.

The assertion that many warranties are not as clear as they should be is confirmed by the National Consumer Task Force, which examined in excess of two hundred warranties used by fifty manufacturers and found more than thirty-four exceptions, disclaimers, and exculsions. The task force concluded that "in some instances the exclusions, disclaimers, and exceptions so diminished the obligations of the manufacturers that it was deceptive to designate the document as a warranty, because the remaining obligations were lacking in substance."

If the warranty seems unclear, insist on an explanation before you buy the items. Questions to ask are: Does the warranty entitle you to a full money refund if the product is defective? What parts are specifically covered by the warranty? What is the length of the refund period? What is the extent of the labor coverage?

With the purchase of expensive items, most of these questions must be answered in the warranty. A federal law, effective as of January 1, 1977, provides that warranties on products costing $150 or more must indicate what parts are protected. If one of the parts under warranty is defective or breaks and cannot be repaired within a reasonable time, the entire product must be replaced or the company must return your money.

MAIL-ORDER FRAUD

Mail-order fraud is prevalent and costly. In one recent year, mail inspectors investigated over 8,000 cases of alleged mail fraud, arrested 700 suspects, and put more than 5,000 fraudulent schemes out of business. Americans lost more than $1 billion through mail-fraud schemes in 1978. That is nearly double the $514 million lost during 1977.

Consumers lose hard-earned money through mail fraud in a variety of ways. Often the advertised product is never delivered by the company. When it is delivered, the product is frequently worthless. Occasionally, consumers face severe consequences if they believe advertising claims. For example, one advertisement offered to sell a birth control device through the mails. The advertisers were marketing an antipregnancy pill that supposedly originated four centuries ago in the Ming dynasty of China and was just now being offered in the United States. The advertisement cited medical authorities testifying to the effectiveness of the pill. It also provided testimonials from purported users of the pill. Unfortunately, many women who responded to the ad became pregnant. Complaints to the postal service finally prompted the postal authorities to cut off mail to the pill operation.

Postal authorities report that citizens complain about mail-order businesses for several reasons. One is false or deceptive advertising. Watch out for promises that seem too good to be true. Vanity items (such as bust developers, hair restorers, reducing pills, and skin-blemish removers) are the subject of most complaints. The magic pill advertised to cure your particular problem will probably do nothing at all except cost you money and cause aggravation.

Too many people believe that because an ad is published in a magazine or newspaper, the product must be trustworthy. Nothing could be further from the truth. Postal authorities don't have the time or the authority to approve products in advance. The postal service acts only when consumers complain — when it is too late.

Consumers also cause themselves extra problems by accepting merchandise before they have inspected it. Be sure to unpack and check any item delivered to your door before you sign the receipt. The delivery person may say that signing the receipt merely indicates that you have received the goods. Don't listen to him. Signing such receipts often signifies that the product was ''in good condition'' when you got it. The receipt carries the legal weight of a binding contract. If you sign it, you will be out of luck if the item is broken when you finally open the package and attempt to make a claim against the company.

Also, make sure you check the amount of time you have to return the merchandise. If you wish to return the item, send a written notice to that effect postmarked on or before the expiration date.

Whenever you respond to a mail-order advertisement, save a copy of the advertisement. It will be useful if you are swindled. If you are cheated by a company that refuses to satisfy your complaints, state the facts in a letter to your local postmaster. Include in the letter a copy of the mail-order advertisement so the post office can begin to investigate possible mail fraud.

The Federal Trade Commission has ruled that you have the right to know when the merchandise you ordered will arrive, and manufacturers must live up to their promised delivery dates. If the seller states no specific date, the company is required to deliver the goods within thirty days. If the company fails to deliver the goods within the required time, you can cancel your order and demand a full refund within seven business days. However, some merchandise is exempt from this safeguard, including film processing, magazine subscriptions, and seeds.

Another source of consumer discontent is receiving unsolicited packages in the mail. Some mail-order companies may try to trick you by mailing you products without your specific request. The typical scheme is to mail first installments of books, records, or magazines from clubs and then urge you to pay for future installments. You may also be sent an unsolicited product and then receive harassing letters demanding payment.

Never accept a package C.O.D. if you didn't order it. Let the sender pay for the return of the item. If you accept the package, you will probably discover a worthless product. And once you've paid the delivery person, you'll never get your money back. Also, never pay for a neighbor's package, unless of course the neighbor asked you to do so. The package may turn out to be unordered junk.

The Federal Trade Commission has clearly stated that a company or charity that sends out unordered products does so at its own risk. Consider unordered merchandise a gift. You have no legal obligation to pay for it or even return it. (You must, however, return packages delivered to you by mistake.) Simply ignore any bills coming later. And don't pay any attention if the company sends you notices threatening to harm your credit rating or tap your salary. These threats are made only to intimidate you. The company has no legal standing to do either of these things.

If you decide to order a product by mail, consider the following tips:

1. Make sure your name and address are neatly printed or typed on the order form. When ordering a gift, be sure you clearly indicate the name and address of the recipient.

2. Never send cash through the mail. Pay by check or money order so that you have a record of your payment. Remember that C.O.D. orders will cost more.

3. Keep a copy of your order form and any correspondence with the company. Keep a copy of the company's address for future reference.

4. Start with a small order. If the company responds promptly and provides a good product, you can feel more confident about placing larger orders.

5. Some people pay for unordered items simply to stop a company from pestering them. Don't make this mistake. The company will immediately give your name to the "sucker lists" used by other companies that send out unordered merchandise. If you pay for unsolicited goods, you are only encouraging this unethical business practice.

If you think you've been cheated through the mails, notify the company of your complaint. If you don't get satisfaction, inform the company that you'll take your grievance to the U.S. Postal Service. The post office department can take away mailing privileges from businesses that defraud throught the mails. Mail-order cheats know this, and they want to avoid it.

DOOR-TO-DOOR SALES

Each year thousands of consumers are tricked into buying worthless merchandise by door-to-door sales representatives. To avoid door--to-door swindles, be leery of strangers who come to your door. Some high-pressure sales representatives may misrepresent who they are and the purpose of their businesses. Knowing that many citizens are suspicious of salesmen, the representative may claim he is in "marketing research," "public relations," or "advertising."

Always ask to see the salesperson's identification. Many communities require door-to-door salespeople to possess a solicitor's license issued by the police department. Also check the salesperson's credentials with the company he claims to represent. If you are not familiar with the company, call the Better Business Bureau to determine if any complaints have been filed against the company.

It is safest not to let the salesperson into your home. Many burglars and other criminals use door-to-door sales as a cover. Moreover, many companies don't screen carefully the people they hire. Undesirable or even dangerous people may represent reputable companies.

Many consumers regret being talked into the purchase of something they didn't want or couldn't afford. Some door-to-door sales representatives may try to pressure you into buying something on the spot. They may tell you that the fantasic offer is being made to only a limited number of people and that you must decide immediately or you will not qualify. Or they may say that the company will not be coming into your area again for a long time. Don't be swayed by these lines. Sales people are trained to close the deal on the spot, before the buyer has a chance to think clearly and make an informed decision. Your best course of action is to wait, think the matter over, and investigate the product and the company. Time is your greatest ally. By waiting a few days, you will have time to study the terms of the contract and you will avoid buyer's remorse.

Before you buy from a door-to-door salesperson, compare prices for the same or similar items at local businesses. You will probably discover prices at local retail stores are just as low, if not lower, and it is much easier to return an unsatisfactory product to an established retail firm than to find an elusive door-to-door salesperson. Never let a salesperson leave a product at your home on approval because he may not come back and pick it up. Instead, you may recieve a bill for the merchandise.

If you are the slightest bit suspicious about signing a contract, wait and think it over. If you decide to sign, follow the rules listed earlier in the section on contracts. Pay for a product by check and make it payable to the company, not the salesperson. And always get a receipt.

If you think you've been cheated or acted too hastily, don't panic. Both federal and state truth-in-lending laws allow a buyer to change his mind and back out of certain door-to-door sales transactions. You normally have three days (some states allow more) after you sign the contract to cancel the sale. At the time you are closing the deal, the salesperson must inform you about your right to cancel within three days, and he must write on the contract the date it was signed and the date by which you must cancel. If this information is not supplied, you may cancel at anytime until the seller gives you the correct information.

In most states, there are several restrictions on the three-day cancellation rule. First, the sale must be worth twenty-five dollars or more. Second, the sale must take place in the home, not in the seller's business office. And, finally, this law does not apply to some sales transactions, such as those made by lawyers or real estate brokers.

If you cancel a sale, all you have to do is notify the company in writing of your decision. You do not have to state the reason for the cancellation; simply say you've changed your mind. It is a good idea to send the letter by registered mail, since you get a receipt to prove you've sent the cancellation notice within the allotted time. The extra postage is well worth it. The company is required to return all the money you paid, and it cannot impose a charge for your cancellation. Naturally, you are required to return the merchandise you purchased.

As the consumer protection laws become more restrictive, some companies attempt to circumvent them. For example, some door-to-door sales contracts now contain a clause in which you waive the three-day cooling-off period — that is, you give up your right to cancel the deal within three days. Always read the contract carefully and don't give up any of your legal rights.

TELEPHONE SOLICITORS

Your best bet is not to listen to telephone solicitors. The easiest and wisest thing to do is to say you're not interested and hang up.

If a telephone offer interests you, investigate the company before you agree to a purchase or divulge any personal information. Ask the solicitor for his name and the name of his company. Don't bother to get the company's phone number from the caller — he may give you the number of his partner in fraud. Instead, look up the company's number in your telephone directory and call to verify the identity of the sales representative. If the company is not listed in the phone book, report the incident to the police. Also check with your local BBB or consumer fraud unit to see if any complaints have been lodged against the company.

Telephone solicitors use a variety of gimmicks to catch your attention and trick you into a sale. One of the most common gimmicks is the free prize scam. If you have not entered a contest, be especially leery of notification by telephone that you have just been picked as a lucky winner. The caller will say that all you have to do to collect the free prize is let a sales representative visit your home or order a product at a reduced price. Winning a free prize should *never* cost you money. And crediting a small amount of money toward the purchase of a more expensive item is usually worth nothing, because the price of the sale item is normally raised to offset the company's giveaway. The normal result of the free prize trick is that you're duped into paying good money for overpriced or worthless products or services.

Another common telephone trick is the test-marketing fraud. You may be informed that you can buy a product at a small fraction of the cost because you were fortunate enough to be chosen as a member of a test market sample. You are supposed to test the product and then report the results to the company. Once you pay for the overpriced merchandise, the item never arrives or, if it does, it is not worth what you paid for it.

Finally, be watchful of anyone who claims he is not selling anything but is conducting a survey. Never divulge any personal information over the phone to a stranger.

SERVICES AND REPAIRS

Consumer protection agencies throughout the country report that the most common complaint is dissatisfaction with repair work. The complaints generally fall into one of three categories: The fee was too high for the work rendered; the work was not performed on time; or the work was unsatisfactory.

The complaints voiced are often valid. Consumer protection groups have repeatedly attempted to test the honesty of repair businesses. Each time, a shockingly high percentage fail the test. In the most common ploy, a consumer advocate will remove a small part from a perfectly good appliance or a properly running car and take the machinery to a repair shop. A surprisingly large number of repairmen claim that the appliance or car requires substantially more work than necessary.

Because service or repair frauds are so extensive in number and variety, we can review only those most frequently perpetrated and costly to the consumer. However, you can apply the following general tips to less common schemes you may encounter in the future.

Home Improvement Schemes

Never employ a contractor who solicits your business over the telephone or at your door. Reputable firms seldom seek customers by telephone or door-to-door canvassing. Swindlers are forced to use these methods because they must rely on a continuous supply of new customers; crooks rarely have repeat customers. It's safest and cheapest in the long run to deal with reputable local firms for home repairs. Local businesses have a stake in their reputation and rely on acquiring new customers by word of mouth. If their reputation is tarnished, they go out of business.

On extensive home improvement jobs, check the company's credit standing. A contractor who undertakes a large project must have good credit to buy materials. Some contractors "work on a string"; that is, they take the advance payment from the current job to pay the bills for the last job. A contractor who works on a string often has a poor credit rating, which may mean he would be unable to secure the materials needed to complete the work on your house.

Be sure to follow all of the rules found in the Contracts section of this chapter. In home improvement contracts, it is particularly important to get all promises in writing. The contract should detail all parts and materials to be used in the work. Failure to spell out the fine points is the reason so many home improvement customers are dissatisfied. The contract should be detailed to avoid deception and to prevent confusion and misunderstanding. You and the contractor may simply have different ideas about what materials are to be used.

A home improvement contract should always have a closing date, specifying the date by which the work must be completed. Include in the contract a clause that provides for fines if the contractor goes beyond that date. Never sign an open-ended contract — for example, one that states the work will be completed "when the workers have time." Otherwise the home improvement company can finish the work at its convenience.

Because of the high cost of major home improvements, be particularly careful about the company you choose and the contract you sign. In many states contractors who make improvements on your property or supply materials can incur lien rights. If you do not pay for the work at the designated time, the creditor can force you to sell your property in order to collect his money — sometimes even if the home improvement company defrauded you or did not satisfactorily perform the work it was hired to do.

One way to protect yourself against home improvement swindlers is to finance you home repairs through the Federal Housing Administration (FHA). The FHA tries to keep track of fraudulent home improvement businesses, and your loan won't be approved unless the work is to be done by a reputable firm.

Swindlers frequently try to earn a fast buck in less expensive home improvement schemes. Be leery of offers of free inspections, particularly if the offer is made over the phone or at your door. Free inspections of furnaces, chimneys, roofs, trees, and termites are all common ploys.

Three of the less serious and expensive home improvement swindles you are likely to encounter are: termite inspection, furnace inspection, and the gas leak scheme.

Termite inspection. The termite inspection swindler will come to your door posing as a pest control company representative and offer you a free inspection of your home. He'll search in all of the cracks and crevices under your house, and will suddenly appear with a board swarming with termites, roaches, or some other destructive bug. Naturally, he will claim that his company can exterminate the insects at the lowest possible price. In this situation you should never sign a contract without getting another inspection from a reputable exterminating service firm.

Furnace inspection. This swindler will offer a free inspection of your furnace. Invariably he will find something drastically wrong with your furnace and will tell you that if you don't get it fixed immediately, it may explode and destroy your home. The imposter will point out that he already has the furnace dismantled from the inspection. If he completes the repairs now, he claims, you will save a lot of money on labor costs. Concerned about the explosion and wanting to save money, you will be tempted to give in and pay the crook for the unnecessary repairs.

Gas leak scheme. In this scam, one or more uniformed men will come to your door and report that a gas leak has been discovered in the neighborhood. They will want to check the pipes in your basement or garage for a leak. While you are not looking, one of the men will squirt a little lighter fluid on one of the gas pipes, then summon you to watch. He will place a lighted match next to the pipe to show you the "leak." When the lighted match touches the lighter fluid, there will be a tiny explosion and a small fire. The men will then offer to repair your gas leak for the standard fee.

All of these potential swindlers will appeal to your emotions. When you hesitate about having the work done, one of the con men will say something like: "Would you endanger your home and your children by not getting the work done?" Don't be swayed by emotionalism. Always get a second opinion, even when the problem seems pressing.

These swindlers are able to survive because of public ignorance. Houses rarely deteriorate overnight. Of course, a gas leak or faulty electrical wiring can be dangerous, but there is almost always time to have a reputable business doublecheck the problem. For every person who has been sorry for waiting a day or two, thousands have regretted acting too hastily.

Auto Repairs
The U.S. Department of Transportation estimated that Americans now spend $50 billion each year on auto repairs, roughly $500 for every new car in the country. With such an enormous amount of money up

for grabs, dishonest or incompetent repairmen naturally compete for their share.

Repairmen who intentionally try to cheat customers are a second source of dissatisfaction. Cheating usually takes the form of overcharging for auto repairs or parts or performing unneeded repairs. Most of this section is devoted to helping you avoid intentional cheaters.

Although complete protection against fraudulent repairmen is next to impossible, there are several things you can do to lower your chances of being cheated. The best general advice is to patronize a local repair shop recommended to you by people whose judgment you trust. The local auto repairman who repairs the car himself or closely supervises his employees is the most likely person to provide the service you deserve. Because the small independent repair dealer depends primarily on repeat customers, he needs a good reputation to stay in business and will probably try to do a good job.

The local gas station you frequent may seem like a good place to have your repair work done, but a service station has limitations. Often gas station repairmen are not as experienced as mechanics employed at automotive repair shops. Limit your gas station repairs to minor services, such as oil changes and minor tune-ups, and have a professional mechanic handle extensive or complicated repairs.

Some shops are franchised and specialize in one type of auto service, such as muffler or transmission repairs. Since these shops do volume work, their prices may be lower than prices at a small shop. But remember that franchised specialty shops are not necessarily better. The franchised shop is operated by an independent businessperson and the quality of service you receive will depend primarily on his standards and style of business, rather than on the advertising claims make on TV by the parent company. Before going to a franchised specialty shop, check with your local BBB to see if any complaints have been filed against it.

No matter what type of repair shop you choose, find out if it is registered with the Division of Automotive Repairs or a similar agency in your state. Also check to see if the mechanic is industry certified. The National Institute for Automotive Service Excellence offers voluntary tests. Mechanics who successfully complete these tests are considered competent in most auto repair work.

Another piece of advice applicable to all repair work, but particularly to automobiles, is to know as much as possible about the machinery you want repaired. If you show complete ignorance about cars, the mechanic is more likely to feel he can put one over on you. If you know what you are talking about, or *sound* as if you know something about cars, you are less likely to be cheated.

Talk directly to the mechanic in order to clarify as precisely as you can what's wrong with your car. State only the specific symptoms, not your opinions. For example, you should inform the mechanic only that you hear a "ping" when accelerating, not that you think the car needs a valve job. And be precise in the terms you and the mechanic use. For instance, have the mechanic define exactly what he means by such general terms as "tune-up."

Recently many states have passed laws to protect consumers against auto repair cheats. The repair dealer is required to provide you with a written estimate of the costs of both parts and labor. You can use these estimates to compare prices among several shops. You may find, for example, that the service department of a new-car dealership makes a substantially higher estimate than a local shop for performing the same work. (But remember the requirements of the car's warranty. If the repair work, on a new car is not done by an authorized mechanic, the warranty becomes void.)

Once the work is authorized the dealer cannot charge you more money than was agreed on in the estimate. If the dealer deems it necessary to do more extensive repairs and charge you extra, he must have your written or oral consent before proceeding. Whenever you sign a repair shop work order, the dealer is now required to give you a copy. You can thereby compare the final work done and charges with your copy of the work order.

You can check the charges for your repair work in a variety of ways. Labor costs can be checked for most repairs by examining the dealer's standard repair manual, which indicates how much time each type of repair should take. If the labor cost seems too high, compare the time actually spent on your car with the time it should have taken according to the manual. The time needed to repair your car could also be *less* than indicated in the manual. Make sure that you are charged only for the time spent on your car, and not the standard fee suggested in the manual.

Always request all old parts that have been replaced. The repair dealer is now obligated to return all parts, except those under warranty or those for which you have been given credit on a trade-in. Remember that you are often eligible for an allowance on such items as tires, carburetors, generators, fuel pumps, and other rebuildable parts. Requesting old parts will help ensure that the parts were actually changed. It will also help prevent the dealer from selling your car's old parts to someone else as new merchandise. When in doubt, put an identifying mark on your car's parts before you take it into the repair shop. That way the repair shop can't give you back another car's old parts and leave yours in the engine.

Avoid car trouble away from home at all costs. Keep your car well maintained and have it checked by a mechanic before you go on a long trip so you won't be at the mercy of unknown repairmen. When repairmen in small shops or gas stations see out-of-state license plates, they realize they have a once-in-a-lifetime customer. The American Automobile Association suggests that cutomers stay near their cars, particularly if they are being worked on. Be particularly leery of a mechanic who wants you to leave immediately so he can work on your car in privacy. If possible, stick around and watch how the work is done.

Membership in an automobile club will help offer protection when you travel. Most clubs compile a list of approved service stations and repair shops. Because affiliation with the club brings in business, the approved repairman wants to maintain his good standing with the club by providing high quality and reasonably priced service to travelers.

WHAT TO DO IF YOU'VE BEEN DEFRAUDED

If you think you've been defrauded, go to the person or company against whom you have the complaint. It is possible that you and the business in question can work out a reasonable solution to your problem. Perhaps the basis of your complaint rests on a misunderstanding rather than on an attempt by the company to cheat you. If the company is not in your community, send a letter of complaint. Even if you don't get satisfaction, you can at least state your position in writing.

Don't be afraid to ask for help from your local BBB. Although the BBB has no legal enforcement powers, it can help you in several ways. First, the BBB staff can call the business on your behalf. A call from BBB is likely to be more persuasive than your personal call because most businesses want to avoid a bad reputation with the BBB. Second, the BBB can act as a neutral mediator between you and the business with which you are having the dispute. Through mediation you may at least receive some compensation such as a partial refund or additional services. If all else fails, the BBB can tell you what state agency to contact for further help.

Small claims court is the answer in many disputes. In most states the claim may not exceed a specified sum, usually about $500. To find out the exact dollar amount in your area, check with your local court clerk. A small filing fee is usually required, and neither side is permitted to be represented by an attorney in court. Each side explains his position to the judge, supplying any witnesses or documents necessary to support his case. Then the judge decides who is liable, who must pay, and the amount of the compensation. Settlements in small claims court have satisfied many defrauded consumers.

If the swindle exceeds $500, you should see your private attorney. If you do not have an attorney, the lawyer's reference service of your local bar association can recommend one. You may also qualify for legal aid, which is provided free in many states to poor people with pressing legal problems.

If you are the victim of an obvious fraud, notify the appropriate authorities, particularly your local police and district attorney. Many local prosecutors now have special units for prosecuting consumer fraud cases. These local agencies may give you immediate help and aid you in getting your money back. They may also put an end to the fraudulent business. You should also contact the state attorney general's consumer fraud unit and the Federal Trade Commission.

CONCLUSION

The old saying "Buyer Beware!" is still true today. Even though the government is trying to crack down on consumer fraud, thousands of dishonest business people are waiting to steal your money from you.

Government agencies alone are not sufficient to protect consumers. As the Federal Trade Commission has stated: "No governmental policy is as effective as the purchaser who is willing to shop for what he wants and who is intelligent enough to judge what quality he should receive for the price he pays. Just plain old cold blooded shopping makes it tough on the gypsters."

We cannot have complete government protection in our society. A free market economy requires that there be open choice to the buyer. The consumer must have the right to spend his money on the goods and services he wants, even if he spends his money foolishly. Therefore, you, the consumer, are responsible for protecting yourself against consumer frauds. Be thoughtful in all business transactions. Try to develop a skeptical and inquisitive attitude about business deals. Knowledge is your best protection.

Chapter 9

Bunco Schemes

A separate category of fraud, unrelated to the purchase of goods or services, involves distorting or suppressing the truth to dupe the victim into willingly handing over his money. Known by many names, we shall refer to these frauds as *bunco* schemes. These ploys are also commonly called *con games* and their perpetrators *con men*, referring to the swindler's efforts to gain the *confidence* of the victim. Interestingly, many bunco artists are women, because they seem better able than men to secure the trust of the victim.

Although the variety of bunco schemes devised over the years practically defies the imagination, some generalizations can be made. In some instances the victim expects something in return, such as more money; sometimes he is tricked into giving up his money on the promise that it will be returned shortly; sometimes he is misled into believing that he is doing a good deed. Bunco schemes normally play on human failings or weaknesses, such as greed, vanity, loneliness, or grief. Yet they also appeal to what are generally considered human virtues, such as respect for authority and the desire to help others.

Bunco schemes work best against people who are gullible and naïve. The elderly are frequent targets because they tend to be more trusting of people's motives, and the majority of victims come from the poorly educated segments of society. Yet police files across the country clearly indicate that rich and well-educated people are also commonly deceived by the bunco artist.

The success of bunco schemes does not depend solely on the gullibility of the victims; much of the credit must go to the bunco artists themselves. They are inventive, quick-thinking, and highly persuasive; they are also keen judges of character who can spot human failings in a matter of seconds. Often bunco men are well dressed, friendly and sociable; as consumate actors, they are able to capture the victim's trust and get him to do things against his better judgment.

Criminologists do not know the full extent of this type of fraud because, even more than most crimes, it is vastly underreported. Some victims are unaware that they have been swindled; others are simply too embarrassed to report a crime that resulted from their own greed or gullibility. Despite the lack of official statistics, it is clear that thousands of bunco schemes are carried out every year, costing the victims millions of dollars.

Many of the plots of bunco schemes have remained the same for hundreds of years; only the details change to fit the times. In this short chapter, bunco schemes are divided into three categories, based on the human feelings to which they appeal. We give an example of each type as well as advice on how to avoid it.

SCHEMES THAT PLAY ON THE DESIRE TO MAKE EASY MONEY

Most of the classic bunco schemes appeal to the victim's desire to make easy money. This type of scheme is prevalent in the United States, where so many people are naïve enough to think they can get something for nothing.

The Pigeon Drop

The pigeon drop, sometimes called the "switch," has many variations, but it normally begins in a bank and is committed by a team of two swindlers. The first member of the team approaches the victim, or pigeon, and engages him in conversation. Soon the second member of the team, pretending to be a stranger, walks by and appears to find an envelope, or a purse with no identification, on the ground. The second member asks if the envelope belongs to either the victim or the first member, and they reply that it does not. The second member then opens the envelope and, to everyone's surprise, they discover it contains several thousand dollars in cash.

The trio discuss what they should do with the money. The first member suggests that they split it up evenly, and the victim is enticed at the thought of coming into some easy money. The second member, however, suggests that they first discuss the matter with his best friend, who happens to be an attorney (or some authority figure). All three proceed to a nearby office building where the attorney purportedly works, or they go to a phone booth and the second member pretends to call the attorney. The second member supposedly consults with the attorney and returns shortly with the attorney's advice. Because the amount of money in the envelope is so large, the story goes, the owner probably obtained it illegally or was trying to conceal it to avoid paying taxes. Since there is no identification, it is perfectly legal for the three who found the money to divide it evenly. However, the attorney suggests that each person should put up several thousand dollars of "good faith" money to justify sharing in the profits, that only hard-working people with money in the bank deserve to share in the windfall.

If the victim agrees to put up the good faith money, the second member seals the envelope and places it in his own pocket. The three then proceed in turn to their respective banks — first to the banks of the two swindlers and then to the victim's bank — and finally return to the building where the fictitious attorney works. The second member tells the victim that he can hold the envelope containing the windfall, but in taking it out of his pocket he switches envelopes, giving the victim one filled with phony money. The second member enters the building to see the attorney and, upon returning, claims he has proved his good faith and is justified in collecting his share of the newly found money. The second member then takes the first member's good faith money inside and comes back with the same story. The second member now takes the victim's good faith money inside. The victim might feel uneasy about handing over his money, but he believes he is safe because he has more than enough money in the envelope to cover possible losses. When the second member does not return, the first member goes to look for him; when neither member returns, the victim looks inside the envelope and realizes that he has been swindled.

This scheme sounds so obvious that no one could possibly fall for it, but it is one of the oldest scams on the books, and it continues to work to this day. There are no nationwide statistics on the incidence of this con game, but the Los Angeles Police Department estimated that victims of the pigeon drop lose roughly $500,000 each year in Los Angeles alone.

How to Avoid This Type of Scheme
The pigeon drop is but one of hundreds of bunco schemes that play on the victim's desire to make easy money. You can avoid this and similar con games by remembering that nobody, especially a stranger, wants to help you get rich unless he has a strong financial incentive to do so. Don't be naïve; a stranger will not give you something for nothing.

Avoid discussing your finances or other sensitive matters with people you meet on the street and do not withdraw money from your bank at the suggestion of a stranger. Do not be maneuvered into handing over your money or valuables to a stranger, even for a moment. Many bunco schemes rely on switch tactics, and con artists are particularly adept at sleight-of-hand techniques that leave you with a wad of worthless paper.

Finally, do not rush into any deals that promise to make you rich quickly. Your best bet is to reject all such offers flatly. If you are intrigued tell the person making the proposition that you want time to think about it, that you intend to consult your spouse or attorney, and that you will contact him later with your decision. When you have time, check out the scheme with the police or the district attorney's office to find out if it is legitimate. If the deal is legitimate, you will feel more confident about investing your money. If it is not legitimate, let the police give the swindler a call.

SCHEMES THAT PLAY ON THE RESPECT FOR AUTHORITY

Many bunco schemes play on the victim's respect for authority or his willingness to cooperate with authority figures. In these schemes, the con man assumes the identity of a police officer, government official, detective, or inspector of some sort. Under the cloak of authority, he tricks the victim into turning over his money.

The Bank Examiner Scheme

To put this fraud into motion, the perpetrator visits a bank in search of a likely victim, most frequently an elderly woman. The swindler stands near the victim when she is filling out her deposit or withdrawal slip, looks at her bank book, and notes as much information as possible — at least her name, account number, and bank balance. A few days later, the victim receives a telephone call from a person alleging to be a bank examiner, although he might also claim to be a police officer, detective, or bank auditor. To establish his credibility, he recites the victim's account number and bank balance; quite naturally the victim assumes that only a bank employee would have access to this information. The con man informs the victim that the bank suspects one of its employees, perhaps a teller, of embezzlement. He grabs her attention by telling her that some of her personal savings have been taken.

The ''bank examiner'' asks the victim to help catch the embezzler, and to ensure her cooperation he tells her that anyone who offers assistance will receive a substantial reward. He instructs the victim to withdraw a specified amount of money, usually several thousand dollars, in cash so he can check the serial numbers on the bills. He tells her not to talk about this plan with anyone or else the thief might find out and avoid detection. The victim eventually withdraws the money, takes it home, and waits for the bank examiner or a ''bonded messenger.'' The bank examiner arrives, gives her a receipt for the money, and says that he will take it directly back to the bank. He instructs the victim to come to the bank in a few days and collect her reward. When she does, of course, she learns that she has been defrauded.

How to Avoid This Type of Scheme
No business or public organization will ask a private citizen to use his own money to help trap a suspected crook. Banks and other organizations use their own or government funds in all investigative or police work. If a person approaches you and claims to be some sort of bank investigator, do not discuss your finances until you have checked out his story with the police or district attorney.

Do not discuss your personal finances (or any other sensitive information) over the telephone with anyone you do not know, whether it be with a scientist conducting a survey or a police officer conducting official business. Get the person's name, organization, and the reason for his call, and then ask him to come to your house to talk with you in person. In the meantime, call the organization he claims to represent and find out if he works there and has contacted you on legitimate business.

SCHEMES THAT PLAY ON THE DESIRE TO HELP OTHERS

Bunco artists often use the victim's desire to help people in need or distress to carry out their schemes. They trick kindhearted people into turning over their money to help a wide variety of groups, including religious groups, minority groups, the poor, the handicapped, and even people falsely imprisoned in foreign countries.

Charitable and Religious Appeals
In the classic scheme, the perpetrator saturates a community with letters appealing for donations to a nonexistent charitable or religious organization. Frequently, the letter of solicitation includes a small "gift" that is supposedly handmade by the people the charity is trying to help, such as orphans or the physically handicapped. The letter also includes a list of celebrities who supposedly contributed to the charity. Many people receiving the appeal make a contribution, in part out of sense of obligation for receiving the free handmade gift, but mostly out of a genuine desire to help people less fortunate than they. If a lot of people send in donations, the con man can easily make several thousand dollars in a matter of days and leave town before the postal authorities discover his racket.

Appeals to nonexistent charitable or religious organizations are frequently made by door-to-door solicitors — men, women, or children — who can be highly persuasive. They might be dressed in religious outfits, have a religous book in hand, and pray for your salvation on the spot. They might show you a picture of the starving children the charity is supposed to benefit. These bunco artists will tell you sob stories, will play on your guilt, and will tell you how lucky you are that you have your health, enough food to eat, and a roof over your head. Finally, wanting to help the needy, the well-meaning victim donates a few dollars. After an entire neighborhood or community has been canvassed, the bunco artist, several thousand dollars richer, moves on to the next town.

How to Avoid This Type of Scheme
The simplest way to avoid being defrauded by this scheme is not to donate to any questionable charities or religious organizations. Do not make contributions, purchase any product, or buy tickets to raffles or other games of chance whether the appeal is made through the mails, by telephone, or door-to-door. We do not mean to sound cold-hearted; giving to worthy charities is an unselfish and noble gesture. But if you give, you should be sure your money goes to one of the hundreds of organizations worthy of your generosity.

There are several warning signals that can alert you to questionable charities. All legitimate charities will accept checks made out in the name of the charity. Be suspicious of any organization that insists on cash donations; always make out the check in the name of the organization, never in the name of the solicitor. Most cities require licenses for solicitation, and the licensing agency tries to screen out disreputable organizations. Always ask to see the door-to-door solicitor's license. If you suspect that it might be phony, jot down the person's name and license number, call the police, and check on it. Well-established charitable organizations are in no particular hurry to collect donations; their offices will be operating well into the future. Be suspicious, therefore, of any telephone solicitor who says he will send a messenger over immediately to pick up your donation. Tell the solicitor to wait a few days while you determine if the charity is reputable. And finally, you must even be careful not to be taken in by child solicitors. Some enterprising children go out on their own and try to make some fast money by falsely claiming to represent a local boys' or girls' organization. Children collecting money for bona fide causes are usually accompanied by adults with licenses or identification tags. If the children are alone, do not contribute.

If the charity sounds worthy and you want to contribute, follow a rule that applies to all of your financial transactions: Do not act in haste. Get all of the facts about the organization from the solicitor and tell him to come back in a few days. Call your police department or the fraud division of your district attorney's office and find out if any complaints have been lodged against the organization. It is also a good idea to call the local United Fund office, which screens all of those charitable and religious organizations that apply for a share of the United Fund monies. If you determine that the charity in question is legitimate, we suggest you make your donations directly to the organization's offices and bypass the solicitor.

CONCLUSION

We have mentioned but a few of the many categories of bunco schemes. Others play on the victim's grief, loneliness, or vanity. Some con men read the obituary columns in the newspaper and try to collect fictitious debts recently incurred by the widow's departed husband. Some scheming men pretend to fall in love with lonely and depressed women and then bilk them of their savings. Phony talent agents might collect large sums of money to get aspiring actors into the movies or on stage. The list of schemes is practically endless.

You can protect yourself from bunco schemes by following some simple advice. Be suspicious about deals that promise you something for nothing. Any deal that sounds too good to be true probably is. Do not delude yourself into thinking a stranger is going to help you strike it rich. Never turn over your savings to any stranger, no matter how reasonable his story sounds. Do not be put into a position where your money, wallet, of purse could be switched so that you would be left with worthless scraps of paper.

Do not be taken in by appearances. The bunco artist might be dressed in expensive and fashionable clothing, in an official-looking uniform, or in religious garb. He may pretend to be blind, handi-capped, or injured. You should even be leery of children who try to get your money. Unscrupulous adults often use children in plots to make money because children are so often perceived as innocent.

Bunco schemes are as varied as people's imagination. To learn more about them, we suggest you call your local police department, district attorney, or state attorney general's office and request any literature they have on the subject. Also try to find out if any bunco artists are operating in your area. A healthy and informed skepticism is your best protection against this type of fraud.

Chapter 10

Victim Compensation

Crime is part of the American way of life and the extent of victimization is enormous, but until recently the government has done little to help the victims of crime. Each year over 35 million crimes are committed — *not* including crimes against the public order, such as drunkenness, consumer fraud, and so-called victimless crimes. All crime categories are rising steadily; reported crime has doubled in the past decade.

The growing concern for crime victims is due to efforts from the press and politicians. This attention has resulted in legal procedures, called *victim compensation,* that allow government payment to qualified victims for their losses suffered from crime.

Although proposals for victim compensation can be traced back several thousands years, full-scale government programs are a relatively recent phenomenon. Within the past fifteen years approximately half of the states have introduced or passed some form of state assistance for crime victims. Congress has been debating a federal victim compensation bill for several years and will probably adopt a law in the near future.

Many types of victim compensation laws exist in the United States, varying in scope, procedures, eligibility criteria, and amount of money paid to victims. Before we describe some of these laws, we will discuss the history of victim compensation that falls under criminal law, and the victim's use of the civil suit to recover directly from the offender financial losses due to crime.

HISTORY OF VICTIM COMPENSATION

The criminal law as we know it today did not exist in ancient times. If one person harmed another, the two parties or their families resolved the dispute privately. In the eyes of the law, the victim had been wronged, not the state. Government did not interfere in the personal affairs of its citizens.

In early English law, an offender made direct payments, called restitution, to his victim — not to the government. The idea was to right the wrong that had been done. Specific amounts of restitution were often prescribed for different offenses. For example, if someone knocked out another person's front tooth — a crime we know today as battery — the offender had to pay the victim eight shillings.

Gradually, the king and his government became more involved in the operation of the legal system. Many wrongful acts, previously left to individual citizens to redress, were now considered "breaches of the king's peace." In addition to the victim, the king was also wronged by a breach of the peace, and the offender had to give money to the government as well as to the person he harmed. This system recognized that harmful acts affect not only the victim individually, but all of society. Breaches of the king's peace eventually evolved into crimes, and the king, not the victim, was compensated by fines or other forms of punishment. Crimes — wrongful acts against the state — thereby became separated from civil law, creating a greater legal distance between the criminal and his victim.

Early American law was based on contemporary English practice. During America's colonial period the victim of crime exercised substantial control over the administration of justice. The victim's interests were at stake, not the government's. In theft cases, for example, the offender had to pay the victim three times the amount stolen. If he could not pay, he sold himself into servitude to the victim for a period equal to the value of the goods taken. It was up to the victim to prosecute the case. If the victim wanted to drop the matter, the government was indifferent.

Shortly after the American revolution, new methods of justice, the workhouse and the penitentiary, replaced restitution and servitude to victims of crime. Criminal justice became increasingly the states' responsibility and the victim's restitution became purely symbolic.

At this point we should make clear the distinction between restitution and compensation. Both are intended to provide victims reparation for damages resulting from crime. The difference lies in who makes the payment. With restitution, the offender pays directly for the losses the victim suffered. With compensation, the government pays, much as an insurance company pays a damage claim, and the link between the offender and his victim is lost.

Recent Interest in Victim Compensation

Victims of crime have been largely forgotten in the criminal justice system until the middle of this century. Recent discussion of victim compensation opened in England in 1951, when Margery Fry, a social reformer, published an influential book entitled *Arms of the Law*. Fry maintained that the government has an obligation to protect the well-being of its citizens. If the government does not fulfill this obligation, it should pay for the damage it failed to prevent. In other words, the government should financially compensate victims of crime.

Fry's book aroused a flurry of debate. Countries around the world discussed the extent to which governments are obliged to compensate victims of crime. Eventually, Fry's arguments proved compelling. On January 1, 1964, New Zealand became the first country to put a victim compensation law into effect. England's victim compensation law went into operation seven months later, on August 1, 1964.

Victim compensation has been hotly debated in the United States during the past two decades. Opponents cite several reasons why victim compensation laws should not be enacted. Because our country is based on the principle of free enterprise, opponents claim, the government should not usurp responsibilities from the private sector. Why should government compensate victims when private assistance is available? A sizeable percentage of the population already has private insurance that covers major medical expenses resulting from criminal attack. As of the mid-1970s, approximately 95 percent of the people throughout the country had insurance to cover surgical expenses, 84 percent were for regular medical expenses, and 78 percent had coverage for major medical expenses. The solution to the problem, some argue, is more private insurance, not more government spending.

Cost is another argument against state victim compensation programs. The President's Commission estimated in 1967 that the loss of earnings and medical expenses of victims of violent crime exceeded $800 million per year. Assuming that every eligible victim received an average compensation payment of $1,500, the current national cost of victim compensation would be roughly $4 billion. That is a lot of money.

Finally, victim compensation programs would be even more expensive if the government were held responsible for not protecting its citizens — that is, if the government were left open to civil suits designed to collect payment for the damages it failed to prevent.

Arguments in favor of victim compensation laws are also compelling. The most general argument holds that society and the government have a duty to protect its citizens. If the government fails in its responsibility, the least it should do is pay for the resulting damages. Proponents also point out that victim compensation laws do not necessarily leave the state open to civil suits. Victim compensation could be administered like the social welfare system, in which money is given out to needy individuals. If the government gives public assistance to people in need, it is not admitting failure to protect its citizens or assuming liability for the damages resulting from crime.

Second, supporters of victim compensation argue that the current civil or private remedies are inadequate for many victims. The shortcomings of the civil law will be discussed in detail in the next section.

Third, since the income distribution is so unequal in America, crime does not affect all victims equally. Poor people can't afford insurance; nor can they afford a lawyer to represent them in court. They can't afford medical bills and they can least afford to lose time and wages through absence from work. Victim compensation is necessary, it is argued, for those people who are unable to afford the regular methods of coping with crime. As former Supreme Court Justice Arthur Goldberg said, "It is only right that society, through a program of public compensation, recognize its obligation toward these victims. As a practical matter also, society alone is able to assist victims of crime."

CIVIL SUIT FOR DAMAGES

The distinction between a crime and a civil wrong remains to this day. A crime is a wrongful act against the state, even though the harm may be inflicted on an individual. A crime is prosecuted by the state with public funds. A civil wrong, called a tort, is a wrongful act against an individual, prosecuted by the individual at his discretion and expense.

Many harmful acts are both crimes and civil wrongs. If a person commits a crime, he can be sued by the victim in civil court, as well as punished by the state. If, for example, a man commits a rape, he will be punished by the state, assuming he is apprehended and found guilty in court. Legal theory holds that he has injured society by his act. But obviously he has also caused great harm to his victim. The victim can therefore sue in civil court for the damages incurred in the crime. If found civilly liable, the rapist could be ordered to pay for the damages.

The civil suit has obvious advantages. The victim receives money for damages suffered, and he is paid directly by the offender. Thus, money plays both a punitive and a restorative function in the civil law. The victim does not have to be satisfied with the symbolic justice meted out by the criminal court. Having the offender sent to prison won't pay for medical expenses or make up for lost wages.

Unfortunately, the civil suit has drawbacks. First, the victim, not the state, bears the responsibility for prosecuting the suit. The victim must therefore pay for an attorney, and possibly for court costs. Most victims don't have the time or the money to spend on a civil suit.

Second, a civil suit cannot be pressed unless the offender is identified and apprehended. The circumstances of most crimes, however, do not permit the victim to identify the offender. Even if identification is made, the assailant will probably never be caught. The 1978 *Uniform Crime Reports* states that the police make arrests in less than one-fourth of all reported crimes. In other words, it is impossible to sue someone unless you know who he is and can get him to court.

Third, most offenders cannot afford to pay damages, even if they are apprehended. In 1966 the President's Commission on Crime in the District of Columbia reported that ninety percent or more of the inmates in prison are indigent. Most inmates could not raise sufficient funds to hire a private attorney. Criminals are less able to pay civil damages if they are sentenced to prison or made to pay fines after criminal conviction.

For these reasons, the civil suit is normally not a viable method for collecting payment from an offender. One study of 167 victims of violent crime in Toronto, for example, found that although 75 percent of the victims incurred financial losses, only 15 percent considered suing to recover the money lost, a mere 5.4 percent consulted an attorney, and 4.8 percent tried to collect from their attackers. Only 3 of the 167 victims, or 1.8 percent, actually collected money from their assailants.

Despite these problems, you should consider a civil suit under the right circumstances. We urge you to use a civil suit if you know the offender has the funds to pay damages and he has been convicted in criminal court. In other words, you are limited to those cases in which you are likely to receive more money in damages from the offender than you would have to spend in legal fees.

CURRENT VICTIM COMPENSATION LAWS

Most current victim compensation laws provide public funds to victims of violent crimes or to the survivors of people killed by violent crimes. Payments normally cover only medical costs and loss of earnings, that is, out-of-the-pocket expenses. A minority of states awards compensation for pain and suffering. Most states do not give compensation for the value of property lost except for items taken or destroyed during a physical attack. You would not qualify for victim compensation if a burglar cleaned out your house.

Only innocent victims are eligible for victim compensation. Contributory negligence may mean disqualification. If a person consents to or incites a criminal act, he is likely not to be found an innocent victim. Exposing oneself to a high-risk situation, however, is generally not deemed contributory negligence.

Discussion of all victim compensation laws is beyond the scope of this book. We will therefore describe in some detail the victim compensation programs of two states, California and New York. These two states have the largest programs and they are representative of the other states' laws, which we will mention briefly.

The California Program

California was the first state in the Union to pass a victim compensation law. Enacted during the 1965 legislative session, the program went into effect at the beginning of 1966. The law originally authorized the Department of Social Welfare to administer the program, and the department was instructed to establish criteria and rules for granting compensation to victims. At first, victim compensation in California was considered a form of public welfare with a specialized clientele. The law did not work well under the Department of Social Welfare, and in November 1967 control of the program was transferred to the state Board of Control — the agency currently administering the law.

The staff of the Board of Control prepares cases for review and hearings are held by the board. All decisions made by the board are subject to legislative approval, but in practice this is a routine matter. The law currently provides a maximum possible award of $23,000, which is broken down to a $10,000 ceiling on medical or burial expenses, $10,000 on loss of income or support, and $3,000 for employment rehabilitation expenses. Although not stated explicity, the law is interpreted, as are all other compensation laws, to allow compensation even if the offender is not apprehended, tried, or convicted. Naturally, if the defendent is found innocent of the charges, it is much more difficult, although still possible, for the victim to convince the board to grant compensation.

There are several requirements for eligibility. First, the victim must show that he or she was incapacitated as a result of the violent crime. A victim cannot receive compensation for losses due to theft if there was no incapacitation, nor can the victim receive compensation for pain and suffering alone. If, for example, a woman is raped, she cannot receive payment unless she is kept off her job and the crime otherwise imposes financial hardship. She cannot receive compensation for only the psychological trauma associated with rape. The California law was recently revised to permit victim compensation for injury or death resulting from an automobile accident in which the offender was driving while intoxicated or under the influence of drugs. Previously, California, like most states, had restricted compensation to vehicular crimes in which the vehicle was deliberately used as a weapon.

Next, the victim must show as a result of the violent crime, he or she is suffering serious financial hardship. This provision means that the victim cannot have money in the bank to pay for the injuries. It also means that the victim does not receive money from other sources, for example, from insurance benefits.

The victim must comply with several provisions; if not, he or she may be disqualified from receiving compensation. Conditions for disqualification include the following: 1) if the victim fails to file a claim for compensation with the state Board of Control within one year after the date of the crime (extensions made in exceptional cases); 2) if the victim does not cooperate with law enforcement officers conducting the crime investigation; 3) if the victim in some way was negligent or provoked the criminal attack. Note, however, that Good Samaritans are eligible; that is, a person injured while aiding in the apprehension of a criminal or in the prevention of a crime can be compensated for resulting injuries.

Despite California's large population and high crime rate, the victim compensation program is not used extensively. Through the first eleven months of the 1976 – 77 fiscal year, the state Board of Control awarded 2,284 claims amounting to approximately $4.5 million. Over the past few years each compensation payment, including lawyers' fees, has averaged slightly less than $2,000.

Several explanations may account for the minimal use of the program. First, most people don't know the law exists. Second, the ''hardship'' requirement greatly restricts the number of crime victims eligible for the program. And third, the bureaucracy is hard to penetrate; many people do not want to spend the time or trouble for a modest award.

Because the victim compensation program has been so infrequently used, a new state law requires police departments to inform every victim of a violent crime of the program's existence. Many police departments automatically send victims the forms needed to file a claim. If you are the victim of a violent crime in California and the local police have not informed you about the law, call your local district attorney's office to get all necessary information.

The New York Program

Impetus for New York's victim compensation law came from the widespread publicity about an innocent crime victim. On October 9, 1965, Arthur R. Collins attempted to prevent a drunk from bothering some elderly women on a New York City subway car, and during a scuffle he was stabbed to death by the drunk. Shortly after Collin's death, then Governor Rockefeller established a committee to study the feasiblity of adopting a victim compensation law. The next year, in 1966, the legislature created a Crime Victim's Compensation Board, which began operation in March 1967.

The board originally consisted of three members appointed for seven-year terms, but in 1973, due to an increasing work load, the board was expanded to five members. The board established three branch offices in New York City, Albany, and Buffalo to make it easier for victims to file claims; offices in Syracuse, Nassau and Suffolk County have since added. Staff members initially handle the claims and prepare the cases for review by board members. The decisions of individual board members are then subject to appeal to the full board; approximately 10 percent of all cases are appealed. Victims can be represented by legal counsel, but attorney's fees are paid out of the award.

The board is authorized to compensate all victims of crime, but the word *victim* is carefully defined, and the definition is intended to be restrictive. According to the law, a victim is a person who suffers personal physical injury as a direct result of crime. Note the words *personal* and *physical*. Compensation for pain and suffering is not granted. Compensation is allowed only for out-of-the-pocket expenses paid by the victim, plus loss of earnings and support resulting from physical injury. Compensation can also be awarded to any person dependent for his primary support on a victim who dies as a direct result of the crime.

There are other requirements for eligibility. New York, like about half of the states, has a hardship test. The rules governing what constitutes hardship were developed in 1968 and generally provide that all of the victim's financial resources be considered. However, some items are exempted from consideration, for example, a home, the family car, clothing and other small items. In effect, a standard of living test is used in determining whether a victim is under serious financial hardship. If a board member finds that the victim's medical expenses and loss of income make it impossible to maintain his standard of living, then serious financial hardship exists.

The maximum award for cases of loss of earnings is $250 a week, up to a ceiling of $20,000. There is no limit on payment for medical expenses. The board will also make an emergency award of up to $1,500 when it appears that undue hardship will result if immediate payment is not made, and when it seems likely that the board will ultimately honor the claim.

Specific provisions must be met before the board can give an award. A claim must be filed no later than one year after the crime was committed, or no later than one year after the death of the victim. No award can be made unless the victim reports the crime to the police within one week of its occurrence. No award can be made unless the victim proves serious financial hardship as a result of the crime. Finally, the New York law provides that compensation be reduced by any amount the victim receives from other sources — from the offender through restitution, from public welfare, or from private insurance payments. As with the programs in most other states, the board can reduce or refuse compensation to a victim whose conduct contributed to the crime.

Other States

Victim compensation laws in all states share similarities, yet differ on the specifics. Most states, for example, have a hardship test for eligibility, but Hawaii, Massachusetts, and Washington allow for compensation regardless of the victim's resources, as long as he or she does not recover losses from other sources such as insurance. Similarly, some states do not award compensation for pain and suffering; a handful of states do.

The dollar amount of the awards also varies from state to state. In Maryland, the average value of an award in 1976 was over $4,000, compared with $3,600 in Massachusetts, $3,100 in Illinois, $2,000 in New York, $1,200 in Minnesota, and $1,000 in Washington.

At present, the federal government does not have a comprehensive victim compensation program. Several small federal programs, exist, but they are isolated examples, funded individually by the Department of Justice. A nationwide victim compensation law is expected soon.

WHAT TO DO IF YOU ARE THE VICTIM OF A VIOLENT CRIME

If you are the victim of a crime, particularly a violent crime, we suggest you call your local law enforcement agency or District Attorney's office. These agencies will help you find out whether a victim compensation program exists in your state and whether you are eligible for it. Be sure to check if you think you might qualify. Unfortunately, most eligible people do not apply for compensation. In New York, for example, only two victims out of every ten eligible bother to file victim compensation claims.

Here are some questions you should ask your police department or district attorney about victim compensation:
- Can I receive victim compensation from the state if my private insurance covers the damages?
- Can I receive victim compensation if I have money in my bank account? How much money can I have before I am no longer eligible?
- Can I receive compensation for pain and suffering resulting from the crime? Can my family receive compensation if I am killed in a criminal attack?
- Is hardship a requirement for receiving compensation and how is this defined?
- Can I receive compensation if I was acting as a Good Samaritan?

- Can I receive compensation if the offender was mentally ill?
- Can I receive compensation if I was injured by a vehicle and must the vehicle have been used as a weapon or does a drunk driver qualify me?
- Can I receive compensation if my own negligence contributed to the injury?
- How long after the crime do I have to file a claim?
- Can I receive compensation if I am a relative of the offender?
- Does the offender have to be arrested or convicted before I can receive compensation?
- How much money can I receive for partial or total disability?
- How long will the compensation payments last and what is the ceiling on them?
- Will I receive one lump sum or will the compensation be paid in installments?
- Can I be represented by an attorney at all stages of the compensation proceedings?
- Does the victim compensation board pay attorney's fees?

CONCLUSION

The law has increasingly extended its protection to the poor, to minority groups, and to persons accused of crimes. A just society demands as much. But until recently victims of crime have been largely denied legal protection. A move is now afoot to help some victims of crimes. Although limited in scope and effect, and although the losses and damages incurred as a result of crime cannot be recovered, victim compensation laws are a step in the right direction.

Victim compensation laws are needed because, as a practical matter, only society is able to assist victims of crime. Civil suits or insurance are of little use when the criminal is not caught, when he is poor, or when the victim does not have enough money to pay insurance premiums or hire a lawyer to prosecute a suit. All too often, the victim must bear the burden of medical bills, lost wages, and similiar expenses. Society also pays the costs; lost jobs, unemployment compensation, public welfare, and an inevitable sense of insecurity affect us all. Ultimately, victim compensation programs cost society less than continuing to let individual victims bear sole responsibility for their misfortune.

Chapter 11

Community Crime Prevention

People all over the country are concerned for their personal safety and the protection of their property. According to the latest public opinion polls, the American public considers crime one of its gravest problems.

Citizens generally respond to the crime problem, as they do to most problems, by looking to the government for help. They demand more police on the streets, harsher sentences for criminals, and a greater use of capital punishment.

In response to public pressure, millions of dollars have been poured into the criminal justice system, with most of the money coming from federal grants. Criminal justice agencies have developed new crime control strategies, have broadened training programs, invented new technologies, and acquired modern equipment. State legislatures have reinstated or expanded the use of the death penalty. Despite extensive government action, the crime rate continues to climb.

Law enforcement officials and criminologists are beginning to realize that the criminal justice system alone cannot win the battle against crime. Unemployment, poverty, racial discrimination, and the sense of injustice that pervades our society must be eliminated before the crime problem can be solved. The underlying causes of crime must be eradicated.

Equally important, from a strategic point of view, is the active involvement of the general public in crime prevention. In 1967 the President's Commission on Law Enforcement and Administration of Justice stressed the need for direct citizen action in the crimi al justice system. The commission realized that citizen participation is not only

229

desirable, it is mandatory. Today, more people are taking the advice of the president's commission and they are making crime prevention *their* business.

If crime prevention is defined broadly, citizens can participate at many levels. Efforts by citizens may be directed, for example, at strengthening the crime prevention activities of criminal justice agencies. Individuals can volunteer to work for the police, courts, probation departments, or other law enforcement agencies. They can volunteer to tutor underprivileged delinquents; they can attend community relations meetings conducted by local police departments. Individuals can fight crime by bolstering the anti-crime efforts of the private sector. As the National Advisory Commission on Criminal Justice Standards and Goals stated in 1973, private agencies and organizations outside the criminal justice system greatly influence the rise and fall of the crime rate.

Recently, more citizens have become involved in community crime prevention. In cities throughout the country, organized neighborhood associations and other community groups, working together and with criminal justice agencies, are making progress in combating crime, promoting neighborhood security, and maintaining order.

The importance of community crime prevention cannot be overemphasized. Your own neighbors provide one of the best forms of security. In many neighborhoods it is next to impossible for a criminal to enter a building without being spotted. Unfortunately, in our fast-paced and alienated society, many people do not know their neighbors. When suspicious activities are noticed, people are reluctant to report them because they don't want to be considered nosy. Yet if crime is to be beaten, all citizens must participate more actively in protecting their neighborhoods and communities.

In this chapter we will discuss the two roles that you, as an individual, have in fighting community crime. In the first role, the individual, acting alone, has a minimal responsibility to help law enforcement agencies do their jobs more effectively. Second, the citizen has a role as *part* of the community. This second responsibility — the efforts made by private individuals joining together in their neighborhoods and protecting each other's interests — is the focus of this chapter. Studies now available explain the operation of community crime prevention efforts and show the importance of individuals working together in their neighborhoods. Mostly volunteers, these people use limited funds to run their own crime-prevention programs, usually with the consent and cooperation of the police.

THE INDIVIDUAL IN THE COMMUNITY

All of us must do our share to combat crime. We must use good locks on doors and windows, and keep our homes well lighted and our property marked. We have to spend more time keeping abreast of new crime prevention techniques. Most importantly, we should maintain a sense of civic responsibility and concern for our community. By taking our civic duties seriously and by translating our fear and anger into active participation in crime prevention, we will accomplish something more important than helping the police directly. We will create a climate in our community which will not tolerate crime, and we will foster an attitude on which more tangible crime prevention programs can be built.

Most people acknowledge that crime prevention is everybody's business, but too many fail to fulfill their civic responsibilities. One obvious example is the lack of citizen cooperation in reporting crime to the police. Victimization surveys show that at least half of the crimes in the United States are never reported. It may not seem important for you to report a small crime in your neighborhood. However, when half of the victims in the country take that same "who cares" attitude, all of those unreported crimes accumulate to an astounding total.

Many people have seemingly valid reasons for not reporting crime. Some fear retaliation from violent offenders, some want to avoid vandalism by juvenile delinquents. Others feel it is not worth the trouble to report minor crimes because the police can't do anything about them. And, as incredible as it may seem, some simply don't know how to report crimes. Yet most people don't have a valid reason for not reporting crime. Apathy is the major cause of people not fulfilling their civic duty, and it is dangerous, because it contributes to the spread of crime.

Who can forget the infamous Kitty Genovese case? Thirty-five New

Yorkers stood by for two hours while Ms. Genovese was raped and killed. Not one person came to her rescue, not one even called the police.

Criminals are becoming increasingly daring; they know most people don't want to "get involved." Criminals count on citizens not to report crime or to be witnesses in court. To a large extent, the lawlessness in our society results from our attitudes. The unwillingness to take a little extra time to help our neighbors and the lack of faith we place in the criminal justice system help to breed crime.

Acting alone in your community, you can fight crime in several ways. First, report all crimes — even minor ones — to the police as quickly as you can. The police are hampered in their operations when they lack knowledge about where and when crimes are being committed. If all crimes were reported, the police would have an accurate picture of crime patterns in different parts of a city. They could deploy more patrols, in cars or on foot, to areas with the highest crime rates. Quite often, one crime is followed by another in the same neighborhood. With complete crime information, police could alert citizens in a given area to possible danger.

It is important to report crimes *quickly*. The police have the best chance of catching criminals moments after the crime has occurred. Studies reveal that crime victims often wait too long to report crimes — sometimes hours after the crime has been committed. The longer you wait to call the police, the lower are their chances of apprehending the offender.

If you fear retaliation, you don't have to identify yourself when reporting a crime. If you don't want to talk directly to the police, you can call other crime fighting organizations that will report the crime for you. For example, a program that began a few years ago in San Diego takes anonymous calls concerning any criminal activity. Called WETIP (We Turn In Pushers), the program originally took calls from people who had information about narcotics pushers in the neighborhood. WETIP was so successful that it spread to other parts of California and expanded its concern from drugs to all major crimes. Through anonymous calls to law enforcement agencies or programs like WETIP, the police can know where the crimes are being committed and they can react accordingly.

Another thing you should do is report all suspicious activity in your neighborhood, even if you are not sure it is a crime. Because the police are often unfamiliar with the people or cars in a neighborhood, they need constant help from an alert and cooperative citizenry.

Train yourself and your neighbors to be on the lookout for strange vehicles. If you notice an unfamiliar car, truck, or service vehicle prowling around the block, jot down the vehicle's license number, make, color, number of doors — as much information as you can. If you ever see a strange vehicle containing TV sets, stereos, or similar items, call the police immediately. Do not assume that because the vehicle is a service van it has legitimate business in the neighborhood. Burglars often pose as repairmen — with white coats and all — to trick unsuspecting people.

Don't be afraid that your call may be a false alarm. Police realize that they must check out all tips and are fully aware that many will be of no help. But many tips pan out. Often, people give tips that lead to the arrest of someone who has committed dozens of crimes — and who would have committed dozens more. If one crime is prevented, one criminal caught, then the time spent investigating tips is worth it.

If you observe a crime, you should serve as a witness. Although serving as a witness is admittedly inconvenient and frustrating, it is a necessary element of the criminal justice process. One of the biggest obstacles to successfully prosecuting a criminal is drumming up sufficient evidence — evidence that is usually supplied by witnesses. Without them, there are no convictions and the criminals are right back out on the streets.

You should also be willing to serve on a jury. Many people do not register to vote specifically because they do not want to be called for jury duty. This attitude lowers the quality of justice in our courts, and ultimately hurts us all.

Finally, every citizen should cooperate with the professionals who maintain law and order. The police have been the brunt of much criticism over the last two decades. Sometimes they deserve it. But by and large, the police want to help you — and they want to help you help yourself.

THE INDIVIDUAL AS A MEMBER OF THE COMMUNITY

Although necessary, the individual action discussed in the previous section is not sufficient to stem the tide against crime. An individualistic approach to crime prevention causes citizens to transform their homes into fortresses and families to become isolated from their communities. Social isolation in turn means that neighborhoods are less able to form a united front against crime.

Members of our society must begin to feel responsible not only for themselves, but also for the general welfare of others. If individuals unite, neighborhood crime prevention will become more than the sum of its parts. An attitude of community concern and involvement is your best security. We must act together, not react individually.

Community responsibility for law enforcement and crime prevention has a long history. Before the eighteenth century, professional law enforcement organizations, as we know them today, did not exist. Each person was responsible not only for his own actions, but for those of his neighbors. A citizen observing a crime had the duty to summon his neighbors and catch the criminal. Town sheriffs forced citizens to help in law enforcement efforts. If citizens refused, *they* had to go to jail. Peace was kept, for the most part, not by officials, but by the whole community. Mutual responsibility was the rule, not the exception.

By the beginning of this century, local citizens began to delegate crime-fighting responsibilities to professional law enforcement officers. Municipal police departments developed and law enforcement evolved into a specialty. As the police became more professionalized, citizens gave up even more of their peace-keeping duties. The police took over the field of crime prevention, and for a long time they felt they had the exclusive expertise to combat crime.

Yet increased police specialization and the decline of citizen involvement obviously did not solve the crime problem. Criminal justice professionals began to admit that more money, manpower, and technology would not win the war against crime unless citizens again joined the battle. Today, crime prevention needs a greater balance between the duties of the police and those of the citizenry.

You can begin to build a community crime prevention system by becoming better acquainted with your neighbors and your neighborhood. Get to know your neighbors' everyday living patterns. By knowing when they work, go on vacation, and so forth, you will be better able to determine whether someone has legitimate business at your neighbor's home. You don't have to be best friends with your neighbors to look out for each others' interests. Talk to your neighbors informally. Many of them undoubtedly want to help, but they are waiting for someone with drive to start the ball rolling. Take the initiative. Get together in groups and discuss your problems. Arrange for a law enforcement expert to address your discussion groups. The police will gladly give you ideas for feasible community action. The U. S. Department of Justice is currently making citizen involvement in community crime prevention one of its highest funding priorities. If you belong to, or want to start, a civic organization, check with your local police department or regional criminal justice planning board to find out how it might qualify for funds.

Community or neighborhood crime prevention programs vary in size and organization. Some have formal leadership and rigid structure, others are informal and flexible. Some have large memberships and meet regularly, others are small and meet when the need arises. Some try to root out all crime in the neighborhood, others attack one specific type of crime.

Crime prevention programs may be initiated either by the police or by the citizens themselves. Normally it makes little difference who starts the project, as long as both the police and the citizens agree on basic principles and procedures of the program. Police commitment will depend in part on having the interest expressed in crime prevention come from different parts of the community. Community crime prevention programs are therefore more likely to succeed in areas where all racial, ethnic, and income groups participate. Race and ethnic background make no difference in the desire to eliminate crime or in the effectiveness of doing so.

Although experts now acknowledge the need for greater citizen action in crime prevention, neighborhood groups must never resort to "vigilante justice." Vigilantism is not tolerated because it is illegal. It is also dangerous, and often ineffective. Vigilantism merely adds to the existing atmosphere of lawlessness. No matter how well motivated, citizens must not take the law into their own hands. Crime prevention and the preservation of order must be balanced against the protection of those values and rights the neighborhood groups are supposed to protect — the safety and well-being of *all* citizens.

COMMUNITY CRIME PREVENTION PROGRAMS

Block Clubs

Citizen fear of crime has prompted an enormous growth of private self-help crime prevention groups throughout the country. These groups are usually found at the neighborhood or block level, and are known by many names. In this chapter, we will use their most common name, block clubs.

Block clubs are associations of neighbors who join ranks primarily to fight crime. In general, block clubs do what individuals acting alone would do, only they do it in an organized and united manner. Block clubs vary in size, organization, leadership, funding, and crime fighting techniques. Yet they have common threads, they get citizens to know each other, to look out for each others' interests, and to make crime prevention a group enterprise.

The sheer number of block clubs will give some indication of how popular they have become. Over 7,000 block clubs exist in New York City, over 3,000 in Los Angeles, and over 1,000 in Oakland. Thousands more exist all over the country, in big cities and small. The number of block clubs has doubled in the past few years.

Block clubs have been one of the most effective means of bringing people together and of instilling a sense of community. The majority of block club members state that they did not know most of their neighbors before joining the club. Some neighbors rarely spoke. But fighting crime was an incentive to get together, and block clubs provided a way to do it. Getting to know each other has helped people to appreciate their mutual problems and reduce their fear of crime. Moreover, many delinquents and criminals admit that it is much more difficult to victimize people they know than strangers they don't care anything about.

Block clubs increase neighborhood security in a variety of ways. First, members disseminate crime prevention information to every person in the neighborhood. The entire neighborhood learns about locks, alarms, and the basic security techniques. When the clubs get together, members also discuss broader issues related to crime prevention, such as slum clearance, drug rehabilitation, and general community improvement. Next, attitudes change when people join block clubs. Members become far more concerned about their fellow neighbors, and their community as a whole. Some of the ways these attitudes are put into action will be discussed shortly.

Block clubs also increase security by improving relations between the community and the police. Although the police are supposed to treat all people equally, there are not enough police officers and other resources available to achieve this idea. Police departments must set priorities. They must decide what areas of the city will have more patrols and better service. They must determine neighborhood problems and establish reliable communication channels between themselves and the citizens they serve. Block clubs help in these efforts. Police interest is enhanced in neighborhoods where residents become organized, know beat officers by name, and report all crimes and suspicious activity. A spirit of cooperation emerges when block clubs invite beat officers to their meetings. In many communities both the police and residents report that some areas get better service than others because block clubs have more effectively communicated their problems and their needs.

Block Club Activities

Block clubs engage in hundreds of activities for the improvement of their communities. We will list only a few of the possibilities. If you join a block club, you can bring along these suggestions. But we're sure your club members will be able to think of many more activities on their own, depending on the special needs of your community.

1. Distribute crime prevention literature to every resident in the neighborhood. The crime prevention literature can be written by the block club itself, or some of it may be secured from your local law enforcement agency. Call your police department to find out if they have extra copies.

2. Write and distribute a block newsletter. The newsletter should contain the time and place of all upcoming crime prevention meetings. It should also describe the crimes that have recently been committed in the neighborhood and the reasons for those crimes (such as unlocked doors, or an open window).

3. Draw a block map with people's names (including children), addresses and phone numbers.

4. Encourage all people on the block to become involved in crime prevention.

5. Inform all people on the block engaging in injurious and illegal activities that you are aware of what they are doing and how the block feels about it.

6. Welcome new neighbors personally, and invite them to the next block club meeting.

7. Arrange meetings with other block clubs in the community to discuss common problems.

8. Identify the causes of block deterioration (potholes, rape, drugs, abandoned houses, bad street lighting, etc.) and ask a representative from the appropriate city or county agency to come to a block meeting.

9. Organize block parties or outings. These can be of many types, including: a barbecue or potluck supper, a trip to the zoo or a museum, a craft or art show, recreational or athletic games, or raffles to raise money.

10. Report all crimes to the police. Keep a record of the time and date of your call and follow through to see if appropriate actions have been taken.

11. Report all suspicious activity to the police. Keep a record of a suspicious car's license number, a description of the person, and other pertinent information.

12. Look out for the elderly citizens of the neighborhood. Set up escorts for the elderly — to the bank, shopping centers, clinics. Arrange periodic telephone calls to the elderly to see if they need anything.

13. Arrange for residents to watch each other's houses, yards, cars, and other property.

14. Plan to watch neighbors' homes and property when they are on vacation. Take in the mail, newspapers, circulars. Engage in the other crime prevention techniques discussed in Chapter 1, pages 43 – 46.

15. Establish a committee to follow up and try to mediate neighbors' complaints concerning dogs, trash, loud music, landlord neglect, and so forth.

16. Invite the beat police officer to a block club meeting.

17. Invite the crime prevention officer of your police department to a block club meeting to speak about the latest crime prevention techniques. Request the officer to conduct home security surveys on block homes.

18. Invite an expert on health services (drug programs) to a block club meeting.

19. Invite a person working with the juvenile justice system or the local school system to a block club meeting.

20. Invite judges, district attorneys, public defenders, and other people working in the criminal justice system.

21. Request your district supervisor or city councilman to discuss problems in your neighborhood.

22. Organize community walks or mobile patrols to spot criminals in the area. (See next section in this chapter.)

23. Organize a property identification program, like Operation Identification. (See Chapter 1, pages 41 – 43.)

24. Provide support and counseling for victims of crime in the area. Help them get cooperation from the police and learn about victim compensation.

25. Arrange for first-aid instruction.

Block Club Effectiveness

Block clubs have helped reduce crime in countless neighborhoods. While the crime rate has been rising in cities as a whole, it has been declining in neighborhoods where block clubs operate. In many of these neighborhoods, the formation of a block club has been the only

noticeable change. Other factors, such as police patrol and the unemployment rate, have stayed the same over time.

Both law enforcement and community officials agree that the crime
rate can be lowered when block clubs participate more actively in
crime prevention. Individual block club leaders agree. A 1974 survey
of block club leaders conducted by the Center for Governmental
Studies indicates that block clubs have reduced both crime and the fear
of it. The results of the survey's questionnaire from three cities are
shown in the following table.

EFFECTIVENESS OF BLOCK CLUBS*

Question #1:   Have block clubs reduced crime?

	Yes	No	Could not tell
West Philadelphia, Pa.	70%	11%	19%
Oakland, Ca.	64	24	12
Compton, Ca.	92	4	4

Question #2:   Have block clubs reduced fear?

	Yes	No	Could not tell
West Philadelphia, Pa.	64%	24%	12%
Oakland, Ca.	34	55	11
Compton, Ca.	60	32	8

Question #3:   Have block clubs been effective?

	Yes	No	Could not tell
West Philadelphia, Pa.	79%	17%	4%
Oakland, Ca.		*Not compiled*	
Compton, Ca.	85	4	11

*Source: Center for Governmental Studies, 1974.

There appear to be several reasons why crime has been reduced in
block club neighborhoods: a) heightened awareness among residents
of criminal and suspicious activity, b) enhanced citizen cooperation in
reporting crime, c) better working relationships between police and the

community, d) increased residential security (locks, marked property, alarms), e) more community activities, such as meetings and workshops, and f) greater citizen commitment to work together and look out for each others' interests. Word spreads quickly that some neighborhoods are not good places to engage in criminal activity.

The reduction of crime in block club neighborhoods also has indirect benefits. Because more people want to live in these areas, property values go up. West Philadelphia presents a good example. During the Block Association of West Philadelphia's first year of operation, property values jumped over 50 percent, compared to only a 12 percent increase for the city as a whole.

Neighborhood Patrols

Neighborhood patrols are organized to watch over their neighborhoods, to act as additional ''eyes and ears'' for the police. Members of patrols should be thoroughly familiar with their neighborhood, enabling them to report criminal or suspicious activity quickly to the police. Beside their own neighborhoods, patrols should cover shopping centers, parking lots, bus stops, schools, and other frequently used areas. Neighborhood patrols can be started by any private or public group. Block clubs, for example, are excellent organizations for sponsoring foot patrols around the neighborhood.

Neighborhood patrols can walk on foot or use vehicles such as cars, motorcycles, or even bicycles. Foot patrols are best for covering small neighborhoods, but are usually inadequate for larger areas of the city. A group of block clubs, or other areawide organizations, is needed to organize mobile patrols, that is, neighborhood patrols that use vehicles.

Civilian mobile patrols can be particularly effective these days, because so many cars are equipped with CB radios. There are usually many volunteers for mobile patrols. Amateur radio operators like to put their hobby to good use, while also learning more about their favorite subject. Mobile patrols don't have to rely on residents alone. Trucking companies, taxis, delivery service trucks, and city vehicles are all in a good position to aid mobile patrol in spotting criminal activity.

Although block club foot patrols can be set up on almost any block, and in any neighborhood, mobile patrols are much more complex. It is best to check with the police before your club sets up a mobile patrol. In some of the highest crime districts, it may be too dangerous for civilians to patrol, in cars or on foot. This is especially true where organized youth gangs roam about.

Under proper supervision, civilian patrols offer extremely effective protection in most areas of the city. In many cities, for example, neighborhood patrols have been used to discourage street prostitution. Members of block clubs, churches, and other civic groups cover the streets where prostitutes congregate and take photographs of the men who speak to the prostitutes or jot down the customers' car license numbers. This surveillance deters potential customers from coming into the neighborhoods, so the prostitutes — and the people they associate with — go elsewhere. The same methods can be used to keep burglars, muggers, rapists, and drug dealers out of your community. Criminals don't want to have encounters with private citizens or the police. If lawbreakers believe their criminal behavior will be discovered, they will go to another part of town.

Police departments often issue rules governing neighborhood patrol activities, in large part to guard against vigilantism. As we have said, vigilantism is illegal, and the police will put an end to all vigilante groups immediately. The most common police rules are:

1. Patrol members must be at least eighteen years of age.

2. No firearms or other weapons are allowed on patrol.

3. No member will leave his or her car to investigate any criminal or suspicious activity.

4. Members will assist the police officer *only* upon the officer's specific request.

5. Members are never to pose as police officers.

6. Members are never to engage in an automobile chase.

7. No member will detain anyone unless ordered to do so by a police officer.

8. No member shall question any suspect.

9. Members with a radio monitor are not to respond to police department transmissions.

Patrol members should be properly trained. Training lowers the chance of error on the job, and it instills greater trust among patrol members. Training, often provided by the police, should cover at least the following areas:

1. Fundamentals of criminal and civil law.
2. Review of basic municipal ordinances.
3. Conditions under which members should call police for assistance.
4. First aid and emergency care.
5. Auto safety and general vehicle maintenance.
6. Proper radio language and communication procedures.

Neighborhood patrol members should constantly vary their patrol routes and times to preserve the element of surprise. Obviously, patrol schedules should not be published. However, general announcements through the mass media about the existence of patrols in specified neighborhoods are effective deterrents to criminals.

Protecting Children—The Block Parent Program

Crimes against children arouse deep emotion in everyone. Protecting children, therefore, is an aspect of crime prevention that produces many volunteers. With police cooperation and with properly trained citizens, child protection programs are effective in reducing crime, in addition to providing parents with greater peace of nind.

Hundreds of child protection programs operate throughout the country. One of the most common and effective is the Block Parent program, which tries to have one or more members on every block. The primary duty of a Block Parent is the protection of children going to and from school. Block Parents are also responsible for reporting any criminal or suspicious activity to the police. They must therefore be alert for violations of the law, particularly those affecting children.

The Block Parent program can be set up with the assistance of the P.T.A., local service clubs, improvement associations, or similar organizations. Information about the program is usually distributed to parents through schools and the P.T.A.

A Block Parent is first screened for acceptability by the police, but may be married or single, old or young, employed or not working. The main consideration is that the Block Parent be at home when children are walking to and from school. The central Block Parent office issues a "Block Parent" sign which is put in a consipicuous place in the home, usually in the front window. Children are instructed at school to look for the Block Parent sign if they get lost, are bothered by a stranger, or need help of any kind.

There are several rules to follow if you become a Block Parent.

1. You must not take the law into your own hands. If a child should come to your door, find out any important information, and, if necessary, call the police.

2. Do *not* transport children in your car. If the child's parents cannot be located, call the police department or school.

3. If the child has been molested or frightened by a stranger, or if a child has witnessed an incident of exposure, call the police department immediately.

4. Do not offer children food or beverages.

5. Do not administer first aid in case of injury except to stop excessive bleeding or to restore breathing.

6. Do not call an ambulance, since you become responsible for payment if the parents refuse to pay. Call the police or fire department for emergency service.

If you are interested in becoming a Block Parent, contact your local police department or school district for information.

Special Crime Prevention Projects
Less common crime problems often require special crime prevention projects. Special projects are occasionally part of a block club's general plan, but they freqaently develop when particular interest groups face unique crime problems and want them solved through group action. We will mention but a few of the many possible projects.

Antirape Programs
Increasingly, crime prevention programs concentrate on protecting women against rape. (See Chapter 5, page 139 for details.) The

programs provide counseling, self-defense training, and general crime prevention education to women in their communities.

An example of a community's effort to fight rape is found in Berkeley, California. A rapist identified as Stinky (because of his peculiar smell) was responsible for over fifty rapes, most of them occurring in one part of town. After several of Stinky's sexual assaults, an anti-rape program, working with a block club, instituted foot patrols to guard several square blocks after dark. The program members also gave instruction on general crime prevention techniques, to lower the chances that Stinky would enter a residence at night. The patrols continued for a month or so. Although Stinky was not captured, he was at least deterred from committing any more rapes in the area.

High-Rise Tenant Security

Although block clubs and neighborhood patrols are excellent ways to combat crime in the streets, they are less effective for people living in high-rise buildings. Special crime prevention methods are needed to protect these people from attack inside their buildings.

Organizing residents in many high-rise apartments is as necessary as organizing homeowners in the community. Residents can arrange to have floor captains, newsletters, guest lecturers; and hardware security and other familiar crime prevention methods are as valuable in large apartment buildings as they are in the single family home. Many high-rise tenant security programs have proved successful. The key to their success, as in all crime prevention programs, is motivating residents to take action.

Protecting Employees

The fear of crime is especially prevalent among people who have to commute long distances to and from work in hours of darkness. Many businesses, plants, and factories, with the help of both unions and management, have started special crime prevention programs for such employees. Employee security programs usually have workers use the buddy system — traveling together and looking out for each other. Some programs have also acquired better lighting outside factories; others demanded shuttle-buses to and from parking lots or public transportation.

One effective program using the buddy system is the Maintenance

Employees Night Protection Alert Corporation (MENPAC). Their statistics prove that traveling in groups does reduce chances of attack: 18 percent of women employees who traveled alone to work were attacked, whereas only one percent of those who traveled with friends were.

CONCLUSION

The tolerance Americans have for crime is amazing. Perhaps it is because they feel helpless to do anything about it. Whatever the reason, too many people fail to join the fight against crime.

We are now beginning to realize that any solution, short or long range, to the problems of crime and violence must involve private citizen participation. Numerous national commissions, as well as criminologists and law enforcement officials, urge the formation of local citizen groups to combat crime at the most basic level — the neighborhood.

The ultimate solutions to crime are not obvious, but it is clear that little will ever be done to reduce crime without the active involvement of all citizens. Citizen initiative is needed to organize groups, to provide general crime prevention education, and to stimulate a concern for the well-being of the community.

Bibliography

Abrahamsen, David. *The Psychology of Crime*. New York: Columbia University Press, 1960.

Amir, Menachem. *Patterns of Forcible Rape*. Chicago: University of Chicago Press, 1971.

Astor, Gerald. *The Charge is Rape*. Chicago: Playboy Press, 1974.

Brown, Brenda. "Crimes Against Women Alone." Mimeographed. Memphis, Tenn.: 1974.

Brownmiller, Susan. *Against Our Will*. New York: Bantam Books, 1975.

Cartwright, Joe and Jerry Patterson. *Been Taken Lately?* New York: Grove Press, Inc., 1974.

The Challenge of Crime in a Free Society. Report by the President's Commission on Law Enforcement and Administration of Justice. Washington, D.C.,1967.

Clark, Ramsey. *Crime in America*. New York: Pocket Books, 1970.

Community Crime Prevention. Report by the National Advisory Commission on Criminal Justice Standards and Goals. Washington, D.C., 1973.

Cramer, James A., ed. *Preventing Crime*. Beverly Hill, Ca.: Sage Publications, 1978.

Crime Prevention Officers' Handbook. Santa Rosa, Ca.: California Crime Prevention Institute, 1978.

Crimes of Violence. The Staff Report to the National Commission on the Cases and Prevention of Violence. Washington, D.C. 1969.

DeFrancis, Vincent. *Protecting the Child Victim of Sex Crimes Com-*

247

mitted by Adults — Final Report. Denver, Colo.: The American Humane Association, 1969.

Fontana, Vincent. *Somewhere a Child is Crying*. New York: Macmillan and Co., 1973.

Gebhard, Paul H. et al. *Sex Offenders*. New York: Harper and Row, Publishers and Paul B. Hoeber, Inc., Medical Books, 1965.

Gorman, Robert. "Home Burglar Alarms." *Popular Science,* March 1979, pp. 114 – 17.

Hayman, Charles R. et al. "Rape in the District of Columbia." Paper presented to the 99th Meeting, American Public Health Association, Minneapolis, October 11, 1971.

Hunt, Morton. *The Mugging*. New York: The New American Library, 1972.

Jeffery, C. Ray. *Crime Prevention Through Environmental Design*. Beverly Hills, Ca.: Sage Publication, 1977.

Jelley, Herbert M. and Robert O. Herrmann. *The American Consumer*. San Francisco, Ca.: McGraw Hill Book Co., 1973.

Kanin, E. J. and C. Kirkpatrick. "Male Sexual Aggression on University Campuses." *American Sociological Review*, Volume 22 (1957), pp. 52 – 58.

Kinsey, Alfred C. et al. *Sexual Behavior in the Human Female*. Philadelphia: W.B. Saunders Company, 1953.

Kinsey, Alfred C. et al. *Sexual Behavior in the Human Male*. Philadelphia: W.B. Saunders Company, 1948.

Lewis, James. *The Consumer's Fight-Back Book*. New York: Award Books, 1972.

MacDonald, John M. *Rape Offenders and Their Victims*. Springfield, Ill.: Charles C. Thomas, 1971.

Medea, Andrea and Kathleen Thompson. *Against Rape*. New York: Farrar, Strauss and Giroux, 1974.

Offstein, Jerrold. *Self-Defense for Women*. Palo Alto, Ca.: National Press Books, 1972.

Pekkanen, John. *Victims: An Account of Rape*. New York: Popular Library, 1976.

Scarr, Harry H. *Patterns of Burglary*. Washington, D.C.: United States Department of Justice, Law Enforcement Assistance Administration, 1972.

Skolnick, Jerome H., Martin L. Forst and Jane L. Scheiber, eds. *Crime and Justice in America*. Del Mar, Ca.: Publishers Inc., 1977.

Statistical Report. Federal Bureau of Prisons, Washington, D.C., 1978.

Storaska, Frederic. *How to Say No to a Rapist and Survive*. New York: Warner Books, 1976.

Uniform Crime Reports. Washington, D.C.: United States Department of Justice, Federal Bureau of Investigation.

Willwerth, James. *Jones: Portrait of a Mugger*. Greenwich, Conn.: Fawcett Publications, Inc., 1974.

Wittier, Tinker. "Secrets of a Car Thief." *Money Magazine*, October 1978, pp. 64–68.

Wolfgang, Marvin E. and Franco Ferracuti. *The Subculture of Violence*. London: Tavistock, 1967.

Index

251